INCEST
FANTASIES
& SELF
DESTRUCTIVE
ACTS

INCEST FANTASIES & SELF DESTRUCTIVE ACTS

Jungian and
Post-Jungian
Psychotherapy
in Adolescence

edited by
Mara Sidoli
Gustav Bovensiepen

Transaction Publishers
New Brunswick (U.S.A.) and London (U.K.)

Copyright © 1995 by Transaction Publishers,
New Brunswick, New Jersey 08903

All rights reserved under International and Pan-American Copyright Conventions. No part of this book may be reproduced or transmitted in any form or by any means, electronic or mechanical, including photocopy, recording, or any information storage and retrieval system, without prior permission in writing from the publisher. All inquiries should be addressed to Transaction Publishers, Rutgers—The State University, New Brunswick, New Jersey 08903.

This book is printed on acid-free paper that meets the American National Standard for Permanence of Paper for Printed Library Materials.

Library of Congress Catalog Number: 93–43159
ISBN: 1–56000–152–6
Printed in the United States of America

Library of Congress Cataloging-in-Publication Data

Incest fantasies and self-destructive acts : Jungian and post-Jungian
    psychotherapy in adolescence / edited by Mara Sidoli, Gustav
    Bovensiepen.
        p.   cm.
    Includes index.
    ISBN 1–56000–152–6
    1. Adolescent psychotherapy.   2. Jung, C. G. (Carl Gustav),
1875–1961.   3. Psychotherapist and patient.   I. Sidoli, Mara.
II.   Bovensiepen, Gustav.
RJ503.I53 1994
616.89'14'0835—dc20   93–43159
                                                          CIP

Contents

Preface

In 1983 an international group of Jungian analytical psychologists came together at a conference in Jerusalem to create a forum for the discussion of the theoretical and technical issues involved in working with children and adolescents. Since the tradition in the international Jungian community, both in Jung's day and now, has been to work primarily with adults, resistance to tackling the problems of young people has been strong, and only a few analysts of the older generation have taught child analytic psychotherapy. The Jerusalem conference, however, yielded a fertile exchange of ideas among the Jungian and post-Jungian therapists who attended. The result of this exchange was a collaborative volume, *Jungian Child Psychotherapy,* compiled and edited by the English analyst, Miranda Davies, and myself, which appeared in 1988. The response to this book was so encouraging that I have undertaken, along with my coeditor, Gustav Bovensiepen of Berlin, to compile the present volume on adolescents. The team of contributors to our first volume has remained here largely the same, with several welcome additions.

Very little has been written by Jungians on the subject of adolescent psychotherapy. The intent of this book is to remedy a serious omission. The papers presented here illustrate a number of psychotherapeutic methodologies that the various authors have developed in the course of their practice. Of particular importance are the discussions of the therapeutic relationship that emerges between the inner world of the adolescent and the therapist. The unifying element among the authors' widely divergent perspectives is the emphasis on the transference/countertransference process, a process which involves the continuing analysis of the relationship between the young patient and the therapist as the therapy proceeds. The papers concentrate on severe neurotic disturbances, psychotic illnesses, psychosomatic disorders, and other behavioral problems that can occur in adolescence. Most of the psychological disturbances in this age group originate in the body, where dramatic changes and powerful instinctual discharges—related to hormonal discharges for which the adolescent must develop mental representations—create violent psychological upheavals. These upheavals can result in such destructive behavior as self-mutilation, sexual abuse, psychosomatic illness, and suicide.

Addictive and antisocial problems that need a more educational approach are not discussed here, unless they are considered in specific cases to be symptomatic of deep traumatic disturbances. Rather, the focus is on pathological situations that derive from incest fantasies and acts. These are considered from a Jungian theoretical standpoint. Our approach differs from the Freudian insofar as Jung understood the activation of incestuous fantasies in adolescence not just as genital phenomena, but as a "regression" to the pregenital images of the unconscious in search of wholeness and rebirth. He saw "incest" as a metaphor for regression to pre-oedipal object relations. Other post-Jungian views, especially those of the British analyst, Michael Fordham, and the Israeli analyst, Erich Neumann, form part of the theoretical underpinnings of many of the articles in this collection.

The strength of the present volume lies in the diversity of the therapeutic approaches—both theoretical and technical—adopted and presented by this international group of contributors. These differences are naturally influenced by national training, work experience, and the prevailing tendencies in different countries. The purpose underlying our selection of these papers is to form a synthesis of these ideas. The book represents a collective attempt to formulate and conceptualize a "post-Jungian" way of working with adolescents. This integrative approach makes the volume a unique contribution to psychoanalytic literature.

Although both Freudian and Kleinian concepts are interwoven in these psychoanalytic constructs, the theoretical framework of the book is rooted in Jung's conceptualizations and their application to childhood and adolescence by Michael Fordham. Fordham lives in London, where the major movements in child psychoanalysis first developed, and hence he has been influenced by object relations theory and by Melanie Klein's views of the child's inner world and unconscious fantasies and the post-Kleinian developments of Wilfred Bion. Although Fordham has developed a great interest in the study of infancy, he has not focused his attention specifically on adolescence.

Fordham's theoretical and clinical approach is primarily taught in the child training program at the Society of Analytical Psychology in London, but his ideas are now spreading throughout Europe and the United States. In Germany, child analysis is taught in the institutes that represent the three main psychoanalytic schools in that country: the Freudian, the post-Freudian, and the Jungian. Child analytic training has been an amalgam of post-Freudian and Jungian elements, especially in Berlin. Only recently have the Kleinian-influenced ideas of Michael Fordham influenced child analytic thinking of Jungians in Germany.

Kleinian and object relations terminologies are widely used in the papers, along with Jungian child analytic language. All the authors focus on the clinical setting where the blending of archetypal and primal self theory takes place. While the post-Jungian attention to detail and technique gives the book a unique approach, the emphasis on severe pathological states makes the work very "Jungian" in its own right.

As the interest in child analytic work has steadily increased among Jungians in the last few years, child analytic training programs have been recently established in Italy, France, and Switzerland. However, before such official programs emerged, Dora Kalff, the Swiss therapist, had been offering training sessions in her sandplay method of working with children, and this approach has become very popular with therapists from the different Jungian schools. Many have found the sandplay method easy to master and suitable for working with children and adolescents, since often many of the patients are only able to reveal their inner experiences through nonverbal means. A paper on the clinical use of this method and an illustrated case study has been included here, as well as papers on psychodrama, group therapy, and other technical approaches to adolescent treatment in outpatient and inpatient units.

Implicitly or explicitly, the approach of each of our contributors is based on the premise that disturbances in adolescents are often connected to their pre-oedipal development. Early emotional experiences are dramatically relived in the analyst's office, and can lead to well-known technical difficulties in the course of treatment. The case histories in this book serve to promote insight and further understanding of the highly charged relationship that develops between the analyst and his young patient.

The principal aim of this book is to assist psychotherapists working in clinical settings. It will also be informative and useful to therapists who work in institutions such as schools, hospitals, and children's homes. Although the language is technical, the concepts are sufficiently defined so that the book will be helpful to teachers, students, and beleaguered parents as well.

Joining me as coeditor of this volume is Dr. Gustav Bovensiepen of Berlin, who brings with him extensive experience and expertise working with adolescents both in clinical settings and in private practice. In addition to the authors published in *Jungian Child Psychology,* Dr. Francesco Bisagni and Dr. Gianni Nagliero have joined us from Italy. Dr. Nagliero, head of the Adolescent Department of the Bambin Gesu Hospital in Rome, is well-known for his work with anorexic patients. From England, Dr. Geoffrey Brown of the London Society of Analytic Psychology contributes his experience as director of the Adolescent Center at St. Luke's Hospital in London.

Finally, this collection of papers does not claim to be a comprehensive manual on adolescent psychotherapy. Rather it presents the ideas and techniques originating from our working experience and interest in young patients. There is no single, uniform theoretical system in analytic psychology. Analytic practice embraces a wide spectrum of approaches, which we believe this book richly demonstrates.

MARA SIDOLI

Acknowledgments

We would like to express our gratitude to our colleagues whose contributions have made this book possible. A special thanks to Miranda Davies of the London Society of Analytical Psychology for her patient and competent assistance with the early editing of the book. Our many clinical and theoretical discussions with her formed an important background for the analytical concepts presented here.

We also want to thank Marianne De Pury for help with the German translations. For their many hours of excellent professional editing of the final manuscript, we would like to thank Leslie Haynes and Marigay Graña.

Finally we would like to express our appreciation to the many patients who have provided us with the clinical material contained in this book.

MARA SIDOLI
GUSTAV BOVENSIEPEN

Notes on Contributors

HELGA ANDERSSEN-PLAUT is a Jungian training analyst at the Berlin Institute of Psychotherapy She works both in a child guidance clinic and in private practice. She studied psychology at the Sorbonne in Paris and later trained at the Berlin Institute where she now teaches. Her special interests are analytic work with very young children and adolescents, and she has published several case analyses on these age groups.

FRANCESCO BISAGNI is a psychiatrist and Jungian analyst member of the Milan Centro di Psicologia Analitica (CIPA). He is principally interested in developmental child and adolescent object relations theory, combining post-Kleinian and post-Jungian approaches. Dr. Bisagni has published widely in both Italian and English and has lectured in Jungian Institutes in San Francisco, Chicago, and Santa Fe. He is the former editor of the Milan-based journal *Analysis.*

GUSTAV BOVENSIEPEN is the medical director of the Max Burger Clinic of Child and Adolescent Psychiatry in Berlin and a training analyst at the C. G. Jung Institute of Berlin. He is the honorary secretary of the International Association of Analytical Psychology and a founder of the International Workshop on Analytical Psychology in Childhood and Adolescence. Dr. Bovensiepen is a lecturer at the Berlin Free University and has presented papers in many institutes in Europe and the United States. He has published widely in German and English and is the coeditor of this volume with Dr. Mara Sidoli.

GEOFFREY BROWN is an adolescent psychiatrist and Jungian analyst member of the Society of Analytical Psychology in London. He is the director of the Adolescent Unit of Saint Luke's Woodside Hospital in

London, and is well-known for his pioneering work with adolescent patients in the National Health System. Dr. Brown's chapter included here, "Borderline States, Incest, and Adolescence" is a revised and expanded version of a study published in the *Journal of Analytical Psychology*.

JANE BUNSTER has worked for many years in child guidance clinics and private practice, where her specialty is autistic pathology in children and adolescents. She is a senior member of the British Association of Child Psychotherapists and is chair of Child Analytic Training at the London Society of Analytical Psychology. Bunster is a popular lecturer both in England and abroad; she is a leader of Infant Observation Seminars and a visiting lecturer at the University of Bristol.

MIRANDA DAVIES is a member of the Association of Child Psychotherapists and the London Society of Analytical Psychology, where she worked for many years with Dr. Michael Fordham. She works both in child guidance clinics and in private practice. Davies's analytical approach is fundamentally Jungian, strongly influenced by post-Kleinian theories. Davies is a founder of the International Workshop of Analytical Psychology in Childhood and Adolescence. Davies's chapter included here, "Heroic Deeds, Manic Defense, and Intrusive Identification" is an expanded version of an article that appeared in the *British Journal of Child Psychotherapists*.

BRIAN FELDMAN is a member of the teaching faculty of the C. G. Jung Institute of San Francisco. His analytical work has been strongly influenced by the object relations school and by his work with Dr. Michael Fordham at the London Society of Analytical Psychology. Dr. Feldman is a past chairman of the Department of Psychology at Stanford University, and a frequent lecturer at Jung Institutes in the United States and Europe. He works with adults as well as children and adolescents in private practice in Palo Alto.

JANET GLYNN-TREBLE is a Jungian analyst at the London Society of Analytical Psychology and a member of the Association of Psychotherapists and the British Psychological Society. She has worked for many years as a therapist for children and adolescents in residential institutions. Glynn-Treble is a well-known lecturer in psychology and child development, and maintains a private practice in London.

HEIDI HEIDTKE is a Jungian child psychotherapist and member of the C. G. Jung Institute of Berlin. She is a colleague of Dr. Bovensiepen and Mr. Neumann-Shirmbeck at the Berlin Max Burger Clinic, where she specializes in group therapy and psychodrama techniques.

GIANNI NAGLIERO is a Jungian analyst and member of the Italian Association of Jungian Analysts (AIPA). He is the director of the Adolescent Psychiatric Unit at Bambin Gesu Hospital in Rome. His therapeutic interest is the blending of sandplay techniques with transference interpretations. Dr. Nagliero is a member of the Jungian Childhood and Adolescence International Group, and has a private practice in Rome for adolescents and adults.

MICHAEL NEUMANN-SHIRMBECK is a lecturer at the C. G. Jung Institute in Berlin where he is a member of the Child and Adolescent Training Committee. He is a colleague of Heidke and Bovensiepen at the Max Burger Clinic. Both Neumann-Shirmbeck and Heidke have a specific expertise in group psychodrama therapy for adolescent patients.

MARA SIDOLI is a Jungian child and adult analyst in private practice in Santa Fe, where she is president of the C. G. Jung Institute of New Mexico. She is a senior member of the British Association of Child Psychotherapists and has worked for many years with Dr. Michael Fordham at the London Society of Analytical Psychology. She has been a leader of Infant Observation Seminars in Milan, London, Berlin, and the United States, and a founder of the International Workshop on Analytical Psychology in Childhood and Adolescence. Dr. Sidoli is a former faculty member of the Child Psychiatric Department at the University of New Mexico. She has published a number of articles and books on child and adult psychotherapy in which she emphasizes a developmental post-Jungian object relations approach to psychoanalytic practice. Dr. Sidoli is coeditor of this volume with Dr. Gustav Bovensiepen.

Glossary of Terms

ALPHA ELEMENTS (See *Alpha function.*)

ALPHA FUNCTION A theory of learning developed by Wilfred Bion to describe the unknown, but presupposed process by which raw sense data (*beta elements*) are transformed into mental contents which have meaning, and can therefore be used for thinking. The resulting products of alpha-function are *alpha elements.* The accumulation of alpha elements (thoughts) creates an apparatus for thinking, rather than, as in other theories of learning, the apparatus for thinking creates thought. The failure of the alpha function gives rise to the accumulation of unassimilated beta elements, which the mind expels, often violently (projective identification).

ARCHETYPES A term given by Jung to those universal structures of the psyche that occur in the collective unconscious and that regulate or order conceptual thinking. Jung postulated the existence of these unconscious psychic structures from the observation that myths and fairy tales of diverse, and in many cases, unrelated cultures throughout the world contain definite motifs or personifications that are repeated again and again. These same motifs occur in the fantasies, dreams, and delusions of people living today. They appear to be preexisting psychic forms or primordial images that are inherited in the unconscious

---

These definitions are paraphrased and edited versions of those found in C. G. Jung, *Memories, Dreams and Reflections* (New York: Vintage Books, 1965); Mario Jacobi, *Individuation and Narcissism* (London: Routledge, 1990); R. D. Hinshelwood, *A Dictionary of Kleinian Thought* (London: Free Association Books, 1991); H. B. English and A. English, *A Comprehensive Dictionary of Psychological and Psychoanalytical Terms* (London: Longman, 1958); A. Samuels, *Jung and the Post-Jungians* (London: Routledge and Kegan Paul, 1985); D. Meltzer, *The Claustrum* (London: Clunie, 1992).

of each individual. Papers in this volume use such archtypal images as the Hero, Punch, the Trickster, the Terrible Mother.

BETA ELEMENTS (See *Alpha function.*)

CATHEXIS The investment of emotional significance into an activity, object, or idea and the affective, energizing value of that activity, object, or idea. Cathexis of the libido: a psychic energy that has been fixed upon or invested in an object (object cathexis).

CLAUSTRUM Donald Meltzer uses this term to describe the physical geography and qualities of the internal object (see Object) and traces the metapsychological implications for the self of the phenomena of projective identification (Klein and Bion). He has developed the concept of "intrusive identification" as an aspect of severe psychopathology, narcissistic organization, and perversion. The claustrum is the "geographical" compartment of the body where these pathological phenomena take place.

COMBINED PARENT (See *Primal scene.*)

COMPLEX Jung defined complex as a "psychic fragment" that has split from consciousness. Complexes disturb conscious performance, interfering with memory and blocking the flow of associations. They can temporarily obsess consciousness, or influence speech or action in an unconscious way.

CONTAINING This term derives from Melanie Klein's theories of projective identification: a person "contains" a part of another. It is frequently used in the transference situation, where the patient projects parts of him/herself onto the analyst. As well as describing another person "containing" a part of the patient's personality, the term can be extended to a protective institution such as a hospital. The paper in this volume by Bovensiepen. "The Clinic as Container," uses the term in this sense.

INDIVIDUATION Jung uses this term to denote the process by which a person becomes a separate, indivisible unity, a psychological "whole."

In so far as individuality embraces our innermost and incomparable uniqueness, individuation means "becoming one's own self."

INTEGRATION Klein understood the mind as operating in split and unintegrated ways, and the integration of psychic elements was therefore a developmental task. Michael Fordham carries this idea further in his discussion of the primal self of the infant. Fordham, like Jung, sees the self as a totality of conscious and unconscious elements present from birth. He disagrees with Jung, however, that the self should be considered an archtype, since as a totality it already contains all the archtypes of the unconscious and the center of consciousness, the ego. (See Archtype) Fordham sees, for example, the feeding situation as, in a certain sense, a disturbance of the infant's unity through "deintegrative discharges." Once the infant's needs for food, contact, and warmth have been gratified, the process of reintegration resumes; the infant becomes content. Hence integration assumes a process in which parts deintegrate from the self and then reintegrate with it once again. The infant learns that situations of tension can change into gratification and release of tension. Hence deintegration makes possible the "life experiences" that are the basis of maturational processes that are organized in the self.

OBJECT The term was used originally in psychoanalysis to denote the object of an instinctual impulse. It is a person or some other thing that is of interest for the satisfaction of a desire. In the 1930s, object-relations became a major focus of British analysts. Klein modified the concept, considering the object to be a component in the *mental representation* of an instinct. The "part object" is firstly an emotional object, having a function rather than a material existence: for example, the infant is not interested in the breast as an anatomical entity, but in its function: feeding. The "whole object" is a synthesis of the part objects; for example, the mother is the "good" object that satisfies the infant's needs, and also the "bad object" that keeps him waiting. Through the maturational process, these part objects come to be seen as one and the same person, the whole object.

OBJECT RELATIONS SCHOOL The Object Relations School includes a number of different theoretical points of view and generally indicates those British analysts who focus primarily on the state and character of objects. It is to be contrasted with the Classical or Ego-Psychology School, which focuses more on the instinctual impulses that make up the energy of interest. The Object Relations School includes Fairbairn, Winnicott, and Balint particularly, and in general the psychoanalysts of the British Psycho-Analytical Society.

POST-JUNGIAN Andrew Samuels uses the term "post-Jungian" instead of Jungian to indicate both the connectedness and distance from Jung by his followers. Post-Jungian schools represent changes and development in analytical psychology that lay differing emphases on various aspects of Jung's work. Samuels classifies the post-Jungians into three schools: classical, archetypal, and developmental. These are further classified according to three theoretical areas: (1) definition of archetypal, (2) concept of the self, (3) development of personality; and three clinical areas: (1) analysis of transference/countertransference, (2) emphasis on symbolic experience of the self, and (3) examination of highly differentiated imagery.

PRIMAL SCENE Freud used this term to denote the infant or child's experience of the parents in intercourse. Klein's observation of children led her to coin her own term for primal scene: the *combined parent* figure. This figure exists only in the child's imagination. The effects of the fantasy of attacking the mother's body, where the child believes the father (or his penis) constantly resides, are actual in the normal and abnormal development of the child. One of the infant's most profound experiences is the wish to penetrate the mother's body in anger and frustration, partly out of jealousy and partly out of the desire to posses. The fantasy of the combined parent figure is that the parents (or rather their sexual organs) are locked together in permanent intercourse. It is the earliest and most primitive fantasy of the oedipal situation.

REVERIE This term was adopted by Bion to refer to a state of mind that the infant requires of the mother. The mother's mind needs to be in a state of calm receptiveness to take in the infant's own feelings and give them meaning. The mother's reverie is a process of making sense of the infant's fears, a function known as alpha function (See *Alpha function*.) Through introjection of a receptive, understanding mother, the infant can begin to develop his capacity for reflection on his own states of mind.

SELF The self is the central archetype in Jung's thought. The self is a quantity that is supraordinate to the conscious ego. It embraces not only the conscious but the unconscious psyche. Jung did not believe that an individual would ever reach even approximate consciousness of the self, since however much information we may make conscious, there will always exist unconscious material that belongs to the totality of the self. (For an excellent discussion of Jung's concept of the self, see E. F. Edinger, *Ego and Archetype* (New York: Viking/Penguin, 1972) Chapter 1.) The word is used somewhat differently by the post-Jungians. (See *Integration.*)

SELF OBJECT This term is used to denote persons—usually the mother—in a baby's environment who are experienced as if they were parts of it's own self. Because of the initial lack of boundaries of the self, the infant does not differentiate between itself and others; rather its environment is vast and inclusive.

SHADOW Jung uses the archetypal concept of the shadow to denote the sum of all personal and collective psychic elements which, because of their incompatibility with the chosen conscious attitude, are denied expression in life and therefore coalesce into a relatively autonomous "splinter personality." The shadow personifies everything that the subject refuses to acknowledge about himself, and yet is always thrusting itself upon him directly or indirectly.

SPLITTING The concept of "splitting" was taken over by Freud from the older idea of dissociation. The mind was considered to exist in separate parts, explaining the phenomenon of multiple personality. Klein later used the term to describe the way in which objects come to be separated into "good" and "bad" objects (See *Object.*) Klein also described the splitting off of aspects of the self which were feared as bad, usually with the projective invasion of them into an object.

PART I

Individual Adolescent Psychotherapy in Private and Clinical Practice

SECTION 1

A Jungian Approach

Introduction to Section 1:
Jung's Contribution to the Understanding of Adolescence and A Review of the Literature

Gustav Bovensiepen

> *Nothing stirred within his soul but a cold and cruel and loveless lust. His childhood was dead or lost and with it his soul incapable of simple joys, and he was drifting amid life like the barren shell of the moon.*
>
> — James Joyce,
> A Portrait of the Artist as a Young Man[1]

It is only in recent years that the adolescent phase of life has aroused a broad interest among Jungians. Although Jung included in his early writings numerous clinical vignettes from the therapy of adolescents or young adults, his emphasis was on the psychology of the second half of life and on individuation as his key conceptual contribution to the theories of personality development.[2]

Adolescence is often described as a transitional phase from childhood and family life to adulthood and the collective world in terms of ego development and social adaptation. However, the developing and unfolding of the self—what Jung calls individuation—takes place concurrently as an inner process.[3]

In this chapter I will examine some of Jung's writings, especially those from his early and middle periods, because they contain some ideas that help in the understanding and conceptualization of the adolescent individuation process. In our attempt to understand adolescent development and therapeutic approaches to working with adolescents, it is important to distinguish between analytical psychology and psychoanalysis.

Adolescent States of Mind

When approaching adolescents, whether as a psychotherapist, a teacher, a father or mother, we can draw on memories of our own youth as well as our adult experience. Both in everyday life and therapeutic settings, the range of typical states of mind experienced by the adolescent vary in the extreme. The remarks below do not describe psychopathological states of mind, but rather the normal spectrum of adolescent emotional experience. Adolescent moods frequently alternate between high spirits and utter despair; typical is an abrupt change from anxiety and feelings of inadequacy to a form of grandiose certainty of omnipotence. Mindless states are common and lead sometimes to manic behavior that can be interpreted by the parents (who are identified with the adolescents' projected superego) as the adolescent's complete refusal to take responsibility for his actions. At times adolescents suffer also from intense feelings of shame resulting from the fantasized morbidity, ugliness, and insufficiency of their bodies; for the first time they become consciously aware of their own mortality.

Painful pricks of conscience are common when the adolescent simultaneously condemns and idolizes the parents, sustaining the faint hope of being completely understood and accepted by them. In psychodynamic terms, these complex and often confusing states of mind clarify the adolescent's task, which is to separate from mother and father and to leave the infantile relationship behind. In this situation they may feel as if they are "drifting amid life like the barren shell of the moon."

The large majority of adolescents manage to cope with these inner and outer conflicts without any serious signs of mental breakdown. Analytic psychology attributes to the self the forces that hold together the adolescent's inner world, a world threatened by fragmentation.

Whether or not the self will be able to develop with sufficient strength and effectiveness to maintain cohesion depends on a person's early childhood experiences. The adolescent must succeed in maintaining an inner continuity in a phase of life during which many inward and outward changes are taking place.

Thanks to an enormous capacity for acting out, most adolescents manage to cope with these changes. The defensive significance of acting out represents an externalization of an inner conflict and is, therefore, of great importance. Unlike the process of separation in children, adolescents have to separate psychically from infantile parent images and ties that they have, to a large extent, already internalized. It is not unusual for this process of separation to be accompanied by a great upheaval in the ego-self structure, which has already taken considerable shape by the time of adolescence. Acting out is a form of inflation of the ego by collective fantasies.[4] These fantasies are manifest in a personalized form as such archetypes as the powerful hero/heroine, warrior, or victim. If the identification of the ego with these archetypal fantasies is accompanied by feelings of omnipotence and uniqueness, or a sense of unworthiness, the ego is disturbed in its relationship to reality. Most adolescents find these collective fantasies, in their peer groups or in society outside the family, facilitated by the mass media. Adolescents tend to "solve" their inner conflicts by projecting them into the outer world: they identify with these fantasies and often act them out. The adolescent's identification with unconscious collective fantasies disrupts the ego-self relationship, bringing about the archetypal images of death and rebirth, concretely experienced by the adolescent. This disruption can lead to the age-typical increase of psychopathological behavior such as psychosis, drug addiction, severe eating disorders, and suicide attempts.

In contrast to these death (regressive) tendencies, there is an enormous upheaval of libido during adolescence that allows progressive potentialities and "leads the young person into life."[5] This interplay of regressive and progressive energy is, according to Jung, an archetypal activity undertaken in the quest to reach wholeness: it is the dynamic function of the self.[6] Psychically experienced as a rebirth, this process creates images derived from the child archetype.[7] The child as an archetypal image contains the past, the present, and the future potentialities: the unity and the multiplicity.[8]

The Psychology of Adolescence in the Writings of C.G. Jung

In contrast to Freud, who primarily emphasized the psychodynamic parallel between puberty and the oedipal constellation (see "Three Essays on the Theory of Sexuality"), Jung extended this conceptualization of the classic libido theory to include the pre-oedipal aspect of development. In myths and images the youthful ego's battle for a separate identity is symbolized by the "hero's battle." Jung's basic ideas on separation are found in *Symbols of Transformation* (1912); for example, the numerous myths of the "night sea journey" (corresponding to regression into the unconscious) of the sun god/hero (symbolizing the libido of the ego) and his reappearance (representing the expanded, matured ego) are regarded by Jung as archetypal images that represent psychic processes at the collective level.[9] The adolescent externalizes and projects this inner psychic process onto heroes or heroines that popular culture and mass media offer. James Dean was such a hero of the fifties: Madonna is one of the eighties.[10] It seems to be a tendency of the *Zeitgeist* to feature a child or a young person as the hero or heroine in order to transport the artistic message to the collective consciousness.[11]

In Jung's *Collected Works* there are few theoretical comments explicitly concerning adolescent psychology. Jung's first scientific work (1902), was his dissertation entitled *Concerning the Psychology and Pathology of So-Called Occult Phenomena*;[12] it was a case study of a fifteen-year old hysterical girl. In this paper, Jung was interested in the dissociation process as a form of unconscious fragmentation of the personality.

Jung's most important early work, *Symbols of Transformation* is a case study of a young woman, Miss Miller. Here Jung delineates for the first time his conceptualization of the vicissitudes of the libido, which represents a departure from Freud's position on the subject. Jung states that libido is not restricted to sexual instincts; instead he postulates libido as a general psychic energy that is diversely transformed by the symbolic process and becomes manifest in various images. He emphasizes the introverted and extraverted dynamic of the libido, as well as its progression and regression.

In their essentials, these movements of the libido delineate the conflictual dynamics of adolescence. As early as 1910, in his paper "Psychic Conflicts in a Child," Jung compares the movement of libido during the oedipal conflict of four-year-old Anna with the transformation and movement during puberty:

> Here we meet with an important new feature in the little one's life reveries, the first stirrings of poetry, moods of an elegiac strain—all of them things which are usually to be met with only at a later phase of life, at a time when the youth or maiden is preparing to sever the family tie, to step forth into life as an independent person, but is still inwardly held back by aching feelings of homesickness for the warmth of the family hearth. At such a time they begin weaving poetic fancies in order to compensate for what is lacking. To approximate the psychology of a four-year-old to that of the boy or girl approaching puberty may at first sight seem paradoxical; the affinity lies, however, not in the age but in the mechanism. The elegiac reveries express the fact that part of the love which formerly belonged, and should belong, to a real object, is now introverted [in the German edition in italics], that is, it is turned inwards into the subject and there produces an increased fantasy activity."[13]

The "increased fantasy activity" is the introversion of libido which, during early adolescence, can become externally manifested as a puberty depression: the young person withdraws, laments about boredom, loses interest in school performance, takes refuge in daydreams, and becomes passive. The internal conflict arises when the adolescent pulls back his libido from the primal object (the parents) but is still unable to find new objects outside the family that are available for cathexis. Sometimes the adolescent may experience a painful objectless state in which no one can do anything right in response to him.

A large amount of libido is free-floating and oscillates between introversion (fantasies) and extraversion (actions). Adolescents develop different ways of coping with this sometimes painful state. Some manage to integrate their fantasies through, for example, keeping a diary; for others, listening to music seems to have a stimulating effect on their minds and prevents them from falling into a depressive void. Still others develop manic defenses against depression by jumping into numerous extraverted in-group activities. During early adolescence, all of these activities have a primarily hedonistic character.

Using the peer group as a field for experimenting with new object relations is more typical of middle adolescence. In order to allow the peer group to carry this important function, the adolescent has to be more separated from the infantile ties to his parents, and enough extraverted libido must be available to be projected into the group. Jung writes that adolescence (after puberty) becomes more and more a time of extraversion of libido.

In puberty, libido not only oscillates between introversion and extraversion, there is also a regression of libido that is facilitated by the beginning sexual maturation. Jung does acknowledge the enormous effects that the physical changes ushered in by puberty have on the inner world of the child. In fact, he goes so far as to compare the beginning of sexual maturation with the eruption of a catastrophe for the ego when he writes:

> At puberty there is . . . already a certain personality present, which then suddenly is subjected to the shock of sexuality. As a result the conscious position is shaken, at times to a catastrophic degree . . . Something totally new erupts and confronts the Ego which had not suspected its existence."[14]

This comparison seems an appropriate description of the emotional experience of psychotic adolescents, particularly in the beginning of a psychotic breakdown when adolescents experience a "catastrophic change" in their internal (infantile) world.[15] The ego of nonpsychotic children in latency is relatively stable and splitting is rigid. But the eruption of sexual instincts in puberty threatens the cohesion of the ego, because

> there is always the danger of being overwhelmed by an emerging drive to dissolve in multiplicity. The unity of personality is lost. If one is unified, one confronts the other".[16]

As the ego-complex is being weakened by the increasing instinctive needs, the psychic process goes deeper into the personality of the adolescent. Jung refers here to the self ("the unity of personality") as he was to conceptualize it shortly thereafter.

What Jung describes here in abbreviated form is a developmental process similar to the process that Michael Fordham later called the "deintegration of the self." Fordham assumes a primary or original self as existing at the outset of life. The primary self contains all the innate, archetypal potentials that may be given expression by a person throughout life. From the beginning of life the integrated state of the self is changed into states of deintegration by environmental stimuli. The innate, archetypal potentials seek correspondence in the outer world (e.g. the sucking mouth instinctively seeking the nipple). The resultant matching of an active infant's archetypal potential and the mother's responses are then reintegrated to become an internalized object. Deintegration is a state in which the self is open for external or internal experiences; after successful reintegration there is again a state of integration or wholeness of the self. The rhythm of deintegration/reintegration continues throughout life. The sexual maturation in puberty (as do other instinctual needs) triggers the deintegration of the self that initially causes a confusioned state in the adolescent's mind, a state that Jung calls the "inner division with oneself."[17] The deintegration of the self brings the adolescent's ego into relationship with his early (infantile) inner objects. This relationship was described by Jung with the metaphor of incest: in puberty an "incestuous" regression to the infantile mother object occurs. Jung implicitly formulated this idea in *Symbols of Transformation* (1912), sixteen years before M. Klein published her ideas about the "Early Stages of the Oedipus Complex."[18]

For many years psychoanalytic theory stated that during puberty the oedipal conflict is repeated. But this covers only a part of the adolescent psychodynamic. The more important dynamic is the activation of pregenital stages of development in puberty, which evokes infantile anxieties in the adolescent. In *Symbols of Transformation* Jung modifies Freud's understanding of the oedipal complex. He understands regression not only as a defense against genital tendencies, but also as a regression to the pregenital parental imagoes in the unconscious in search of wholeness, the union of opposites, and rebirth. Jung uses incest as a metaphor to symbolize this regressive transformation of libido. Although he emphasized the creative and regenerative nature of regression, he was quite aware of the danger inherent in the regression of libido, as the following quotation illustrates:

> Stripped of its incestuous covering, Nietzsche's "sacrilegious backward grasp" is only a metaphor for the reversion to the original passive state where the libido is arrested in the objects of childhood. This inertia, as La Rochefoucauld says, is also a passion . . . this dangerous passion is what lies hidden beneath the hazardous mask of incest. It confronts us in the guise of the Terrible Mother."[19]

To illustrate his argument, Jung includes a plate showing a shaman's amulet depicting the devouring mother. The incest fantasy is treated by Jung as a special case of regression to a state of merging with the mother of infancy. This regression tendency is unconsciously repeated in puberty, when the accompanying infantile anxieties are mixed up with sexual anxieties and incest fantasies. The pre-oedipal parental images become sexualized. To avoid the emotional experience of this mental state, some adolescents exhibit a strong defense (Jung's "inertia of libido") and fail to separate from their infantile ties. If the unconscious merger wish is too overwhelming, only a constricted ego can be salvaged from adolescence through pathological defenses (e.g. pathological splitting, denial projective identification). The result is symptom formation such as psychoses, eating disorders, borderline structures, and addictions. Adolescents in regression cannot develop a sufficiently stable self-representation for development. The archaic parental imagoes reactivated by puberty, for example, the devouring mother or the penetrating, raping father (as part objects), cannot be integrated into the ego-complex. As a consequence, ego boundaries are not enlarged and the ego remains in fragile infantile dependence.

A Review of the Literature

(The following discussion of psychotherapeutic literature is brief and by no means meant to be inclusive. Some additional authors, beyond those mentioned in the text, are listed in the notes at the end of this paper.)

A review of the literature on analytical psychotherapy for young people might lead one to the conclusion that there is a rich clinical literature in existence. But in contrast to child analysis, there are no clearly demarcated theoretical schools of analysis with adolescents. The writings of Freudians and Kleinians are by far in the majority, while the Jungian literature is skimpy.

The first psychoanalytic treatment report on an adolescent patient was Freud's 1905 study of "Dora."[20] It was during his treatment of Dora that Freud encountered the problem of transference. The early Jungian who developed an interest in working with young people was Alfred Adler. The majority of analysts following Sigmund and Anna Freud were somewhat fearful of treating adolescents because of the moodiness and unstable ego structure during this stage of life. Nevertheless, at the beginning of psychoanalysis there were some pioneers who were interested in working with adolescents, although they tended to follow a more educational approach. Principal among these were Bernfeld, Aichorn, and Zullinger.[21] From the perspective of psychoanalytic ego-psychology, Geleerd, Eissler, Blos, Harley, Fraiberg, and Deutsch have contributed some important ideas about treatment techniques with adolescents.[22] Freudian works on adolescence still tend to exhibit the "educational bias," one which views the "developmental crisis" of adolescence primarily as both an expression of drive conflicts and defense mechanisms of the ego and a recapitulation of the oedipal dynamic. However there are some exceptions among them. The work of D. D. Breckman, Derek Steinberg, Moses Laufer, and Eglé Laufer reflect the influence of the object relations school.[23] Laufer and Laufer work both in private practice and outpatient clinics with severely disturbed suicidal adolescents, using analytic therapy to contain the anxieties of the adolescent crisis. The British psychiatrist, Derek Steinberg, and his coworkers have successfully combined several therapeutic approaches with Freudian analysis in their work with extremely disturbed, hospitalized adolescent patients at the Adolescent Unit of Maudsley Hospital in London.

The London *Journal of Child Psychotherapy* has published some interesting papers by members of both the Kleinian and Freudian schools that focus on object relations and treatment techniques. However from my point of view, Kleinian theory lacks a clear definition of the self. Wilfred Bion's concept of "container-contained" constitutes, in the Kleinian field, the closest approximation to the Jungian concept of the self, whereas the post-Freudian concept of the self is merely an expansion of the view of the earlier ego-psychologists.

Conclusion

From the viewpoint of developmental analytical psychology, a successful separation in adolescence presupposes an emotional and affective revival of the infant's early relationship to the mother, especially to the body of the mother. Adolescence as a phase of the individuation process offers a second chance for integration of those infantile parts (fantasies, emotions, and sensations) that could not be integrated during early development. This integration process cannot be separated from the development of the self. This concept is one of the most important areas of difference between analytical psychology and psychoanalysis. In psychoanalysis the conceptual emphasis is on the ego and its integration, in contrast to analytical psychology, where the emphasis is placed on the self as a totality of the conscious and unconscious personality within which the ego is contained. In Jungian theory, the self maintains the psychic cohesion, which is severely threatened during adolescence. If the course of individuation is successful, the ego becomes differentiated from the self. However the intense psychic upheavals of adolescence activate deintegration of the self and this deintegration becomes manifested in the pubertal turmoil. The deintegration/reintegration of the self during this stage of life facilitates the differentiation of the ego from the self. Analytical psychology defines identity (the main developmental aim in adolescence) as a balanced relationship between ego and self. As Jung discussed in *Symbols of Transformation,* when the self deintegrates, it cannot reintegrate if the rigid defenses of the ego are too strong. In this case, psychic development is inhibited and the result can be disturbances of the neurotic spectrum. If, however, the adolescent ego is too weak, the deintegration of the self can lead to psychotic disturbances resulting from the overwhelming power of unintegrated infantile material and fantasies. As the collection of papers in this volume will demonstrate, Jungian psychotherapy with adolescents focuses more than does Freudian psychoanalysis on transformation and regression of libido to the pre-oedipal level within the frame of deintegration/reintegration processes of the self. Analytical psychology, with its individual as well as collective approach, provides a broader and more inclusive theoretical frame within which to understand and contain severely ill adolescents.[24] The state of mind of these young people often reflects a confusion and destructiveness that is prevalent in the greater social environment that surrounds them, an environment in which we all must struggle—with varying degrees of success—to establish a sense of wholeness and personal identity.[25]

Notes

(The following references to C. G. Jung's work, are, unless otherwise specified, taken from the volumes of *Collected Works* published in London by Routledge and Kegan Paul. Therefore the entries will he shortened to: Jung, title. *CW,* volume, page or paragraph.)

1. J. Joyce, *A Portrait of the Artist as a Young Man* (New York: Penguin Books, 1981) p. 95.

2. A. Samuels, et al, *The Critical Dictionary of Jungian Analysis* (London/New York: Routledge and Kegan Paul, 1986) p. 76.
3. M. Sidoli, *The Unfolding Self,* (Boston: Sigo, 1989)
4. See Jung: "An inflated consciousness is always egocentric and conscious of nothing but its own existence. It is incapable of learning from the past, incapable of understanding contemporary events and incapable of drawing right conclusions about the future. . . . Paradoxically enough, inflation is a regression of consciousness into unconsciousness." (1944) *Psychology and Alchemy, CW* v.12, para. 563.
5. See Jung: "Obviously it is in the youthful period of life that we have the most to gain from a thorough recognition of the instinctual side. A timely recognition of sexuality, for instance, can prevent that neurotic suppression of it which keeps a man unduly withdrawn from life, or else forces him into a wretched and unsuitable way of living with which he is bound to come into conflict. Proper recognition and appreciation of normal instincts leads the young person into life and entangles him with fate . . . " (1928). *The Structure and Dynamic of the Psyche, CW* v.8, para. 113.
6. Jung, *CW* v.5, chaps. 4 and 5.
7. Adolescence is often described in literature as the "second birth." See P. Grotzer, *Die Zweite Geburt. Figuren des Jugentlichen in der Literatur des 20. Jahrhunderts* (Zurich. Ammann Verlag, 1991).
8. Jung, "The Psychology of the Child Archetype," *The Archetypes of the Collective Unconscious, CW* v.9,1 para. 271–280.
9. Jung, *CW,* v.5, chaps. 4 and 5.
10. James Dean was a hero who personified a common adolescent problem, both in his films and in his life. The adolescent's search for identity is often accompanied by attacks on his or her body. See "Suicide and Attacks on the Body as a Containing Object" G. Bovensiepen, in this volume.
11. There is a rich literature on this subject since the beginning of the twentieth century; for example, Alain Fournier's *Les Grand Meaulnes,* Robert Musil's *Die Verwirrung des Zoglings Torless,* Elsa Morante's *L'Isola di Arturo.* The same trend is seen in modern films such as *Dead Poets Society.*
12. Jung, *CW,* v. 1
13. Jung, *CW,* v. 15, para. 13.
14. Jung, *Seminare: Kinderträume* (Seminars: Children's Dreams), (Olten and Freiburg i. B.: Walter Verlag, 1987) p. 223.
15. This term is used by W. R. Bion to describe dramatic transformations in psychotic patients during analysis. See Bion. *Transformations* (London, Heinemann, 1965) pp. 8–11.
16. Jung, *Seminare,* p. 231.
17. Jung: "In psychological language we would say: the problematic state, the inner division with oneself, arises when, side by side with the series of ego-contents, a second series of equal intensity comes into being. This second series, because of its energy value, has a functional significance equal to that of the ego-complex; we might call it another, second ego which can on occasion even wrest the leadership from the first. This produces a division with oneself that betokens a problem." "The Stages of Life," *CW* v. 9, para. 757.

18. M. Klein, "Early Stages of the Oedipus Complex," *Int. J. Psycho-Analysis* 9 (1928): 167–180.

19. Jung, *Symbols of Transformation, CW,* v. 5, para. 253, 254.

20. S. Freud, *Bruckstucke einer Hysterie-Analyse, Gesamte Werke,* v. 5.

21. S. Bernfield, "Uber eine typische Form der maennlichen Pubertät, *Imago* 9 (1923): 169–188; A. Eichorn, Verwahrloste Jugend (1925) (Bern: Huber, 1971); H. Zullinger, *Die Pubertät der Knaben,* (Bern: Hubert, 1969).

22. E.R. Geleerd, "Some Aspects of Psychoanalytic Technique in Adolescence," *Psychoanalytical Studies of the Child* 12 (1957): 263–283; K. R. Eissler, "Bemerkungen zur Technik der Psychoanalytischen Behandlung Pubertierender nebst einigen Uberlegungen zum Problem der Perversion," *Psyche* 20 (1966) 837–872; P. Blos, *The Adolescent Passage,* (New York: International University Press, 1979): S. Fraiberg, "Some Considerations in the Introduction to Therapy in Puberty," *Psychoanalytic Studies of the Child* 10 (1955): 264–286; M. Harley, "On Some Problems of Technique in the Analysis of Early Adolescents," *Psychoanalytic Studies of the Child* 25 (1970): 99–121; H. Deutsch, *Selected Problems of Adolescence* (New York: International University Press, 1968).

23. See for example D. D. Breckman, *Late Adolescence,* Psychoanalytic Studies (New Haven, CT/London: Yale University Press, 1984); M. Laufer and E. Laufer, *Adolescence and Developmental Breakdown* (New Haven, CT: Yale University Press, 1984); Derek Steinberg, *The Adolescent Unit* (New York/London: John Wiley, 1986).

24. See M. H. Stone, "Suicide in Borderline and Other Adolescents," in *Adolescent Psychiatry,* op. cit.

25. Other works of note on adolescent psychology include: E. Erickson, "The Problem of Ego Identity," *Journal of the American Psvchoanalytical Assn.* 4 (1956): 56–121; E. Erickson, "Identity and the Life Cycle," *Psychological Issues,* Mono. 1 (New York: International University Press, 1959); O. F. Kernberg, "Developmental Theory, Structural Organization and Psychoanalytic Technique," in *Rapprochement,* ed. R. Lax et al (New York, Aronson, 1980); S. Levine, "Adolescents Believing and Belonging," in eds. S. Einstein and P. Gioracchini, *Adolescent Psychology* (Chicago: University of Chicago Press, 1979) v.7; E. Kessler "Individual Psychotherapy with Adolescents," in ed. J. Novello, *The Short Course in Adolescent Psychiatry* (New York: Brunner/Mazel, 1979); J. Lampl-de Groot, "On Adolescence: *Psychoanalytical Studies of the Child* 15: 95–103; D. Meltzer, *Sexual States of Mind* (London: Clunie, 1973); M. Klein, "The Technique of Analysis in Puberty," in *The Psycho Analysis of Children* (London: Hogarth, 1932); M. Klein, "Early Stages of the Oedipus Complex," *International Journal of Psycho-Analysis* 9: 167–180; A. Samuels et al, eds. *A Critical Dictionary of Jungian Analysis* (London/New York: Routledge and Kegan Paul, 1986); Gianna Henry, "Difficulties about Thinking and Learning," in *Psychotherapy with Severely Disturbed Children,* ed. Mary Boston (London: Routledge and Kegan Paul, 1983); R. Szur, ed. *Extending Horizons* (London: Karnac, 1991). See papers in Part II: Patients Treated in Adolescence; M. Harris, "Depression and the Depressive Position in an Adolescent Boy," in *Melanie Klein Today,* ed. Elizabeth Bott-Spillius. (London: New Library of Psychoanalysis, 1991)

1

Notes on Technique and the Personality of the Analyst

Gustav Bovensiepen and Mara Sidoli

In the course of our work with adolescent patients over the years we have been struck by the lack of contribution by the Jungian analysts to the literature on the subject. Jungian child analysts have oriented themselves toward infancy and early childhood, and they have almost completely bypassed the area of adolescence. However, we feel that the increasing interest among Jungians in the developmental approach, including infant observation, has placed new emphasis on adolescence as a fundamental developmental phase of life. Dramatic bodily and emotional changes create in adolescence a specific psychological instability that needs to be dealt with by specific treatment techniques that differ from the ones applicable to children and adults. Furthermore it is necessary to develop appropriate techniques for dealing with adolescents who perceive the therapist as a representative of a society against which they are often in rebellion.

The First Encounter

It is rare for adolescents to seek therapy on their own, but when they do, the prognosis is more favorable. This is why adolescent walk-in psychotherapy clinics should be more available. In general adolescents exhibit greater resistance to therapy when they are sent to it. They tend to experience therapy as a punishment or as an abuse of authority on the part of adults, which then immediately sets up conflictual parental transference projection onto the therapist.

Usually from the very first encounter adolescents let one know whether or not they will allow the therapeutic relationship to develop. However there is also an autonomous unconscious immediacy that can be difficult for the therapist to detect because the relationship between the unconscious motivation and the observable behavior does not always fit. The adolescent appears to hesitate, to put on airs and perform a series of tactical maneuvers until the moment when he comes to a decision about the therapist. The internal conflict between ego and superego becomes externalized and projected onto the therapeutic situation. The Austrian psychoanalyst, Ernst Federn, noted that these dynamics are to be attributed to the fast development of the ego in adolescence.[1] In fact it is a part of the ego complex (not the superego) that seeks help and connects with the therapist. Thus, in our view the decisive criterion for assessing whether to get involved therapeutically with an adolescent lies in having succeeded in establishing a good contact with that part of the youngster's ego that is looking for help.

There is another reason why the adolescent quickly decides for or against the therapist: the instability of the self's deintegration-reintegration dynamics in adolescence. Meeting and deeply connecting with a powerful potential "helper" activates earlier infantile object-relation fantasies which, from the very first meeting, are projected onto the helper.

Before reaching a therapist's consulting room, usually adolescents have undergone lengthy assessment procedures by a variety of professionals (such as schools, doctors, and counseling systems). These assessments may hamper the treatment, even making it impossible at times. In the course of the assessment the youngster's striving towards autonomy may not have been taken seriously or sufficiently respected. Hence a part of the adolescent's initial resistance may be created by the system.

When individual psychotherapy is recommended, the analyst should insist that the first consultation take place with the adolescent alone. It should be explained to the parents or the institution by phone that it is advisable for the young person to contact the therapist herself or himself. In principle this arrangement is possible even when the parents are very worried or disturbed. For the adolescent, setting up an appointment by one's self with the therapist is an important step toward autonomy.

(An exception would be the cases of those adolescents who have been committed to a psychiatric institution). Beginning the therapeutic relationship in this way gives the therapist a "down payment" towards trust. The therapeutic frame can then be outlined to the adolescent in the course of the successive sessions. It may also need to be discussed with the parents, the teachers, or the institutions. However all these steps should be brought up at length with the adolescent before hand in order to clarify why it is essential to make the framework of the therapy clear to those responsible for him or her in the external environment.

In spite of all that has been said so far, adolescents do often sit in front of us looking skeptical, or denying altogether that they have any problems. This behavior is an attempt to conceal the severity of their problems and to deny the length of time they have been struggling with them. Often suicidal ideas, severe depressions, or various forms of self-destructive behavior are so concealed that parents or intimate friends have no inkling of them. This can even extend to actual suicide attempts, several of which may have been carried out without the youngster revealing his behavior to anyone. In the course of the diagnostic assessment, one must pay a great deal of attention to the less "clamorous" symptoms. The careful scrutiny of the countertransference body sensations, feelings, and fantasies can lead the therapist to greater insight into the situation. Attention to countertransference reactions will help the therapist to recognize the infantile parts of the patient that have remained unchanged in the course of the developmental process. It is extremely important to take into account one's countertransference responses because parameters such as the developmental level of the patient's ego and the maturity of object relations or capacity to master anxiety will become much easier to assess. When one glimpses primitive pre-oedipal states of mind in the course of an initial diagnostic session, one can only significantly evaluate them through bodily manifestations in the countertransference.

Because of the rapid developments and changes occurring at this age, diagnosis is difficult, especially in the case of severe depressions or psychoses that require an ongoing observational period. From the point of view of diagnosing adult psychopathology, one might define many adolescents as psychotic or as presenting borderline traits. However, one needs to take into account such serious phases of disturbance in adolescence within the context of outer reality and the fluctuating mental organization typical of adolescence. Although these phases should not be overemphasized in themselves, they are often of great importance. Thus it is incorrect to diagnose adolescents according to traditional psychiatric classifications while the patient is still in this transitional phase.

The Psychotherapeutic Frame

As we have described above, the structure of the analytic frame has to be clearly defined from the start. By the frame we mean the number of sessions per week, the time of the sessions, payment, absences and breaks.

The frequency of sessions with adolescents is a controversial question among analysts of different schools. The Kleinians for instance are of the opinion that in general adolescents should be seen in intensive analysis. However, the authors tend to adopt a more flexible approach. In principle, an analytical psychotherapy aiming at reaching into deep regression and working through pre-oedipal material is best achieved with a frequency of two to four sessions per week. If the adolescent feels that the frequent sessions interfere with commitments such as school or sports, one may start with lesser intensity and try to encourage the young person to come more often. At times the adolescent himself may suggest this. On the other hand we know of many successful therapies with adolescents that have been conducted on a once-weekly basis, when the adolescent's ego is relatively stable and shows a certain capacity for introspection and containment. The authors would agree with the Kleinians in the case of more regressed patients, who should be seen four to five times per week until they reach the level of development appropriate to adolescence.

Adolescents tend to attack and mercilessly manipulate the frame. The function of the therapist is to hold, to keep the frame together, and if necessary, to rebuild it. Thus the most important and difficult aspect of the therapeutic work is to make the patient stick to the contract. If the therapist is too accommodating, that is to say unconsciously colludes with the patient, the adolescent may experience the therapist's collusion as a way of breaking the frame. He may feel uncontained and may break off the treatment. The initial phase consists in establishing the therapeutic setting, while the adolescent tests out the therapist's capacity for containment, flexibility, and strength.

Attacks on the Frame

Missed appointments, forgotten sessions, or late attendance are all forms of attack on the frame. Young people can be incredibly creative in these matters. There is always something else going on at the time of the session. Often they fail to understand how the therapist can be so mean as to stick to their fifty minutes, when they have arrived half an hour late; they tend to assume that they are automatically entitled to extra time. Whether they have a date with a boyfriend or girlfriend or have tickets to a pop concert (where they want to go ahead of time), sports practice or an important assignment for school (a particularly powerful tool for putting pressure on the therapist) one should insist that they keep their appointment, or, in cases out of their control, offer them an alternative appointment. However this will not work out unless the "acting out" is promptly confronted within the transference and clearly understood by both patient and analyst. The same confrontation is necessary when the adolescent has missed several sessions in a row without notification. The therapist is expected to sit in the consulting room and wait for the adolescent to turn up. This is an acting out of the infantile wish for dependency, the other side of the coin that we call autonomy.

How is one supposed to deal with the financial loss that results from such behavior? Notwithstanding the fact that the treatment may be paid by insurance or by the parents, we believe that the youngster should take financial responsibility for the lost appointments. We recommend that the adolescent be told this rule at the beginning of the treatment. One should inquire about his weekly allowance and set out an affordable fee for missed sessions. The adolescent will tend to forget the rule agreed to at the beginning, so when he misses the first time, we should remind him of that agreement; this is an appeal to the reality-connected part of the ego. It is of utmost importance that the adolescent settle the financial matter with the therapist and that the parents not be charged for his misbehavior. At the same time it is necessary and more effective to interpret this particular form of acting out within the analytic situation.

The financial burden of such an arrangement is not ideal for the therapist, but we feel that the advantage of keeping the analytical situations as free as possible from any external interference in order to help the young person in his striving towards autonomy outweighs the inconvenience. Of course this sort of financial arrangement is not necessary when the patient is seen in an institutional setting, as is more often the case.

Management Problems

Much of a youngster's behavior, especially what we often designate as "acting out," raises specific management problems that tend to deter therapists from wanting to get involved with adolescent patients. We disagree with Freud's initial understanding of acting out as a substitute for memories related to transference and resistance; we feel that this view cannot explain many forms of acting out typical of adolescents.[2] The authors are in agreement with Bion that acting out is a preferred way to recapitulate totally preverbal experiences and occurrences exceptionally saturated with ambivalence (beta elements).[3] Body experiences or sensory perceptions cannot be "remembered" in so far as they are not yet physically represented. But they can be repeated or re-enacted. The therapist has to know these ambivalent states and be very comfortable in dealing with them, because the defensive testing out and acting out of the adolescent patient can become extreme. The acting out is aimed at "actually" making the therapist behave as a controlling parental authority, reinforcing discipline and hard rules. By using massive projective identification mechanisms, the adolescent pressures the therapist to behave in violent, aggressive, and out-of-control ways.

Another trap often laid out for the therapist is that of the boring, "know-it-all" adult. In this role, the therapist is not to be listened to because he or she is old-fashioned and out of touch with what is going on with young people and cannot possibly understand or be interested in the patient or his problems. In order to counteract this attitude, the therapist needs to be unpredictable and a "step ahead" to avoid the mold of the patient's negative expectations. These expectations conform to the rigidity of the adolescent's parental projections onto the therapist. Once these basic management problems have been successfully dealt with and a positive therapeutic alliance has been established, the therapy can begin to unfold. Compared to adult defenses, it is surprising how in many cases even the most rigid adolescent defenses will give way to a genuine capacity for psychological work. This element makes working with adolescents rewarding.

Sometimes it may be helpful to let the adolescent engage one in general discussions or respond to his curiosity about the therapist's personal life. However these responses should not be given as advice or suggestions but rather aimed at eliciting the adolescent's capacity for self-reflection and insight.

The therapist's capacity to tolerate high levels of anxiety without acting on them is also challenged by the adolescent's self-destructive or delinquent behavior, such as drug taking or promiscuity, as this behavior is aimed at drawing the therapist into action. This can be difficult because by not taking action, it may seem that the therapist is colluding with or not taking seriously potentially dangerous behavior. It makes a difference whether such behavior appears occasionally during therapy or whether it is habitual, underlying fierce anxiety states. These coping mechanisms need to be spotted in the diagnostic phase because their implications may influence the decision whether to recommend therapy or a more educational or behavioral approach. When such undesirable behavior comes up in treatment and the adolescent requests absolute confidentiality, an arrangement can usually be worked out within the containing therapeutic relationship. Whenever possible, it is better not to break the therapeutic frame by calling the parents, teachers, police, or the staff of an institution, even though legal requirements for reporting vary from country to country. Even when the adolescent reports experiences of abuse, the matter of disclosure should be dealt with extreme sensitivity and discretion in relation to the parents or public authorities. This aspect of working with adolescents is extremely taxing because the therapist must be able to be very present, assess the danger, communicate it to the patient, and mobilize the patient's sense of responsibility while containing his or her own anxieties. We find that the ability to contain anxieties, together with a nonpunishing superego structure, are essential if the therapist is to be successful in working with young people. Adolescents are specialists in arousing high levels of anxiety in adults and then feeling persecuted by the "worried adults" who are frantically trying to prevent disasters. The only justification for breaking confidentiality is the recognition of a high suicidal risk. In an inpatient setting, the reasons need to be discussed with the adolescent so that the patient understands the necessity of informing the staff for his or her own safety. The same applies to outpatient therapy when one feels that the suicidal impulses of the patient are getting out of control. Often the problem is not what to do about it, but how to spot the suicidal tendencies early enough to prevent them from being acted out.

Breaks in the Therapy

The treatment of adolescents is often fragmentary, either because help was only accepted to alleviate the immediate psychic distress and receive temporary solace, or because of the quick changes in the cathexis energy of adolescents. This means inner conflicts are externalized by other conflicts, or "solved" by a new object libidinally cathexed. Adolescents tend to externalize the inner situation and project intrapsychic conflicts into the peer group, and as a result, they break off therapy more often than children and adults do. Sometimes they write to the therapist after discontinuing treatment. The therapist can decide to maintain contact by replying, thus leaving the way open for therapy to be resumed at a later date. If therapy was begun through latency and is carried out into early puberty, the youngster is more likely to return to therapy in late adolescence. By that stage it may be easier for the adolescent's stronger ego to work through infantile conflicts.

Ending the Therapy

As in the beginning of therapy, the ending, too, has some characteristics peculiar to adolescence. Often the youngster will stop very suddenly, leaving no time at all for working through the separation. This often resembles a turbulent separation from the actual parents, so the therapist may never know the outcome of his work. It is particularly distressing when work is broken off just at the stage when the analysis has finally begun, and the adolescent has started to open up and reveal some of his or her anxiously guarded transference fantasies. Unlike psychotherapy with children, where the child returns from the session to the heart of the family, work with adolescents aims at sending them out into the wider world, even when they are still living at home. This may tempt the therapist to make false claims about the therapy, for instance describing it as the last chance for the youngster to reach real change. These claims may be misleading and may cause the therapist serious narcissistic disappointment.

Management of the Therapist's Relation to the Parents

Even though the central developmental task of adolescence is to separate from the inner parents as a preparation for separation from the actual ones, we should not forget that most adolescents live at home and depend on their parents, at the very least financially. This means that one cannot ignore the influence of the real parents, even though we prefer the adolescent's therapy to bypass them when counseling sessions with the parents are not necessary. As previously stated, this aspect of the therapeutic frame needs to be clarified both with the youngster and his parents at the start of treatment. Yet the worries of parents whose children are having difficulties are legitimate and cannot be ignored. Thus, a talk with the parents, perhaps in the presence of the young person, may be helpful to support the therapy.

If the parents telephone about a particular worry, it is important to talk about it with the adolescent and find a way, if possible, to resolve the problem without calling the parents into the actual session. There are some young people who want you to speak with the parents. These wishes may represent disguised attempts to turn the therapist into an ally in such superficial endeavors as a raise in allowance or a later curfew, but they may also represent a way of holding onto the infantile dependence and a transference resistance. In the diagnostic phase, after the first meeting with the adolescent, it is advisable to see him with his parents. Such a meeting may be extremely difficult at later stages in the course of therapy. Even for experienced therapists it may be difficult for the therapist to separate the transference to the patient from the transference to his parents. In such cases it would be easier to have another therapist work with the whole family, even if this solution should prove less optimal for individual therapy. In the case of inpatients and day hospital therapy, other arrangements can be made. With severely disturbed patients, in addition to the individual sessions, regular family sessions led by two therapists should take place: The individual therapist acts as a passive agent who will represent the adolescent, and a colleague leads the family session. Working in this way requires a high level of confidence in team work. What applies to parents also applies to other adults in the psychological environment of the adolescent. Only if the youngster can trust the safety and protection of the analytic frame can the analytic therapy take place.

A Personal Approach Is Needed

What motivates one to work with adolescents and what personal attitude is required to treat adolescents? In general, one could say that the prerequisites necessary for working with adolescents are firmness, authenticity, readiness for confrontation, flexibility and consistent analytic attitude. We recommend that before working with adolescents, a training candidate be experienced in working with children and adults.

In the course of the therapy, the adolescent inside the therapist comes into direct confrontation with the young patient. Thus some unresolved issues for the therapist may need to be worked out in his or her own analysis. Frequently this cannot take place because, as the Dutch psychoanalyst, Lampl-de Groot pointed out, the adolescent stage is not always sufficiently worked through in adult analysis.[4] The pre-oedipal material that emerges in these adolescent stages is more difficult to contain than early childhood material within a similar frame of transference dependency. The adolescent in the adult, as the adolescent in flesh and blood, is vehemently opposed to dependency because of the need for autonomy typical of this developmental stage.

In the psychoanalytic community one can find two conflicting tendencies that then tend to become narrow ideologies. One supports the value of dependency in the analytic relationship, the other supports the individuation process as leading towards autonomy. Thus the adolescent conflict constellates one of the major collective conflicts of analysis and analytic training. Psychoanalysis today has become institutionalized, and risks losing its initial creative and subversive power. Metaphorically speaking, it would be auspicious for psychoanalytic schools in general to recover some of their adolescent vigor; that is to say, the potential for creativity, curiosity, vision, and intolerance of prejudice and dogma.

Notes

1. Ernst Federn, "Anteil der Ich-Storing in der Pubertatskrise," in *Adoleszenz: Biologische, Sozialpadagogische und Jugentpsychiatrische Aspekte,* ed. R. Lempp (Bern: Huber, 1981) pp. 77–83.
2. S. Freud, *Remembering, Repeating and Working Through.* Standard edition. v.10.
3. W. R. Bion, *Learning from Experience* (London: Heinemann, 1962) Maresfield Reprints, London, 1984, p. 6
4. J. Lampl-de Groot, "Zur Adoleszenz," *Psyche* 19: 477–485.

2

Experience of Time and Death Fantasies in Adolescence

Mara Sidoli and Gustav Bovensiepen

Desire itself is movement
Not in itself desirable;
Love is itself unmoving,
Only the cause and end of movement,
Timeless, and undesiring
Except in the aspect of time
Caught in the form of limitation
Between un-being and being.
—T.S. Eliot,
Burnt Norton

The purpose of this chapter is to explore the specific experiences of time in adolescence, which often conflict with the adult understanding of time. For instance, in working with adolescent patients one important aspect focuses on their interminable negotiations about time. It starts with the negotiation of the first appointment and carries on until the end of the treatment: the time is never right. It is always too soon or too late, too short or too long. Unpredictability is the name of the game. It takes patience and a great deal of flexibility on the part of the therapist to work out a time structure to which the adolescent patients can agree. And then as soon as an agreement is reached, the adolescent breaks it or candidly "forgets" about it. Something else crops up at the time of the appointment that absolutely must be attended to there and then. More appointments are missed than attended. When patients do turn up on the right day, it is often at the wrong time and they are surprised and frustrated if the therapist cannot see them. When they arrive late they tend to linger on at the end of the session, trying to stretch the time beyond the hour, and feel rejected and resentful about having to leave.

As J.A. Arlow, the American psychoanalyst, puts it,

> Time thus becomes the representative of realistic necessity and the thwarter of infantile omnipotence. Subsequently, the inevitable frustrations experienced at all levels of development intensify the connection between time and reality. Accordingly, the roots of rebellion against the tyranny of time go back far into the individual's early development.[1]

Sometimes an adolescent turns up at the door of the consulting room with some dramatic issue that he feels cannot wait: it is a matter of life or death, it must be dealt with just at that specific moment or it will be too late. At other times the adolescent falls through time into a timeless state and then no urgency is experienced "time can wait," "time can be wasted." The adolescent seems to be lingering, floating, endlessly absorbed in fantasy and day dreaming.

Hence working with adolescents, whether as teachers or therapists, we cannot avoid becoming aware that, more than any other age group, adolescents live between the intrapsychic subjective sense of time and objective time. Time can be lengthened or made to pass quickly, compressed or extended beyond the boundaries of reality and, as George,[2] a sixteen-year-old very graphically put it,

> With most of my time games I can make it pass, stay, slow down and mean as much as I make it. But mostly I can make it go quickly. By seeing myself in the future, it makes the getting there not so real, and it makes the present less purposeful and changing by looking at the past. Only after the milestone has been reached can I look back and actually *feel* what happened to me.

This boy appears to have been in an omnipotent state where he needed to control time because he felt it slipping away. A year later, during a break from therapy this boy wrote,

I have done nothing since July . . . I have not lifted a finger and feel things slipping away. Also the day is so unstructured, things crop up and I am never able to get down to things, except to what my father would call a waste of time. I keep putting things off, like this letter . . .

Poetry lends itself to the expression of similar states of mind, as in T. S. Eliot's following verse:

Time present and time past
Are both perhaps present in time future
If all time is eternally present
All time is unredeemable.[3]

For several months before coming to me, George had been playing unconscious suicidal games such as getting drunk and riding on his bicycle late at night, or running drunk into the middle of a busy road with some peers, twice being just missed by cars. He felt that his actions did not really matter, since nobody cared about him anyway. His parents were very busy and successful professional people. George had a brother three years older, but in George's mind he was too good to care about him. Being the younger was intolerable because it meant feeling unimportant, uninteresting, and unattractive—an unwanted stupid "baby." When he felt like this, he wanted to die. However it took a long time in the sessions for him to become aware of these feelings. Initially he projected them onto a girlfriend who used to get drunk with him, and who actually had attempted suicide. This event, which had scared and concerned him, was the motivating factor that led him into therapy. We spent many sessions in which he described to me his girlfriend's extreme feelings of emptiness, despair, and bleakness. Nobody cared for her at home, nobody knew her; she felt lonely, confused, hopeless about the situation ever changing. This was the tone of a note she had written to him the night she had attempted suicide. In Jungian terms, we could say that his destructive baby feelings were projected onto the girl, his anima, which in the boy's unconscious was merged with his shadow; and this involvement had prevented him from consciously attempting suicide so far.

Whereas George was confused about time, another sixteen-year-old boy, Peter, was preoccupied mostly with time and death. He came to therapy in a suicidal state. He had attacked and destroyed his capacity to think. Like George, he was the son of intellectuals and the younger in the family. He had a sister four years older who was academically gifted and of whom he was very jealous. He acted out his unconscious suicidal wishes by participating in subversive political activities, demonstrating and throwing molotov bombs at the people or groups he considered the "Establishment."

Peter spent many sessions arguing about death and time. He said that he was fatalistic, and tried to convince me that time did not really exist in itself. It only existed in relation to actions. So if one did not act, time would not exist.

Thus whenever he felt overwhelmed by fear of death he would shift into "no-action," that is to say, he would retreat to bed and lie there in total inactivity for days on end. In this way he felt that he was safe; and by obliterating time, he was also denying death, withdrawing into a mindless state. Obliterating time was his attempt to rebel against death. According to Arlow,

> The most significant rebellion against time is the one that man is always fated to lose, and that is the struggle against death. Death is the epitome of narcissistic mollification. For each individual, death is the end of his time, the moment of death the extinction of the self, the final experience of self-awareness.[4]

Development of the Sense of Time

Time is experienced in one's life, from infancy onwards, as an inborn sense of the biorhythms of the body. The British analytical psychologist Lola Paulsen writes:

> In the earlier of these stages, the baby over and over again experienced the cycles of needs and satisfactions, of frustrations and fulfillments, of discomforts or comforts. Time sequences are inevitably associated, for the baby, with the tensions inherent in these experiences. His growing sense of time comes partly from the mother and partly from his physical experiences and his emotional responses. It is as though time becomes, for him, tangible in his body.[5]

Here, in our view, the concept of primal self and deintegrative processes is of utmost relevance. If we assume that instinctual drives (the instinctual pole of the archetype) are mobilized from the very beginning of life for the purpose of survival, we could define the infant's earliest experience of time (and space) as clustering around integrated and deintegrated states. In integrated states one might assume a state of infinity of being in "the present," like an out-of-time state or a pre-time state where before, after, and next have no reason to exist. By contrast, if we hypothesize deintegration as a moving outwards, an opening up in order to reach out, we have to assume that the deintegrative movement carries within itself the potential for time and space experiences (limitedness). One might say paradoxically that due to a state of expectation (having to wait), concepts of present, past, and future begin to develop because the drive to meet satisfaction breaks down the out-of-space-and-time state of the self (uroboric state), whereas the state of limitedness leads to anticipation of drive satisfaction (psychosomatically based). Limitedness leads also to the experience of unpleasure and thus creates time. As the German poet Novalis puts it, "time comes into being with unpleasure" ("Die Zeit entsteht mit der Unlust"). The whole process is archetypally determined, and belongs to the dynamism of the primal self. In our view it is at this point that an experience of time begins as one expression of ego-structuring in a broad sense. However, the anticipation has at first to rely automatically on some sort of archetypally determined sense of trust (the certainty of finding an object) that makes the deintegration possible. The infant's rudimentary ego cannot yet know what will actually happen. For instance, if we hypothesize infantile autism as a disorder of the self, we may say that in such infants the trust that makes deintegration possible is absent or dysfunctional.

It is at this point, when the meeting with the object does or does not occur at the needed time, that satisfaction or frustration color the infant's experience of time. Then pleasure and pain begin to inhabit the infant's sense of time. Between these two states, and indeed in both of them, we believe that the infant experiences a state of infinity as we have described above, from which, we may assume, the concept of eternity develops in later life. For instance, it is as if the primal inertia of the self (the state of integration, the infinite), disturbed by the motion triggered by the drives, were being seduced into space and time and must let itself be transformed by the (maternal) object into temporal experiences. We imagine that adult fantasies of eternal pain in hell or bliss in heaven come from these very specific experiences within the primal self that are not interspersed by and punctuated with maternal interventions.

These interventions and their timing contribute to the creation of a sense of rhythm within cycles and of harmony or disharmony that we define as "being in tune" with someone else or with the world in general. Given this hypothesis, it follows that the "timing" of the interventions is just as important as the intervention itself. The case that follows illustrates very clearly the problems originating from the lack of rhythm in the mother-infant dyad, the infant falling into a "no-time" state.

Case Study

Carla was a seventeen-year-old girl who lived under a constant threat of disintegration. She lived in an altered rhythm of deintegration and reintegration which she constantly seemed to lose. She had not yet reached the state of typical adolescent conflict between a wish for timelessness and unlimitedness, and the necessity to experience time as limiting and structuring. She could not wait a single moment to satisfy her instinctual needs; nor could she trust, in moments of satisfaction, that she would be able to contain and internalize the pleasurable experience. Therefore she was unable to establish a relationship between past and present. Her manipulations and interests focused completely on the future, on trying to control anticipated time, because she equated it with death through illness and physical deterioration. Carla refused time altogether, so to speak, because she felt she was not allowed to have endless time. In the endeavour not to remain stuck in a timeless, uroboric self (an integrated state of the self) and because she felt persecuted by its demands, she tried to annihilate time. Time took everything away; in time she had nothing. To have time meant that she could be thrown into a void and seized by panic. She was in a state of permanent manic action. She busied herself with a thousand things and people; she meddled with everyone and everything and took no care of herself. In the sessions she talked nonstop. In order to be able to put in a word, I had to interrupt her abruptly. I did not have, nor could I develop, a feeling for the timing of my interventions. I often felt I intervened arbitrarily and did not feel that a smooth rhythm of distance and closeness or of give-and-take could come about between us. Our connection could not develop and acquire any degree of continuity. She experienced my interventions as manipulative because she was trying to manipulate me. She was using talk to manipulate me and others, like a toddler does with his body products.[6]

Carla demanded from me constant reassurance that she would not suffer from cancer, that her innumerable hypochondriacal anxieties would not actually happen. She wanted me to tell her there and then what she should do about these fears. At the same time she complained that she could not remember a few minutes later what I had told her. "All is gone lost," "I don't know," "I don't care" were her pet phrases. At night she would sit for hours in her room and write detailed reports about what had happened to her during the day or what people had said to her. And she would be seized by panic if she thought that she could not remember the conversations word for word. She held on to each word as if it were an anchor that she felt was constantly slipping out of her hands. She would write hundreds of pages, and she treated me as a diary in which she told everything in full. In me and in her diary, which she used as a container, she seemed to need to evacuate her uncontainable and nameless "parts" (beta elements) that her disturbed mother had not been able to help her with in her infancy and childhood. It is as if in her infancy she had experienced mother as nonempathic: cold and hard, made of stone.

Each session began as if it were the first. For a long time I had the feeling that Carla did not internalize any of her experiences with me in the session or that she reintegrated. In the course of the therapy it became clear to me that Carla's problem manifested itself as an insufficient internal separation from her mother, and that this relationship was caused among other things by a deeper disturbance of the "Mother Time."

Shortly after Carla's birth her mother had suffered a serious depression which was diagnosed as manic-depressive and had required a long stay in a psychiatric hospital. During Carla's early infancy and childhood her mother was again often hospitalized. During this time Carla had developed a close relationship with her father, who had taken care of her as well as he could given the fact that he had a full time job. When she was nine years old her younger brother was born, and Carla had to take care of him because her mother was frequently unfit. At the time that she came to me for treatment, her relationship with her father was much too affectionate. She fought to have her father all to herself and she managed to go on holidays alone with him to the seaside. They slept in the same room, and later she told me how happy she was when they had walked on the beach and had drawn a big heart in the sand. The parents had not had sexual contact for a long time. They reported to me that they had had intercourse only when they had conceived the children, but they enjoyed eating out together. Carla and her mother often had very bad arguments and her father was always busy mediating between them. Carla hated her father when he went on and on about her mother, and she maliciously "diagnosed" that I went on and on just like that too.

According to the American psychoanalyst, C.A. Colarusso, the development and differentiation of the ego in the first months of life allows the infant

> to become aware of his mother's relationship to his experiences of frustration and gratification. According to Erikson (1956) her failure to relieve frustration quickly leads to moments of impotent rage and an obliteration of time sense, while the perception of each approaching satisfaction from her gives time in infancy a highly condensed quality of intense hope and feared disappointment which contributes temporal elements to the formation of basic trust . . . *mother becomes the conveyer of time and timelessness* . . . Through her power to relieve hunger and painful time, she is the giver and controller of time sense; *she becomes Mother Time.*[7]

In Carla's case her development of the sense of time was severely distorted by her mother's illness. Carla's "Mother Time" had been influenced by two factors: the manic-depressive illness of her mother and the amount of time she had to spend on her own. Her mother's manic-depressive illness was characterized by repetitive cycles of extreme depression, lethargy, and longing for death, alternating with phases of manic activity, irritability, and aggressive arbitrariness. This situation had constituted the unpredictable daily experience of baby Carla. She had to adapt to her mother's rhythms because her mother was unable to respond and tune in to the baby's needs, which she found alien and irritating. Therefore Carla treated me in the transference as an object that might suddenly disappear, as somebody seen and met for the first time who will no longer be there tomorrow, an object that could also be angrily attacked and fought against. She would try to repeat with me in the transference the bad arguments that she usually had with her mother. She often managed to make me very angry, to want to grab hold of her to shut her up, or to kick her out—as she frequently invited me to do. Carla used to tell me in the cool style of a social worker's report about numerous situations in which she and her mother had had physical fights, had screamed and thrown things at each other, and then had come together in a tearful heartbreaking reconciliation.

One day she brought several files full of letters and messages that she and her mother had exchanged; there had been times when the two of them had communicated several times a day only through written messages. These were always assertions that they still loved each other, and reassurances from Carla that she would be a "good girl." These written communications had started before Carla could read or write, so they had sent drawings to each other. Carla's drawing confirmed that her mother used to lock herself up in a room, often for many hours, and that she often slept until the afternoon so that Carla was left in the apartment by herself.

The fact that she had spent so much time by herself was the second factor that, had shaped Carla's "Mother Time." Not only was she left alone, she had also to be very quiet for fear of waking her mother, who would then go into a frenzy. Carla was sometimes made to sleep in the parental bed with her mother while her father slept on the couch in the sitting room. Her mother would lock the bedroom door because she did not want to be disturbed. When Carla would wake up. she could not get out. Her subjective experience was of lying down for long stretches in bed unable to move for fear her mother would hit her. The same anxiety would overcome her when going to bed in her own room, where she felt persecuted by confused shapes and would begin to panic. So she began to read or write in her diary for hours, and in this way lost all sense of time. In order not to feel overwhelmed by the absense of the mother's concerned attention (the "maternal reverie") she had had to split off her destructive impulses and fantasies about her mother, which then, as untransformed beta elements, persecuted her as the "confused shapes" on the wall. In the transference/ countertransference, Carla's reports of these experiences had a dream-like quality to them.

At other times, when she felt overwhelmed by unbearable affects in relation to the mother/therapist, she had to split off and displace them onto other staff members, particularly onto a male colleague of mine on whom she had a "crush." I think it is important to mention here that before I started treating her, Carla had started therapy with a female colleague in the day unit who, after about two months, had to be hospitalized for a physical illness and was away for several months. This unfortunate event was an uncanny repetition of Carla's infancy when her mother had been hospitalized shortly after giving birth, and it reinforced her omnipotent infantile fantasy about her destructiveness. Her fear of abandonment was reflected in the mother transference with me: she constantly had to attack and reject me to test out my resilience.

In order to defend herself from becoming aware of her destructiveness, she took refuge in timelessness. Such timelessness seems to me to be a typical manifestation of a strong defense system in adolescence, like timelessness in defense of the self in the psychotic transference, as described by Michael Fordham.[8]

Discussion

In this chapter we have explored conflicts about the experience of time when working with adolescent patients. We need to keep two main factors in mind, one related to the primal self dynamism and the deintegration-reintegration rhythms of the self, and the other related to treatment techniques. The development of a time sense (subjective as well as objective) is considered to be a lifelong process in the course of individuation. There are characteristic differences in infancy, childhood, and adolescence.[9] In treating disturbed adolescents, the use of time and the intrapsychic experience of time lead us directly to the body-based experience of the adolescent's infancy.

The adolescent's state of timelessness, the clinging to the belief that one need not submit to time, that one can be independent from it, serves the need for autonomy and the omnipotent denial of death. On the whole, this attitude is part of normal development in adolescence. However, in disturbed youths it can become a fitting defense against any further development, as in the cases described above. Each of the adolescent patients exhibited a way of dealing with time: George became confused in time, Peter tried to annihilate time, and Carla would get lost in time.

Thus one could say that the process of acquiring a personal, realistic sense of one's own time may be experienced by some adolescents as being trapped in a space between being and nonbeing; that is to say, in a twilight area between life and death.

We view the interminable negotiations about session times, the attacks on the analyst, and the attempts at manipulating the analytic frames as testing-out behaviors. These attempts on the part of the adolescent aim at assessing the analyst's capacity to function as a containing, flexible "good enough object," and his or her reliability and ability to empathize. For the adolescent, the analyst can only become a good containing object when he or she is able to meet the young patient's rhythm of deintegration and reintegration.

Notes

1. J. A. Arlow. "Psychoanalysis and Time." *Journal of the American Psychoanalytical Association* 34:522.
2. The boy discussed in this paper was treated by Mara Sidoli; the girl by Gustav Bovensiepen.
3. T. S. Eliot, *Burnt Norton, Four Quartets* (Orlando, FL: Harcourt Brace Jovanovich, 1971) p. 13.
4. J. A. Arlow, p. 525.
5. L. Paulsen, "The Unimaginable Touch of Time," in *Analytical Psychology: A Modern Science* (London: Heinemann, 1973) p. 191.
6. The toddler "identifies with the mother and through increased activity gradually assumes her powers, the child recognizes that time can be used to manipulate the environment." C. A. Colarusso, "The Development of Time Sense from Birth to Object Constancy," *International Journal of Psycho-Analysis* 60:247.
7. Ibid., p. 246. See also E. H. Erickson, The Problem of Ego-Identity," *Journal of American Psychoanalytical Association* 4 (1957):56–121.
8. M. Fordham, "Defences of the Self," *Explorations of the Self* (London: Academic Press, 1985).
9. C. A. Colarusso, "The Development of Time Sense in Adolescence," *Psychoanalytic Studies of the Child* 43 (1988):179–97.

SECTION 2

Incest Fantasies
and Separation

Introduction to Section 2

In *Symbols of Transformation* Jung described incest fantasies as a special form of regression of libido to pre-oedipal objects. Unlike Freud, he did not understand incest impulses from a literal perspective but rather as a metaphor for a way of psychological growth and a search for wholeness, the union of opposites, and rebirth. When Jung wrote that the "incest taboo makes the creative fantasy inventive," he stressed that the prohibition prevents literal, physical expression, but that the sexual element in the incestuous fantasies of a child deepens the child's emotional and symbolic relationship to the parents. Jung viewed the problem from the perspective of a man and focused on the son's entanglement with and regression to the mother. But his model could be applied as well to the relationship of a daughter to her father. The case of Martina in Bovensiepen's chapter, "Incest Fantasies as a Defense Against the Analysis of Pre-Oedipal Object Relations," illustrates some psychopathological aspects of the incestuous elements in the daughter-father relationship.

The Freudian approach stresses the repetition and final consolidation of oedipal conflict during puberty. From the Jungian point of view this approach has to be revised by work done by Mara Sidoli in her chapter, "Oedipus as a Pre-Oedipal Hero." Starting from Jung's remarks about the archetypal hero motif in "The Psychology of the Child Archetype"[1] Sidoli links hero-like behavior in the service of psychic survival to early disturbances of the mother-infant relationship. When the fit between mother and infant does not occur and the maternal "reverie"[2] doesn't develop, feelings of abandonment, danger, and persecution are likely to be experienced by the infant to varying degrees. The infant may feel he is being surrendered to the various part-object monsters. Then the child has to protect himself, and the hero quality arises "from the infant's need to deal with his larger-than-life enemies." Referring to Melanie Klein's ideas about the oedipal situation in infancy, Sidoli links her observation about some infants' heroic behavior to the early separation-individuation process. She writes: "But what is to be endured by the infant is the awareness of being separate from the love object." This first step in the lifelong separation-individuation process continues into the oedipal situation, and these very early experiences color the separation experiences during adolescence.

Sidoli treats the Oedipus myth as a case history in which the adolescent young man Oedipus leaves his "good" adoptive parents in order to find his own identity. She shows that Oedipus psychologically was a child whose childhood wasn't contained within a nurturing and protecting relationship to his parents. As an abandoned and exiled child he had to develop heroic qualities to survive. In some respects Sidoli understands Oedipus as the typical adolescent runaway, trying to cope with the vicissitudes of life. Distressed adolescents often end up pregnant or in some form of pathological regression such as using drugs. By acting out his unconscious incestuous search for the "real" mother (the "good" internal mother unlike the "bad" abandoning mother) Oedipus fails to separate.

Sidoli gives us a very convincing presentation on the importance of linking the early infant-mother experience to incestuous fantasies and incestuous situations in adolescence. Recognition of this connection is important to understand adolescent psychopathology and developmental breakdowns. The revival of these early emotional experiences often is not bearable for the adolescents and they use strong defenses to avoid these painful states of mind. Some adolescents act out pseudo-oedipal fantasies as a defense against having to work through the pre-oedipal material.

This is illustrated by two cases in Gustav Bovensiepen's chapter. The first case is a less disturbed boy called Peter, who suffered from neurotic separation anxieties and some obsessional symptoms. Although his infantile experience with his mother was not too bad, she treated him as a self object,[3] and he became dominated by an inner mother of very intrusive quality. Reaching puberty, this very mother-bound boy couldn't separate. He experienced her in therapy by splitting the mother image into a threatening monster, "Wasp Woman," on the one hand, and into a seductive and sexy "Wonder Girl," like in the comics, on the other hand. The pseudo-oedipal incestuous fantasy about the "Wonder Girl" could be understood as a defensive fantasy against the pre-oedipal part object monster, the "Wasp Woman," who represented the intrusive, dangerous part of Peter's inner infantile mother.

Whereas Peter used pre-oedipal fantasies as a defense against pubertal separation anxieties and the anxiety of becoming a man, more severely disturbed adolescents defend against further development by perverse sexualization of early objects. An obsessive clinging to the sexual elements of their incestuous fantasies, which are confused with split off part objects, can be observed especially in adolescents with psychoses or borderline functioning.

The second case in the chapter concerns the seventeen-year-old Martina, who had a severe borderline structure with anorexic and bulimic behavior. In a positive father transference she replaced her longing for the "good" mother of infancy she never had, by a violent erotization and sexualization of her relationship to her father, her elder brother, and the therapist. Thus she could defend against the despair and emotional abandonment of the baby part in herself.

Notes

1. C. G. Jung, "The Psychology of the Child Archetype," *Collected Works*, (London: Routledge and Kegan Paul, 1959).
2. See Glossary.
3. See Glossary.

3

Oedipus as a Pre-Oedipal Hero

Mara Sidoli

Introduction

Some archetypal motifs that surface in the course of treatment of adolescents can be linked with Jung's view of the child archetype. At issue is the process of separation and individuation in early adolescence. Jung's writings about the child and the hero archetypes provide a basis for my own writings about early infantile states in which I explore the idea that heroic behaviour in adolescence and later life results from early disturbances in the mother-infant bond. In addition, Michael Fordham's views of early infancy, influenced by Melanie Klein, form part of the theoretical foundation for my views.[1] Outside the Jungian field, I refer to W.R. Bion's views on resilience in infancy, which he postulated as the infant's capacity to tolerate frustration and to hold thoughts in the absence of the mother, to his concept of "maternal reverie," and of the container and the contained.[2] These theories and the case study presented illustrate the connection between the early stages of life, the pre-oedipal stage of the Oedipus complex, and their connections to the Oedipus myth.

Because of the relevance that later oedipal fantasies and anxieties about regression and incest have in personal development and in the individuation-separation process during adolescence, it is essential to connect the infantile roots with the oedipal development proper. Two aspects are fundamental for a healthy resolution of the Oedipus conflict. The first is to have reached a satisfactory attachment and loving bond with the feeding mother of early infancy because of the implications that this bond has for later relationships. The second is derived from the first because the genital upsurge at adolescence reproposes issues of attachment to the parents of the same and the opposite sex in the light of the child's newly acquired sexual development. Incest fantasies, anxieties, and in extreme cases, incestuous acting out are issues that need to be dealt with to progress in life.

We live in a world where sexual abuse and other forms of acting out between adults and children are painfully brought to our professional attention. These cases are actual incests, often perpetrated in a violent way by disturbed parents in intoxicated states; their destructive effect is long standing. After any physical injuries heal, the psychological damage remains as a permanent scar. A more common, subtle, and invisible form of incest is the psychological one that creates a psychological dependency between the child and the parent.

Jung wrote about this dependency in *Symbols of Transformation* where he describes the regression of the libido in adolescence using the metaphor of incest. This is an apt metaphor because incest prevents psychological differentiation and keeps the young person bound to the parents, thereby preventing individuation. This phenomenon is supported by collective cultural patterns. In certain cultures, dependency beyond adolescence is encouraged and supported by the strength of family systems that are threatened by the individuation-separation process. The family sets out to prevent separation at all costs and experiences it as a betrayal. These collective unconscious incestuous patterns operate in deep ways and are connected to the survival of the species, but they are also deadly for the individual because they oppose individuation.

Infantile Impotence as Related to Heroic Fantasies

In "The Psychology of the Child Archetype" Jung writes that sometimes the "child" looks more like a child god, sometimes like a young hero. Common to both types is the "miraculous birth and the adversities of early childhood abandonment and danger through persecution."[3] He continues, "the motif of 'smaller than small yet bigger than big' complements the impotence of the child by means of its equally miraculous deeds. This paradox is the essence of the hero".[4] If this proposition is applied to the actual child and, in particular, to the infant and its beginning, the last sentence contains the essence of the early infantile situation where impotence is maximal in the face of extreme instinctual needs. In such a state, every achievement must feel like a miraculous deed to the infant.

The empathic tuning in on the part of the mother and her "maternal care" usually alleviates the infant's sense of impotence by meeting his/her needs. This may be experienced by an infant as magical or "miraculous," to use Jung's expression. However, when this "magical fit" does not occur, feelings of abandonment, danger, and persecution are likely to be experienced by the infant in various degrees according to the age and length of the frustration endured.[5]

The "Maternal Reverie"

Infants are endowed at birth with varying individual capacities to tolerate frustration. The optimal level of bearable frustration varies for each infant at each developmental step. What is intolerable is evacuated by the infant and requires the mother to intervene, modulate the excessive edge of the experience, and make digestible what is essential for the baby's well being. In Jungian terms, we would say that the mother in flesh and blood transforms the archetypal experiences of the infant and reduces them to human digestible ones. The primitive archetypal unconscious needs, fears, anxieties, and panic states which the baby is unable to process on his own are disposed of and projected into the mother by psychological mechanisms, called by Klein "projective identification."

The British psychoanalyst, W. R. Bion, defines this maternal function as "reverie." The mother digests the baby's projective identifications, transforming them into meaningful, human communications that form the basis for relationships. The healthy infant is genetically predisposed to make use of and integrate the emotional material made digestible by the "maternal reverie." This capacity is linked to the baby's vitality. It is greater in those babies in whom the life instinct prevails, and is at the basis of human communications. These states correspond to what Jung defined as states of "participation mystique": primitive undifferentiated states between self and other.

The Emergence of the Hero

By definition, the hero is someone who has to accomplish superhuman tasks on his or her own. It is impossible to imagine that an infant could survive without a caregiver. However, even if an infant is attended to by a caregiver/mother who is not attuned to his needs, the infant is likely to experience extreme helplessness and isolation.

When the mother cannot perform the "maternal reverie" for her infant, the infant's experience becomes populated with monsters and gods: the monsters being the experience of total badness and the gods being the experience of total goodness. These early experiences form the substrate of the archetypal imagery discovered by Jung in the adult psyche. For instance, a mother acquires archetypal dimensions and is experienced either as the "bad witch" or the "goddess." The same happens for a father who can become idealized as God, the total good one, or Cronos, the wholly bad ogre. Both archetype extremes are too much for a human psyche to bear, and when unmodified by maternal care, they tend to color all the infant's relationships.

When bad experiences prevail, a couple of bad parents are formed in the child's inner world, and thus a "bad primal scene" is activated and experienced in the form of the bad parents combined in a hateful intercourse against the child. The nurturing, protective parents become murderous and monstrous. Against these evil parents, the infant has to fight in order to survive. Thus the parents undergo a metamorphosis, from being allied to the child for its survival, to becoming a couple of perverse, dangerous foes against whom the infant has to protect itself in all areas of experience. Here the hero quality arises from the infant's need to deal with his larger-than-life enemies.

Eric Brenman, in his paper "Cruelty and Narrowmindedness," describes the contribution of the parents in creating a "good home" in which to grow and enjoy life. He writes:

> with a good home problems of cruelty are humanized by the interaction with good parents ... I cannot help speculating, "Would Oedipus have behaved as he did had he been brought up at home?" His tragedy was that he started life in exile and finished it in exile.[6]

Brenman's idea of a home, symbolizing the infant's early experience in relation to the parents is a helpful image. The home as a "mother's place" is a typical image in dreams and represents the mother's body. The womb-container is where the infant's experience begins to take place. It is also a metaphor for the mother creating a psychological home-place for the baby. According to Brenman's imagery, a poor mother-infant relationship gives rise to an "emotionally exiled baby."

Rhythms and Symbolic Functioning

In Fordham's conceptualization, the "home/container" might be represented by the primal self, which paradoxically is also the contained. From the primal self, following typical rhythms that he called deintegrative/reintegrative processes, the ego emerges. The opening and closing of the psychosomatic unity allows for the individual to develop.[7]

According to Fordham's theory, in the course of the early deintegrations of the primal self, the infant is exposed alternatively to experiences of wholeness and of parts: parts of himself and parts of the object. Thus the infant must work out the relationship and the links between these parts. He also must learn to differentiate between himself and the non-self. In this way, the sorting out of outer- from inner-world objects begins to take place, and time and space begin to be shaped as containers of the infant's experience, his mother, his father, their relationship, and the world in general.

The Oedipal Situation in Infancy

According to Melanie Klein, the Oedipal situation dawns in infancy with the initial recognition of the parents' relationship in whatever primitive or partial form. To start with, it is experienced as a relationship between parts of the parents that stand for the whole parents. For instance, the baby's first connection is with the maternal object; thus the breast stands for what will then be experienced as "the mother." Different sensuous experiences of hardness and softness acquired in the earliest relationship to the maternal object are linked to the proto-experiences of maleness and femaleness: softness usually attributed to the mother (feminine) and hardness to the father (masculine). Of course, these attributes do not, in reality, belong to only one of the genders, but one may say that for the baby it feels so.[8]

On the basis of such experiences of soft and hard and in order to combine them in the infant's first love object. Klein hypothesized the presence of the paternal element (the penis) as part of the breast; she was using both the concrete metaphors that prevail in infancy and the symbolic equation by which all that has similar features is the same.

Pertinent to Klein's theory of the maternal body are Fordham's postulations:

> I place the greatest importance on the imaginative exploration of insides, both of the child's and of his mother's body, for here we have an instrument for understanding how an infant creates an inner world . . . made up of sexual impulses, violence, greed, love, and hate, it is found projected to form the paranoid position.[9]

In infancy, children's preoccupations with the content of the mother's body focuses primarily on the unborn babies and the father's penis which is supposed to feed the babies and make the mother happy. The satiated babies will thus be able to grow inside the mother and be born. In turn, the mother will be satiated and full of milk to make the infant happy. As long as things go smoothly, the infant will feel included and can feel the containment of the good parental couple in love, so that a good primal scene will be constellated. However, when an infant's needs are not sufficiently met and frustration and distress are felt and pain has to be suffered, it feels to the infant as if the good mother has abandoned him. She has deprived him because she is having a good time with the penis and the other potential babies inside her. As Bion has mentioned, this experience evokes rage, despair, envy, and jealousy in the infant who will experience her withholding as an intolerable abandonment and betrayal to varying degrees according to the baby's personality structure. Because of this fear, the "penis inside her," imagined as a rival, will be experienced as damaging and dangerous. In that case, a bad primal scene will be constellated.

One of the major stepping stones in the infant's development consists in letting go of the illusion of being the sole possessor of the breast. This is achieved in due time after a considerable amount of trust in the mother and her love has accrued. If the illusion has to be dropped prematurely when the infant is not ready to accept the presence of another, a delusional defensive organization sets in, thus denying the psychic reality of the parental relationship. The sense of abandonment that the premature realization evokes in the infant is experienced as a traumatic event of which the infant feels the victim. The sense of abandonment also evokes extreme feelings of impotence and exposure to danger. Therefore, the weak infant's ego reacts by defensive splitting, while at the same time the archetype of the hero, as one who has to be brave and perform impossible tasks, is constellated. In the paranoid mode, the parental couple may even be experienced as allied against the infant, and this will be felt as a situation of extreme danger. Thus, the archetypal experience of the withholding, abandoning breast/mother, derived from the witch imagery, is compounded with the image of the persecuting, allied, attacking parental objects, a situation Brenman describes as the "bad home."

However, there is a great deal that the loving parent can do to mitigate the hardship of this mode of experiencing. Empathic tuning in with the emotionally distressed infant will help to restore the good object, but what is to be endured by the infant is the awareness of being separate from the love object. This can only take place after a secure sense of dependency has been established. This awareness, however dim and painful, is the first step in the lifelong process of separation-individuation of which the Oedipal situation constitutes a fundamental stage where the growing child's ego will be the hero. The early infantile experience has extreme relevance to further developmental stages, and particularly to adolescence. Jung himself emphasized the regression of the libido in puberty with the consequent reactivation of the pregenital stages of development underlying regression.

Having explored the infant's expectations and emotions and described the projective and splitting defensive mechanisms the infant uses in dealing with them, it is necessary to consider the relevance of the parents' expectations and their unconscious fantasies that the infant will have to fulfill. The story of King Oedipus, with its negative parental expectations and the hostile, unconscious fantasies contained in the prediction, has relevance here.

The case history I am going to discuss happened in ancient Thebes; however it does not differ much from the stories we hear daily in our child guidance clinics. Usually our clinical stories start with two parents who have conceived an unwanted child and, for a variety of reasons, want to give up the baby for adoption when it is born. Beyond the facts presented, we always find deep unconscious anxieties, emotional immaturity, and dramatic histories of the parents' relationship with their own parents. In the minds of the parents-to-be, the infant's birth is felt to be extremely dangerous to their own survival, either physical or psychological. In brief, the parents feel they cannot cope, and decide to abandon the baby. The baby (who we may call Johnny) then begins his life journey shipped from foster home to foster home in a tragic quest for a good enough home. In the best of cases, the pilgrimage is short. The child is given to some loving, adoptive parents and all ends well. However even in the best of cases, the abandonment and rejection by the blood mother deeply scars the infant. When all does not go well, the stage is set for severe emotional difficulties for little Johnny.

Each child, as we know, is endowed with an inborn resilience, which helps him or her deal with life's traumas. But the trauma of abandonment at birth is a severe one, and very few babies manage to survive it emotionally, in spite of the adoptive parents' loving care. If no maladaptive symptoms show up in early development, then usually disturbances break out in adolescence and the early disturbances are rehashed.

Baby Oedipus had a similar beginning, in spite of being the son of a royal couple. His parents' unconscious negative expectations and their hostile, unconscious fantasies were projected into Apollo's prediction and experienced by them as a message from the god who wanted to protect them from impending catastrophy.

The Myth of Oedipus as a Case History

Oedipus was the son of King Laius and Queen Jocasta of Thebes. Before his birth, Apollo's oracle foretold that Oedipus was destined to kill his father and marry his mother. Horrified by the prediction, the parents decide that the child should die. He is given to a shepherd with the understanding that the baby will be abandoned at the side of a mountain. The shepherd has mercy on the baby and gives him to a friend, with the agreement that he will be taken out of the kingdom of Thebes. The Corinthian shepherd takes the baby to his own king, who is childless and who adopts the newborn. When Oedipus is a young man, he finds out that he has been adopted and decides to leave in search of his blood parents. He goes to Delphi and asks the ministers of Apollo who his true parents are. There he is told the prediction. He decides to go to Thebes, but on the way his carriage hits another, and out of hubris he fights with the driver and kills the passenger who, he finds out later, is his father, Laius. Upon his arrival in Thebes, he finds the city in the grip of the Sphinx. The city can only be released from the Sphinx by the person who solves her riddle: What walks on four feet in the morning, two feet at noon, and three feet in the evening? Oedipus answers: a man. He has solved the riddle, the city is saved, and he is given the queen in marriage as a reward. Thus the prediction is actualized. Oedipus has killed his father and married his mother all without knowing it. When the truth is revealed, Jocasta in shame hangs herself and Oedipus puts out his own eyes and goes into exile, accompanied by his daughter, Antigone.

This tragic ending might have been expected from the start, given the destructive prediction of the god. As a consequence, the "bad parental couple" sets the stage, and the psychological plot begins to unfold. Oedipus is an unwanted baby who becomes the rejected and abandoned offspring of a "rejecting couple." The "good" aspect of the archetypal parental couple, in opposition to the real parents, is projected onto the adoptive parents. Oedipus' survival of these circumstance makes him a hero.

As happens frequently, all goes well for Oedipus in his adoptive home during latency. It is adolescence that brings to the surface the early emotional experiences of abandonment and rejection. Thus, without wanting to, the young person falls into the complex, is gripped by the bad parental primal scene in the unconscious, and is therefore bound to act out the prediction of the gods and become a hero. According to Jung, the unconscious complex exerts the same inevitability as Fate does in Greek mythology. When compared to Oedipus, the ordinary child in everyday situations is a mini-hero. As in the story of Oedipus, when the early attachment has gone wrong, feelings of abandonment and rejection are experienced by the infant prematurely. In adolescence, resentment and rage acquire a murderous quality that pushes the young person to act out, often violently. The necessity of separating from the parents brings about unconscious fantasies of death and murder of the child or the parent.[10] This is the case in the Oedipus story where the young hero left his "good" adoptive parents because of his obsession to find his own identity. The search for identity in psychological terms is the main task in adolescence. In everyday life, the adolescent searching for a sense of identity separate from that of the parents, tends to run away from home. The good parental home of childhood has suddenly turned bad in adolescence. It has become the prison where the internal conflicts are acted out and the parents have to act the part of oppressive authority. Most adolescents feel that living at home is the cause of all their troubles. A craving for independence often accompanies this stage of life, and it is at this point that literal and psychological meanings become confused.

There is an urgency towards action in these situations. In fact, getting into action is a typical adolescent defense mechanism, because acting prevents reflecting on and tolerating the conflict of opposites. It is a way of stepping quickly out of ambivalence, a regressive defense that brings the adolescent back into infantile states. At the same time, through the sense of empowerment that action provides, the adolescent is likely to experience a sense of omnipotent triumph and a great deal of arrogance. This need for action can be seen in the story of Oedipus when he arrogantly starts a fight with the king's driver. Refusing to give way to the carriage and the authority of the old man, Oedipus arrogantly asserts himself and lunges into action. He cannot contain the aggressive drive originating from his hurt pride.

Since Oedipus' sin is one of hubris, Bion's paper "On Arrogance" is significant. In it, he states:

> The term "arrogance" may be indicated by supposing that in the personality where life instincts predominate, pride becomes self-respect; where death instincts predominate, pride becomes arrogance.[11]

Referring to Oedipus, Bion states that this myth can be interpreted in such a way that the sexual crime is peripheral and the "central crime is the arrogance of Oedipus in vowing to lay bare the truth no matter what the cost." Bion notes the ruined elements of the psyche, ones that are typical characteristics of psychological immaturity. In the myth and in adolescence, the urge to act destroys the human capacity to reflect, to make sense of the situation, and to wait for the events to unfold. When reflection is absent, impulses predominate and concern and guilt are overridden. This is the price the adolescent must pay for having acted impulsively.

Oedipus' naiveté is further illuminated in *Symbols of Transformation* where Jung writes:

> It happens that if the attitude to the parent is too affectionate or too dependent [in Oedipus' case too neglecting] it is compensated in dreams by frightening animals, who represent the parents . . . The Sphinx is a fearful

animal of this kind and still shows clear traces of a mother derivative. In the Oedipus legend, the Sphinx was sent by Hera who hated Thebes on the account of the birth of Bacchus. Oedipus, thinking he had overcome the Sphinx sent by the mother goddess merely because he had solved her childishly simple riddle, fell a victim to matriarchal incest. Little did he know that the riddle of the Sphinx can never be solved merely by the wit of man.[12]

Jung's statement about the Sphinx riddle is pertinent to the subsequent dramatic development of the story. Oedipus is only using his intellect to solve the riddle, not a deeper form of thinking that incorporates body and soul and is grounded and steeped in suffering or compassion, i.e. Bion's concept of reverie. Oedipus' way of acting is superficial and grandiose: his action tends to get rid of the problem rather than trying to grapple with its meaning. He is far too eager to become a hero and marry the queen in order to become king.

The eagerness to grow up and usurp the parental position before being ripe for the task is typical of adolescents. They feel a sense of impatience and intolerance, especially since most feel tired of submitting to their parents' authority at a stage of life when they are beginning to experience themselves as fully able bodies. Therefore, being dependent on the parents is felt as most humiliating. The other threat that urges the adolescent to speed the separation process is the fear of incest caused by the intimacy of family life and the sexual arousal experienced in the young person's own body. In this sense, the quicker one gets away and finds a sexual partner, the better the anxiety can be kept at bay. This turmoil of conflicting emotions stirs up considerable archetypal regressive fantasies, as well as age-appropriate ones. Thus, Oedipus acts out his murderous infantile rage against his parents because his early trauma was activated by the regression related to adolescence, together with the dreaded incest brought about by the young man's sexually mature approach to relationships.

As in the toddler stage, the body is mature but the emotional development of the personality lags behind because of the many changes that need to be integrated. This is why adolescents feel a sense of powerlessness alternating with a feeling of being on top of the world. The interplay of feelings of omnipotence and helplessness lead to suicidal fantasies as well as genuinely creative fantasies during this period of life. Nonpathological adolescence is, by popular wisdom, considered an acute illness caused by growing up. Under normal circumstance this "illness" is cured by the passing of time, but like any other illness it leaves a certain number of victims.

Notes

1. See Michael Fordham, "Notes for the Formation of a Model of Infant Development," *Journal of Analytical Psychology*: 38,1 (January 1993):5.
2. See W. R. Bion, *Second Thoughts* (London: Maresfield Library, 1967).
3. C. G. Jung, "The Psychology of the Child Archetype," *Collected Works* (London: Routledge and Kegan Paul, 1959) v. 9, p. 165.
4. Ibid.
5. See M. Sidoli, *The Unfolding Self* (Boston: Sigo Press, 1990) Chap. 1.
6. Erich Brenman, "Cruelty and Narrowmindedness," in *Melanie Klein Today,* ed. E. Spillius (London: Routledge and Kegan Paul, 1988).
7. M. Fordham, 1976.
8. M. Klein, "The Psychological Principles of Early Analysis," *The Writings of Melanie Klein* (London: Hogarth Press, 1926) v. 1.
9. M. Fordham, Seminars on Klein. Lectures for training in child analysis at the Society of Analytical Psychology. (1989) Unpublished ms.
10. For a further discussion of the murderous and violent emotions experienced by the adolescent, see: M. Sidoli, *The Unfolding Self.*
11. W. Bion, *Second Thoughts.*
12. C. G. Jung, *Symbols of Transformation,* (London: Routledge and Kegan Paul,1956) v. 5.

4

Incest Fantasies as a Defense against the Analysis of Pre-Oedipal Object Relations

Gustav Bovensiepen

The Hazardous Mask of Incest

During middle adolescence, the drama of the individuation process reaches its climax. The regression to the internal, pre-oedipal parental images that is triggered by sexual maturation has been characterized by Jung as a "passion which lies hidden beneath the hazardous mask of incest."[1] The adolescent is caught in a conflict between the longing for the paradise of early childhood objects and the pull towards exogamous objects encountered initially in the peer group. Jung describes this inner struggle as a conflict between the extraverted progression and the introverted regression of libido:

> Part of the psyche really wants the external object, but another part of it strives back to the subjective world, where the airy and lightly built palaces of fantasy beckon.[2]

Discussing the revival of infantile love and fantasies for the mother as a regression of the libido to the parental images, Jung emphasizes the creative and regenerative character of regression. However, he underestimates the instinctual side of regression in the case of adolescents. Of course, Jung did not explicitly refer to adolescents but was writing about a youthful "Miss Miller." He treats the oedipal desires of the child for the contrasexual parent as merely appearing to be sexually-incestuously motivated. From our contemporary perspective, it is meaningful that Jung should expand Freud's libido theory to include an appreciation of the pre-oedipal object, yet one should not neglect the sexual instinct in the treatment of adolescents. Jung was quite aware of the overwhelming experience of a malignant regression that can lead to a destruction of the adolescent's connection to reality when he wrote:

> For out of the miasmas arising from the stagnant pools of libido are born those baneful phantasmagorias which so veil reality that all adaptation becomes impossible.[3]

The "stagnant pools of libido," as far as adolescence is concerned, are those aspects of the "positive" Oedipus complex that normally do not become "submerged," or only incompletely so. They are re-experienced during the adolescent developmental phase when they become sexualized: archetypal images of the Great Mother form the predominant symbol. The young adolescent tries to defend against sexualization by projecting images of pre-oedipal part object monsters into his or her parents. This dynamic can be illustrated with clinical material from work with a boy who was not psychotic, but who was dominated by his mother in a very intrusive and narcissistic way.

Case 1: The Wasp Woman

Peter was thirteen and a half years old when I first met him. He was a very imaginative and creative boy. He suffered from phobic anxiety and various compulsive symptoms. In the first year and a half, Peter's inner world was characterized by an unconscious identity with the body of his inner mother.[4] This could be seen in a series of cave dreams. These caves were populated by aggressive classmates, robbers, and bandits who Peter had to fight against or escape. He dreamed of himself in his mother's womb, experienced as a kind of paradise in his mother's cozily decorated car.

The theme of his destructive father-introject emerged when a psychodynamic shift occurred. Peter dreamed of wandering over the clouds. A threatening father figure in the form of a black light-demon pulled him down towards earth. The dream set a process in motion that made it possible for him to come to grips with feelings of sadness and fear of loss, as well as with his aggressive feelings about his own father, a former alcoholic. His ego slowly became stronger and at this time Peter reached puberty. In archetypal terms this point of treatment can be understood as the conflict of the womb/mother and a chthonian light-father inside Peter. The emergence of an inner father figure first was a threatening experience for Peter's ego because it meant separation from his infantile ties to his mother.

After this dynamic shift from mother to father, Peter's dreams and fantasies were marked by exhibitionism and phallic omnipotence. He frequently fantasized that he was a pop star on stage in front of his frenzied fans. At the same time he was quite concerned about the size of his penis, since he thought that his was very "underdeveloped" when directly compared to those of his classmates. The night before his confirmation, Peter dreamed that he was at a big, boozy party as a brilliant and admired "John Travolta," but he wore a bib just like a baby. Peter said that the dream expressed exactly what he had felt like before the day of his confirmation, an initiation ritual. On the surface he felt very grown up, but inside he was greedily awaiting the many presents and the expensive meal. This oppositional pull can be understood in relation to Peter's growing sexual impulses which bring the deintegrates of his self into association with his early childhood objects. The image of the pop star represents Peter's identification with the exhibitionist and phallic side of his mother's animus and, at the same time, is the orally greedy infant inside Peter. The more Peter became aware of his sexual fantasies and spoke about them during our sessions, the more he was beset by fantasies of both pre-oedipal and oedipal origins.

A few sessions after the Travolta dream Peter related the following dream:

> For Christmas I was given a small rectangular incubator. I put some corn seeds into it in the hope that they would sprout. Two days later I opened the incubator and looked inside. There were three wasps. I killed two of them but one got away. I started to scream in terror. My father went after the one that got away. All of a sudden the electricity went off, and I ran screaming into my room. Then the lights went on again and on my hand there was a black mark with blood coming from it.

After relating the dream, Peter told me about "The Wasp Woman," a horror film he had seen the previous evening on television. The woman was a beauty queen who turned into a man-murdering monster when she drank a rejuvenating elixir a scientist had developed. Peter was reminded of his biology teacher, a woman whom he liked very much and who had recently carried out experiments with the class on germination with various kinds of seeds. Then he started to speak about his mother. According to him, she was a very anxious person too, and couldn't bear the sight of blood. She had also originally wanted to study biology. He remembered the anxiety he had experienced at night as a four and five-year-old child when he imagined that the house was on fire. He told me that he had lived in constant fear of losing his mother because she would frequently run out of the house in a rage after fighting with her husband, threatening to get a divorce and never come back again.

I told Peter that I had the impression this anxious side of his mother was in him too, as shown by the dream. His terror in the dream was perhaps not so much the fear of losing his mother but the fear of being emotionally locked up inside with her and his "sex fantasies," as he had once called them. He chose to ignore this part of my comment. Instead he maintained that his sex fantasies had nothing to do with fantasies about his mother; instead they were a product of his fascination with the language used in comics. He was an ardent collector of comics about Amazons and female warriors such as "Wonder Girl." In our sessions he could not demonstrate often enough to me how it went "crack" and "zip" when the "sexy" Wonder Girl's brassiere split at the seams while fighting her enemies. This aggressive form of sexual fantasy was, on one level, typical of his neurotic defense system. At this point, however, its purpose was to help him master his panic fear of regression that was triggered by his awakening sexual impulses. Unconsciously these defense fantasies were bringing him very close to his mother again as symbolized by his fantasy of being kept by the Wasp Woman.

There is a build-up of instinctive aspects as well as elements of infantile object relations of an archetypal nature in Peter's very dynamic dream fantasy. If one considers the archetypal background, the "Wasp Woman" becomes an instinctual representative of the "Great Mother." This is the archetypal component of early infantile part-object experience that gives rise to unconscious fantasies related to the deintegrates of sucking and teething. At a later stage these fantasies are projected onto images that the child finds in the culture and that represent the dangerous aspects of the negative breast/mother (like vampires, devouring monsters, and werewolves). These images relate to Peter's inner world, where sexualization of the negative infantile breast/mother creates castration anxieties and guilt feelings about masturbation (the blood on the hand). They are experienced as an attack on his penis and as fears of being sucked out. This response is a "typical" male projection into a negative maternal part object. Peter fantasizes his mother's womb as dangerous, symbolized by the incubator which is full of wasps instead of growing corn plants. His ambivalent feelings about the infantile part object breast/mother and his unconscious incestuous fantasies are defended against through his fascination with the "Wonder Girls." These androgynous comic figures seem to be precursors of anima images during early puberty. Peter can project onto them his attacks on his mother's breasts, and at the same time be sexually fascinated by them as the breasts of a girl, not of a mother.

In a collusive transference/countertransference relationship, Peter identified with the father/therapist and tried to split off the reproductive part of the mother. This impulse may have its roots in Peter's relationship to his mother when he was a baby and had had difficulty getting attuned with her.

Peter's difficulties are typical of the problem of boys in early adolescence that stem from their attempts to deny both the oedipal conflict, in the sense of striving to have exclusive sexual possession of their mother on the one hand, and the pre-oedipal need to re-experience themselves unconsciously as not separated from mother's body on the other. This conflict, however, arouses anxiety since the mother's body is also sexualized by the fantasies of the pubescent boy. If infancy does not run smoothly, then the child who is reawakened within the adolescent is much more vulnerable when confronted with sexual instincts. The adolescent may then have to resort to defenses that impair his ego and his capacity for relationships to an even greater degree, thus making analytic treatment very difficult at this age.

Regressed narcissistic or psychotic adolescents vehemently defend against further development by sexualizing early objects to a much higher degree than Peter did. These adolescents cling stubbornly to concrete, sexualized incest fantasies, thus deintegration of the self cannot happen. An obsessive focus on incest fantasies can defeat all treatment efforts and usually prevents the unfolding of age-appropriate heterosexual relationships with peers. The ego of these adolescents is so preoccupied with pseudo-oedipal fantasies that its adaptive functioning is quite restricted with regard to reality contact. The next case illustrates this defensive clinging to pseudo-oedipal fantasies in an anorexic girl as a resistance against the working through of pre-oedipal material relating to the mother.

Case 2: "Black Emptiness" and Dreadful Greed

Martina was seventeen years old when I first met her. Her father was a vicar and had a position of some responsibility with the church administrative authorities. She loved and worshipped her father and missed him very much when he had to travel for almost half of the year because of his job. Her mother devoted herself totally to the household and to her family, which included caring for two grandmothers. In addition to her anorexia nervosa, Martina suffered from deep depressions with self-injuring impulses and had no contacts with her peers.

During the initial interview, which I carried out jointly with Martina and her parents, her mother introduced her in a low, despairing voice. Her mother uttered, "Martina has always been shy" with such unquestionable certainty that it sounded like a death sentence. During the interview Martina sat in front of me, her legs twisted almost into a knot. For a long time she did not take off her coat and sat gazing into space with grieved, owl-like eyes behind the lenses of her glasses. She spoke hesitantly, her words scarcely audible between long, oppressive silences.

The first phase of treatment lasted a year. Martina then broke off the therapy, only to come back six months later and continue treatment for another year and a half until she broke off again; this time, however, under much more auspicious circumstances. The first phase of treatment was marked by a total denial and splitting off of the experience of her body. She derived her sense of identity above all from a projective identification with famous religious political leaders such as Martin Luther King, Gandhi, and a number of Indian chiefs. She tried to spin me into the web of this idealizing transference. I was not at all happy about this because it enabled her to keep me at a distance. Furthermore, the idea of competing with Gandhi did not appeal to me.

When she came to see me the second time, after breaking off the therapy six months before, her difficulty in introjecting good objects became increasingly clear. Something inside her vigorously refused to take in and digest the understanding and sympathy I tried to give her in the way of commentary or interpretations. She accepted most of my comments by smiling briefly. This was her form of defense. Although Martina did eat again, eating did not seem to have any emotional or psychic significance for her. However, during this period she did begin to talk more about her experience of her body. More and more explicitly she began to relate to me incestuous fantasies concerning her elder brother and her father. At the same time she developed bulimia quite seriously, something which she had never had before. She was increasingly overcome by mental states of complete emptiness and diffuse anxiety. In these states she began to raid the refrigerator at night; she indiscriminately stuffed herself with anything she could lay her hands on and afterwards took handfuls of laxative pills in order to rid herself of everything she had eaten. These psychic states of emptiness also occurred during our sessions, and when they did, she spoke of a "black emptiness in the head" and froze into a numb silence. She said that in my consulting room she was not stricken with the panic and fear she was at home when she was alone in her room. When she was in one of these states, I felt completely helpless and cut off from her. It became apparent that these states of emptiness occurred when I tried to turn my attention to the abandoned little girl inside her, a side I only glimpsed occasionally. She told me about her dog which the family left behind when they returned from South Africa, where Martina lived until the age of eleven. She gave me the impression that her dog was her most important object of love when she was a small child. But Martina's stories about her time with this dog served as a memory to cover up the early loss of her emotional relationship to her mother. There were a number of indications of this emotional loss: one was her mother's depression and exhausted withdrawal after Martina's birth. It was only rarely possible, however, for her to feel any grief about this loss during the sessions. She experienced herself merely as a greedy, ugly monster who was never content. Unlike some bulimia patients. Martina never vomited, but only purged herself. Patients who vomit seem to be unconsciously equating food with an early component of their mother complex that must be expelled and projected. However during the period of the erotic father transference, I regarded Martina's purging orgies as symbolic attempts at abortions. She described how she gazed at herself, naked in front of a mirror, with a fat belly full of food, and was filled with disgust and loathing at the thought that this was exactly how women must feel when they were pregnant.

In our sessions she related dreams and fantasies of men and sinister figures who persecuted her and threatened her sexually. She began to speak of how she compulsively thought of the ugly, frightening penis of her father. She remembered occasions on holiday at the beginning of her illness when she had eavesdropped on her parents having intercourse at night. She was filled with anxiety and above all shame that I was able to see the "dreadful greed" that she felt inside her.

Gradually we both began to understand that, within the positive father-transference, the little girl, who she still was inside, fantasized that she was being made pregnant orally. This is a common fantasy of procreation among children. I now began to realize, too, why Martina felt her bulimic attacks and above all her greed and her "loathing of her mother," as she put it, to be so utterly immoral and abhorrent. Her unrealizable greed as a baby was fused with her sexual desires. The child that she had borne with me or, rather, her father in her fantasy, had to be aborted as a shameful product of incest. She acted out this fantasy through the reckless abuse of laxatives. At this point she broke off the treatment. As is often the case with adolescents, it was a planned termination: she was moving to another town to start a vocational training course which she had planned many months before.

In her inner world this termination can be understood as Martina's refusal to accept the revival of her inner baby within the mother-transference to me. The pain about the loss of the emotional relationship to her mother was so strong that unconsciously she replaced her inner child by the "incest-child" which she had in fantasy with me acting as her father in the transference. Both "children" raised too much pain in her to bear.

Martina writes to me three or four times a year, and she has successfully finished her professional training. In her letters she tells me much about her inner world. Writing letters is something that I often encounter after courses of therapy with adolescents. It is apparently easier for them to disclose in a letter the transference fantasies that they have anxiously kept to themselves during therapy. From the letters that I received there were certain indications that Martina had partly internalized me as good mother object in the sense of a container within her.[5] She experienced me as a container into which she could deposit everything bad, destructive, and shameful that she presumed to be inside her, without being immediately stricken with panic and unconsciously fantasizing that she would get it back from me undigested and intruding, like her father's persecuting penis. She wrote, "After I have written to you, there is a salutary emptiness inside me." This emptiness indicates a more relaxed deintegrated state of mind in contrast to the disintegrative states of "black emptiness" that seemed similar to Fordham's "defenses of the self."[6] This black emptiness had occurred when the incestuous sexualization of her early objects threw her into confusion, and there was no inner space left for the reintegration of the persecuting, greedy penis-deintegrate.

Conclusion

Eighty years ago Jung developed the modern idea that incest fantasies are a special form of regression of the libido to early, pre-oedipal objects. When treating adolescents, one is constantly confronted with this regression "under the hazardous mask of incest." The core of psychoanalytic treatment of adolescents lies in working through the sexualization of the infantile part object relations. Difficulties in treatment techniques result from the permanent oscillation of the adolescent's mind between infantile, pre-oedipal fantasies and oedipal, sexual desires. Adolescents develop a strong resistance against the working through of these states of mind. The two case studies show that sexualized incest fantasies can be used by the adolescent to defend against threatening infantile emotions and fantasies. As a defense, adolescents also try to desexualize the therapist prematurely either by making him or her pals in their group or by forcing them to remain sexually neutral mums or dads. Premature desexualization is also a form of splitting. As long as the "mask of incest" remains a totally unconscious fantasy, its function will continue to be defensive and hamper the development of a mature ego and a sense of identity.

Notes

1. C. G. Jung, *Symbols of Transformation, Collected Works* (London: Routledge and Kegan Paul, 1956) p. 254.
2. Ibid. p. 253.

3. Ibid. p. 254.
4. A detailed report of this treatment appears in M. Sidoli and M. Davies, eds. *Jungian Child Psychotherapy* (London: Karnac, 1988) pp. 245–264.
5. W. R. Bion, *Attention and Interpretation* (London: Tavistock, 1970) Represented in Maresfield Reprints, 1984, pp. 72–82.
6. M. Fordham, "Defences of the Self," *Explorations into the Self* (London: Academic Press, 1989) pp. 152–160.

SECTION 3

Acting Out Incest Fantasies

Introduction to Section 3

In her chapter "Heroic Deeds, Manic Defense and Intrusive Identifications," Miranda Davies explores, in a very original and perceptive way, the relationship between heroic deeds, manic defenses, and intrusive identification. She sees heroic deeds, as does Mara Sidoli, as a manic defense against severe early split-off infantile depression derived from faulty mother-infant attachment. Davies has been powerfully influenced by Melanie Klein and, following Michael Fordham, she highlights differences and similarities between Jungian and Kleinian concepts. These clarifications are extremely important in elucidating the considerable confusion of tongues in the analytic world today. Miranda Davies takes on this task with masterly skill. She weaves her discussion back and forth between the views of Klein, Bion, and Meltzer on projective and intrusive identification and Jung's concept of empathy.

The most interesting and original element in Davies' chapter is her connecting rape fantasies and sexually abusive behavior to the psychological mechanism of intrusive identification. She follows Meltzer's definition of intrusive identification as underlying the violent, aggressive components aimed at exploding uncontainable destructive elements inside a helpless object. The case of Micha is a vivid account of the pain, abuse, and distress experienced by the analyst in the countertransference as she attempts to contain and make sense of extremely perverse sadistic fantasies projected onto her by this very disturbed boy.

Micha, Davies tells us, was desperately in need of containment. After her husband's departure, his mother used to hold onto him as a young child, provoking him with seductive, eroticizing behavior. Then he was suddenly rejected at the arrival of her new husband and, later, their baby daughter. Micha's mother and new stepfather apparently felt no concern for his misery. Rather he was subjected to systematic rigid punishment and outright rejection. His distress turned into explosive rage; he acted out his vengeance in ruthless attempts to push his way into people emotionally. His sexual abuse of his young step-sister represents a vicious, degrading attack on the mother's "good child" at the cost of his own destruction.

This perverse, destructive acting out continued until his complete expulsion from the family. Micha's behavior exhibited a narcissistic, perverse quality which is found in sexual offenders who feel they cannot be redeemed, and who appear to be caught in the compulsive repetition of abuse that they themselves suffered as children. The long, painstaking work done by Miranda Davies and her constant attention to and analysis of her countertransference feelings and reactions made it possible for Micha to feel more contained and for his sexual and emotional intrusive actions to subside.

In "The Trickster and the Terrible Mother," the theme of sexual abuse is treated in a very different way by Janet Glynn-Treble. Her work shows characteristics typical of the Fordham London group. Although she comes from the same training school as Miranda Davies, her style is completely different. Her language and frame of reference is totally rooted in Jung's archetypal conceptualizations, enriched by Michael Fordham's theoretical development; however, Kleinian and essentially post-Kleinian (Bion) influences are clearly visible.

Glynn-Treble's chapter deals with the case of Pat, a sexually abused preadolescent girl with whom she worked in a residential setting. Glynn-Treble focuses on the mother-child relationship and the early infantile disturbances in this relationship that have led the child to focus on negative aspects of the parental archetypal constellations.

The work of Miranda Davies and Janet Glynn-Treble shows clearly the broad spectrum of the theoretical approaches that is characteristic of the Jungian world. Yet the accuracy of the clinical work and the level of containment, empathy, and compassion provided by both Glynn-Treble and Davies is astounding. Glynn-Treble describes her struggle in the countertransference to contain her retaliatory reaction to the vicious, sadistic attacks and the perverse teasing on the part of her very disturbed and tricky patient. She sees the disturbance originating from an identification on the part of the girl with the sadistic terrible mother archetype. The mother in Pat's fantasy was both a trickster and an abuser; trusting her would lead to her being killed. Here Meltzer's concepts of "claustrum," projective and intrusive identification would vividly illustrate and condense the transference projections of hate, love, and deceit enacted by Pat.

This situation raised confusion in the girl between food and poison, love and deceit. She enacted nasty, cruel play in which she regularly abused and tricked the therapist. As the transference/countertransference relationship proceeded, it seemed to illustrate further the intolerable ambiguity of Pat's relation to the breast mother. Her fantasied experience of the terrible mother was then concretized by the oral sexual abuse that she suffered from a maternal uncle, in the course of which she felt trapped and poisoned. Glynn-Treble's sensitivity, her gentle, but persistent interpreting style, and most of all her ability to tolerate and survive unspeakable states of fear, despair, and murderousness in the countertransference, allowed Pat to begin to trust that there could be a mother who cared. She then could allow herself to feel like a child who could play, rather than always expect to be a sexual object for the parent or to be viciously attached by a parental figure. It is important to realize that the analyst in the treatment of abused children has to experience almost unbearable sadistic attacks without retaliating, before the caring, loving aspect of the mother can be constellated in the child and the maturational processes can proceed. In working with abused children, the analyst must give great attention to the analytic attitude and the analytic frame, which need to contain and set boundaries for the violent acting out within them.

In the works presented here by Janet Glynn-Treble and Miranda Davies, special technical skills have been necessary for the analyst in addition to a nonjudgmental analytic attitude.

5

The Trickster and the Terrible Mother: Archetypes Experienced during the Treatment of a Preadolescent Sexually Abused Girl

Janet Glynn-Treble

Introduction

The trickster and the terrible mother archetypes frequently appear as themes in the psychoanalytic treatment of adolescents. Over a period of two years these archetypes dominated my once-weekly individual psychotherapy with an eleven-and-a-half year old girl over a period of two years. The work took place in a residential setting described in the paper included in this volume "Individual Psychotherapy in a Residential School for Girls," to which the reader is referred.

My client, Pat, was placed in the school on two accounts. First, her mother felt unable to cope with her rebellious and difficult behaviour, and second, while on an extended stay with her mother's sister, she was sexually abused by her uncle. Eventually, Pat herself put an end to the abuse by seeking help from her aunt. It was felt that a placement away from home would be helpful in order to put distance between Pat and her family and prevent a reoccurrence of the abuse. As is often the case with girls at school, it was not possible to get a clear idea of Pat's infancy and early childhood experience. Her parents had not been asked to supply details of her early history, since the school's primary purpose is educational, not psychiatric. From information her mother had given to a previous social worker, I learned that Pat was "lent" to relatives for months at a time when her mother felt unable to cope.

The Trickster Archetype

As our sessions took place, Pat seemed to embody many aspects of the trickster archetype as described by Jung in its manifestations in stories and customs of different cultures: the malicious tricks of Mercurius, the destructive orgies of Yahweh, the wildness of the ancient customs of Saturnalia, and certain festivals of the medieval church. Jung concludes that this is an archetypal psychic structure of extreme antiquity, and the myths and stories describing the trickster reflect an earlier stage of consciousness:

> In his clearest manifestations, [the trickster] is a faithful reflection of an absolutely undifferentiated human consciousness, corresponding to a psyche that has hardly left the animal level.[1]

However, stories about the trickster described the gradual humanization of this unconscious bestial being:

> Instead of acting in a brutal, savage, stupid, and senseless fashion, the trickster's behaviour towards the end of the cycle becomes quite useful and sensible.[2]

Jung saw that the trickster manifests itself in the modern personality in the form of the shadow, a summation of all the inferior traits of character in individuals. The function of the trickster stories is to maintain this trickier aspect of the collective psyche within consciousness.

Jung's theory about the trickster archetype illustrates the transformative function of the psychotherapeutic process. The trickster archetype

> holds earlier low intellectual and moral levels before the eyes of the more highly developed individual, so that he shall not forget ... the gradual civilizing, i.e. assimilation, of a primitive daemonic figure who was originally autonomous and even capable of causing possession. [In the process] the conscious mind is then able to free itself from the fascination of evil and is no longer obliged to live it compulsively.[3]

Throughout much of her therapy Pat remained totally possessed by her shadow aspect. Her nastiness erupted into enactments and projections. Allowing feelings connected with the archetypes of the trickster and the terrible mother to emerge without condemnation or repression in Pat's play and transference feelings enabled her to become aware of these parts of herself. She was then able to assimilate them into her idea of herself and manage them. Gradually the projection was withdrawn, and there was less need for her to enact the shadow.

The Tricky, Sadistic Mother

After having met Pat for a few sessions, I began to realize that she was an extremely tricky character. At the end of each session, I was left with the feeling that I had been tricked into believing something was nice, when it was really nasty. Often I felt foolish for having been so gullible. For example, on one occasion she supposedly looked after a fly, putting it in a toy pram and making a plasticine blanket in order to keep it warm. However, the blanket crushed the fly. She called me over to look, and when she revealed the squashed insect, shrieked in a maniacal way. This sadistic abuse of insects was often repeated throughout the first stage of her treatment.

The feeling of having been tricked became transformed in me to an inner state of alertness. I tried to avoid being fooled and felt a continual mistrust of Pat, which made it difficult for me to respond easily to any signs of neediness in her. I was continually in a state of bewilderment, trying to disentangle the kind and cruel elements of our interactions. I was often left with two completely opposing feelings at the same time, uncertain which one was the true response: I found it difficult to bear both. I think my feelings of mistrust and bewilderment mirrored Pat's relationship with her internal breast/mother and her experiences of sexual abuse which concretized her fantasy. The mother of Pat's fantasy was both a trickster and an abuser. This mistrust was correspondingly active in Pat's transference feelings, and her therapy was sometimes difficult to sustain because of this block.

The Terrible Mother Archetype

Intermingled with internalized, sadistic feelings derived from Pat's experience of abuse and neglect was an active negative mother archetypal image. Jung made it clear that he thought the personal mother had only a limited role in the cause of a child's disturbances, since disturbances emanated "from the archetype projected onto her".[4] He noted that Freud eventually thought that "the real aetiology of neurosis does not lie in traumatic effects . . . but in a peculiar development of infantile fantasy".[5] Jung describes the mother archetype, with her loving and terrible aspects. He lists among the negative symbols, the dragon (or any devouring and entwining animal), death, and "the world of the dead, anything that devours, seduces, and poisons, that is terrifying and inescapable".[6]

Food or Poison: The Monster and the Therapist

These fantasies of the negative mother were very alive throughout Pat's psychotherapy. At first they were played out, and then they were re-experienced within the transference where they were recalled as they had been enacted during her experience of sexual abuse. The following example illustrates this process and an oral theme that recurred frequently. Early in therapy Pat made a plasticine pipe that she put in her mouth and announced that her uncle smoked a pipe. She then made a plasticine monster with brightly coloured, toxic-looking spots. Pat told me that the red ones were for eating, and the yellow ones were poisonous. Her figure represented a feeding and poisonous monster/breast/mother. In the game she created involving the pipe, a child came along and tried to grab a red spot, but Pat said he had to wait. When I asked how he felt about having to wait, she picked up the boy and made him punch the monster in the face. His anger mirrored Pat's own infantile rage at having to wait a week for the food of her session. As the game continued, the monster/breast/mother retaliated and killed the child, who became a hard and bony skeleton. Eventually, the child came back to life and took an eating spot off the monster and ate it. This game illustrates the ambiguity of Pat's internal mother and the mistrust she felt within herself and towards me as she projected this fantasy onto me. She could not decide whether or not the monster/mother/therapist feeds good food or poison.

The transference and countertransference material further illustrates the intolerable ambiguity and confusion permeating Pat's experience of her internal breast/mother. It illustrates her possession by the terrible mother archetype, and her corresponding difficulty in arriving at a position of trust with anyone, so that she could acknowledge her painful feelings of vulnerability. Her sadistic omnipotent defenses against these intolerable feelings of confusion, ambivalence, and mistrust were defenses in which she identified with a sadistic, internal breast/mother and attacked "infants" who were external to herself, whether in the form of insects, schoolmates, pregnant members of the staff, or her therapist. In addition, her fantasized experience of the terrible mother was made concrete in her experience of sexual abuse during which she felt poisoned and unable to escape. All this rendered her a potential child abuser in the future.

My work with Pat centered around holding the projections of victim and trickster/abuser and projections of nasty, useless uncaring breast/mother. Together we tried to clarify these issues as they arose within the transference and countertransference process.

The Tricking, Terrible, Abusing Mother

In her early sessions, Pat also made a plasticine road which connected her home to the town where her aunt and uncle live. Along this road sped a racing car, driving far too fast and carrying a frightened black toddler riding astride the bonnet. The allegory of sexual intercourse between a frightening and/or exciting penis and a frightened and/or excited dirty baby is graphically illustrated by this image. Pat then enacted the following scene. A mother stepped into the road, held up her hand, and cried, "stop." Another mother, carelessly wheeling a pram, let it topple over, and the baby fell out. The mother sang, "I don't care about the baby," and Pat gave a high-pitched cackle. This scene also provided a vivid image of the dual nature of Pat's internal mother, the protective and destructive aspects of the mother archetype. In this scene, as in others, Pat found herself having to choose between being the mother inside her who wants to stop the abuse and protect the toddler and the mother inside her who does not care about the baby part of her.

A few sessions later she made plasticine beds and put the whole family in the hospital. One child was swathed in bandages, damaged everywhere: arms, legs, belly, neck, and head. She was put in the emergency bed and had something done to her to make her better, but it was questionable whether this was a good thing or not since she remained damaged. Pat may well have experienced similar sensations in therapy where something that was supposed to help her felt like abuse.

Later some phobic feelings were transferred into her sessions. She objected to coming, sat with her back to me, refused to speak, and was generally hostile and angry. In her mind, I became a depriver and a persecutor. She was clearly testing whether I could stand her anger, or whether I would actually become a person who threw her out or abused her. She was concerned that I did not care about the baby part of her, and so I would become the cruel mother she projected onto me.

In later sessions she repeatedly enacted the ambiguity of her "caring." She took to "washing" my room, making lots of soapsuds and spreading them along the window sill, but contemptuously excluding me from seeing what she was doing. She then "washed" a shelf, the tops of cupboards, and a notice board. When I said it was unclear whether she was cleaning or messing, her cackle revealed the truth. She tricked me into thinking she had dropped the soap-filled sponge out of the window or into thinking she was about to throw it at me. At one point, she thrust the sponge at my face and told me to eat it. The overtones of sadistic sexuality were apparent, and my interpretations could only be attempts to describe my feelings of having to hold all the feelings of being tricked, excluded, tantalized, attacked, and intruded upon. Pat wanted to deny these feelings in herself and so she projected them onto me while she derived obvious satisfaction from being the abuser.

A Glimpse of Softness: The Loving Mother

In her first session after a long summer break, Pat's confusion about what it means to care was reiterated. She played a game where two children in the hospital had something done to them to make them better, but what happened was frightening. There was some indication that some good mothering feelings had been internalized. As a result, some of Pat's hard and bony defenses were beginning to melt. She put some children in a bath with some conditioner which would make them "nice and cosy." However, her confusion reappeared when she began to feed them by pouring water into their mouths, soaking them. Pat said "they feel good," placing the confusion in me.

In subsequent sessions, Pat seemed to care for her dolls. I was reluctant to believe this and did not wish to be gullible, yet I did not wish to be mistrustful, as that would prevent me from being receptive. I had to hold the balance inside me between these two states of mind. I think this experience exactly reflected Pat's state of mind about her therapy. Perhaps the fact that I had returned after a long holiday break rekindled her capacity to hope and be trustworthy, but she still seemed unsure. It was eight months before Pat could allow herself to experience a similar feeling of being cared for in my room.

Abandoning and Cruel Once More

Pat's feeling of damage soon reappeared, perhaps as a result of her envy of the loving mother she felt she could not have or in fear of being abandoned by an internal loving mother she had only just begun to experience. She drew smiley faces with nasty burns on them; she left dolls face down in sinks full of water, saying "I didn't want my baby so I killed it." She drew pictures which she then wet, tore, and squashed. She then refused to come to our session altogether. I had to play the part, for a considerable period of time, of the one who was ignored, hated, abandoned, and rejected.

The following spring, Pat regressed into a toddler state: she complained if I did not fetch her, wanted me to help her make things, and delayed the end of her sessions. Soon after this stage, Pat re-enacted scenes of sadistically abusing insects while pretending to care for them. In the transference, I became the helpless onlooker who could not tell cruel from kind, while Pat remained a cruel, tricky mother figure.

Sadistic Sexuality and the Hurt Baby

Pat's behavior soon took on a more explicitly sexual and sadistic character, intermingled with infantile behavior. She spread a blanket on the floor, lay down and sucked water from a feeding cup. At the same time she flung her legs about and tucked up her blouse in a seductive way. It was unclear whether she was feeding or having oral sex. In another session she was sarcastic and bullying, threatening to throw things out the window or set my hair on fire. The intensity of my feeling was an indication of the sort of internal breast/mother she had projected into me, and I was the first person in her life who was prepared to contain and tolerate the projection rather than act in response to it.

This attempt to bully me was followed in the same session by a scene in which the doll was repeatedly submerged under water and then pulled out gasping. Her identification with the abusing adult was clear. I felt the doll represented the murderous part of her, and she was enacting the retaliatory, murderous mother she felt me to be. I was able to comment on the killing thoughts she had about me, which made her unable to believe I would still be friendly. After repeating the scene and soaking herself with water, she took off her skirt and hung it out of the window. She then lay down and said, "what I need is sex." The implication was clear. My room was for cruel sexuality. She could not believe that I would not abuse her. The whole of the transference relationship felt contaminated with sadistic sexuality.

The following sessions gave me hope that perhaps the baby could be cared for. Pat put two soft chairs together to make a bed. She climbed into the bed and began to drink from a baby feeder. She then asked me whether I had seen any horror films and whether I had a husband. I was able to say that I thought she found it hard to believe I kept a space in my mind for her in order to remember her. She then told me, "I am Cathy today." In reality, Cathy was a girl who had just had an appendectomy operation. Pat told me about Cathy's scar and her stitches. Clearly, she was feeling like the hurt one and wanted to be looked after. At that time she was able to tell me a little about her experience of abuse. She continued to suck from the cup and asked me several times if she was noisy or not or if she was drinking or not, the kind of preoccupations one might have with a baby or the kind of worries a nine year old might have about oral sex. Once again it was unclear whether this was feeding or abuse. The question was starkly alive in the transference. Again, I felt puzzled about what was happening.

After rolling over and pretending to sleep, perhaps in the hope that I would be a protective mother for her, Pat sat up and confided that she first started coming in order to play with the toys. It had taken her all this time to find out whether or not it was acceptable to be a child in my room. Then she asked if I knew why she was there. After telling me her mother could not cope with her, she seemed to want to bring up the issue of sexual abuse. At the same time, she seemed to want to convince me that it would never happen again, that her uncle "did not know what he was doing," that he had forgotten about it, and that she liked her uncle, the confusing part of this entire scenario.

For a few moments she allowed me to be an ally, but suddenly, within the transference, she experienced me as bad and began to complain that she did not like what I had been saying. In her mind, I became the abuser once more. She began to enact some of the scenes of abuse, pouring water into her mouth and gagging. When I tried to say something, she retorted, "Shut up, I am trying to kill myself," and lay still, faking death. She threw the feeding cup away and told me to leave her alone.

Beginning to Love

Pat was very attacking towards me in the following session. Among other things, she splattered the room with water and tore her folder. For her, I had become withdrawing and withholding. My room had become full of abusive sex again, and she was finding it hard to know how to use me. By the end of the session, she changed her attitude and asked me to help her make something. She made paper flowers, which she insisted were for her teachers, but she threw one at me when she left. For the first time, I felt we had done something together that was not contaminated by abusive sexuality.

At this point, Pat avoided coming to her sessions. She spent four months tricking herself out of therapy, thereby proving that I was a horrible person. She returned to her sessions eventually, and it appeared she was trying hard to be friendly. She made many encouraging signs of advancement towards maturity: becoming attached to her therapist, feeling sad at separations, and expressing positive appreciation. In play, she looked after her dolls, another sign of her capacity to look after herself and contain her own confusing feelings. Her increasing concern for others and control of violent impulses was also noted by other staff members. The trickster seemed to be well on the way to being civilized.

Conclusion

Pat's case illustrates the dynamic process of transference and countertransference between patient and therapist dominated by massive projective identifications of an archetypal nature. In early sessions, the patient enacted in her play aspects of the trickster figure and the terrible mother archetype with which she identified. These archetypes were soon projected onto the therapist and became an issue in the transference/countertransference feelings. Interspersed with these projections were fleeting glimpses of positive, nurturing feelings in her play. In time her cruel, sadistic feelings dominated the transference relationship, and I used countertransference sensitivity to interpret what was projected onto me. Months of work containing and interpreting these projections resulted in a dissolution of their power. The patient then began to experience vulnerability, concern, and self-control, which formed a basis for future maturation, thereby providing the keys for transformation within the therapeutic process.

Notes

1. C. G. Jung, "On the Psychology of the Trickster Figure," *Collected Works* (London: Routledge and Kegan Paul, 1959) v. 9:1, para. 465.
2. Ibid., para. 477.
3. Ibid., para. 480, 475, 477.
4. C. G. Jung, "Psychological Aspects of the Mother Archetype," *Collected Works* (London: Routledge and Kegan Paul, 1959) v. 9:1, para. 159.
5. Ibid.
6. Ibid., para. 157, 158.

6

Heroic Deeds, Manic Defense, and Intrusive Identification: Some Reflections on Psychotherapy with a Sixteen-Year-Old Boy

Miranda Davies

In this chapter I examine a particular aspect of adolescence that is one of the main themes of this book: the heroic stance as a defense against impotence, helplessness, dependency, and depression. I also link the heroic flight into action with a particularly active and intrusive use of projective identification by my young patient. Projective identification was first defined by Melanie Klein, the distinguished follower of Freud, whose discoveries through her work with children have immeasurably deepened our understanding of psychic processes. In her 1946 paper, "Notes on Some Schizoid Mechanisms," Klein described a process of projective identification in which parts of the ego are forced into another's psyche in order to take over its contents or control it.[1] This is a deeply unconscious process motivated by envy, and the result is a depletion of the subject and a weakened sense of self and identity.

As an analytical psychologist, Michael Fordham was not working with the same model of the psyche as Klein. Nevertheless, he found her discoveries of the working of unconscious phantasy in children to be inspiring, and her descriptions of her clinical work helped him to gain direct access to the unconscious of his own child patients. Klein, following Susan Isaacs, distinguished between two kinds of fantasy:

conscious fantasy that is directly accessible in daydreams and, for Jungians, in active imagination, and unconscious phantasy that is the psychic pattern that underlies instinctual activity. Two spellings of the word are used by Kleinians to help the reader recognize the distinction between conscious fantasy and unconscious phantasy and I follow this practice. Fordham regards Klein as one of his mentors, and the close correspondence between unconscious phantasy and archetypal patterns was the basis from which he extended Jung's idea of the self and individuation to apply to infancy and childhood. For this reason, the training in child analysis in London under Fordham's direction has assimilated a number of Klein's ideas, but within the context of Jung's model of the psyche.

At the end of his paper, "Some Historical Reflections," Fordham drew up a list showing correspondences between Jung and Klein's formulations.[2] As Fordham points out, the formulations can be compared, but are not identical by any means. The spark that started off my thinking about this paper was the juxtaposition in the list below of the terms heroic feats (Jung) and manic defense (Klein). I have selected and reproduced several of the pairs of formulations in Fordham's list because I have found it helpful to see such a line-up of terms, each of which alludes to a whole area of analytical exploration. In the vast field of analytical theory that we are faced with, such a list helps us to begin to think about the similarities and differences between Jungian and Kleinian concepts. It is a long and difficult task to work on assimilating the approach of these two great analytic pioneers to the same psychic phenomena, but helpful and important for bringing depth and precision to our clinical work.

Jung	Klein
a) Archetypes	a) Unconscious phantasy
b) Empathy and Alchemy	b) Projective identification
c) Inner world primary datum	c) Inner world primary
d) Heroic feats	d) Manic defense

The correspondence between Jung's concept of archetypal patterns and images and Klein's use of unconscious phantasy has often been written about by Fordham and others, and I shall return to the correspondence between Jung's "empathy" and Klein's "projective identification' later in this paper. The emphasis that both Klein and Jung put on the primary position of the inner world is what distinguishes them both from Freud.

Heroic Deeds and Manic Defense

The parallel that particularly struck me in relation to my work with boys was the one between heroic feats, or deeds, and manic defense. I was able to see more clearly the relationship between the heroic myths studied by Jung in *Symbols of Transformation,* for example, and the manic play that is such a common event in my consulting room: little boys charging around declaring that they are Batman, Superman, Spiderman, Luke Skywalker, a Ghostbuster, a Ninja Turtle, and the like. If a boy habitually resorts to this defense in the face of frustration and anxiety, he is bound to come to grief and find himself ill-equipped to deal with reality. Of course, we try to help him get in touch with vulnerable parts of his personality by bringing him back to some awareness of the smallness, dependency, fear, and depression that underlie his omnipotent, and usually noisy, denial.

In his book *Jungian Psychotherapy,* Fordham writes,

> It is known, for instance, from myths that the hero's achievements reach a climax and then a disaster follows . . . The Assyrio-Babylonian hero, Gilgamesh . . . performs many astounding feats in company with his friend Enkidu who eventually dies. Fearful for himself, Gilgamesh determines to seek the herb of immortality. He retrieves it from the bottom of the ocean, only to have it stolen from him by a snake. He returns to his home town, Erech, haunted by the fear of death and the shade of Enkidu. It is the end of his heroic achievements, and the poem recording them finishes in gloom and dejection.[3]

Fordham goes on to say that, on this basis, a prognosis for a heroic dream or fantasy might be made, and this idea helped me in my struggle to understand the material brought to me by a sixteen-year-old boy whom I shall call Micha. At the beginning of our work together Micha was immersed in "role play," a highly organized, commercially produced game that is played out of school hours with a group of like-minded young people. I gathered from Micha that it is capable of endless permutations, while each of the players accumulates degrees of power, according to how long he has been in the game, and in how many battle encounters he has achieved the victory. Although Micha did his best to escape into this "role play" world of heroic panoply, with its colorful and romantic elements accumulated from myth, fairy tale, and medieval chivalry, he always ended up, like

Gilgamesh in the saga, in a state of gloom and dejection. The sense of helplessness and extreme vulnerability that he was trying to expel had its roots in his infancy and early childhood. It could not be overcome by plunging himself into the role of hero, which has as its meaning the separation from the regressive pull to the mother and overcoming the parental imagoes. This was because his infantile rage and intense pain had not been understood, taken in, and modulated in the early relationship with his mother, nor yet in a therapeutic relationship with me. His need for containment was very great; he was not ready to separate.

Linking Jung's study of heroic themes with adolescent states of mind, Fordham has pointed out that

> the study that Jung made of the Miller phantasies [in *Symbols of Transformation*] was recognized by him as being of adolescent conflicts—hence the emphasis on the hero and his demise—but it is clear that adolescence reflects earlier states of childhood and infancy. Jung did not, I think, recognise fully that he was outlining the patterns of infancy, nor did he grasp that this form of conflict was essentially a creative defence that can now be usefully called manic and essentially related to destructive drives and phantasies . . . In his second edition, however, there is a significant passage which shows how he had moved forward in understanding the importance of depression against which the manic defence is directed.[4]

During the early sessions of his psychotherapy, Micha gave many descriptions of his battles in role play, the weapons, the superior strength and cunning he displayed, and trickiness of the traps he set. He often stood up to enact a particular encounter in an excited and intense way, hurling a spear or concealing himself behind a door with a practiced cunning that resulted in many points gained, while the details of the conflict were spelled out minutely. I began to understand the narration of these stories as a manic defense against the meaning of our new, psychotherapeutic relationship. The impact on me of being warded off by these heroic narratives was the same as the impact of the hero-play of my six-year-old patients, and had the same components of violence and aggression. Later in his therapy, it was a small step for Micha to shift from being a heroic combatant to being both hero and narrator, the creator of dramatic scenarios, novels, and poems in which his actions and emotions took center stage. In this way he could perform a double role as hero-actor and hero-poet. His composition of verses and outlines for a heroic-romantic novel can be seen in a literal way as what Fordham calls above a "creative defense."

Projective Identification, Empathy, and Intrusive Identification

When Micha started once-weekly psychotherapy with me, I immediately found myself struggling with my negative feelings. In fact, if my mind wandered slightly during the session before his, I found myself dreading the encounter with him, and wondering if he might be ill that day and let me off the hook. This had to do with the powerfully intrusive effect of his personality. Several times during the first months I had a headache after seeing him, and struggled with angry feelings about being emotionally and mentally invaded. This experience became modified during the time we worked together, because he became increasingly able to use the sessions to stay in touch with painful and depressed feelings about being rejected. But during the early sessions, he pushed material from his fantasy novels into my mind in a powerful way that did not allow me any time to digest, pause, or question, and I was not allowed to point out any parallels between himself and the situation of the characters he described. When I remarked that he was filling my mind in a way that did not allow me any space in which to think, he grinned and mimed zapping me with an electric force and controlling my mind, while he boasted that he had empathy: he knew immediately what people were feeling as soon as he saw their faces. And indeed, his eyes clung to my face, while on several occasions I felt the play of my feelings show more than usually transparently on my features and in the occasional embarrassed rush of blood to my skin.

So it is clear that what Micha regarded as his empathy was having a specific effect on me, bamboozling my mind, making it impossible for me to make interpretations, stirring up my feelings and making me blush. This process was described by Jung in 1921 in the glossary of terms he wrote for his book *Psychological Types.*

As the essence of empathy is the projection of subjective contents, it follows that the preceding unconscious act must be the opposite—a neutralizing of the object that renders it inoperative. In this way the object is emptied, so to speak, robbed of its spontaneous activity, and thus made a suitable receptacle for subjective contents. The empathizing subject wants to feel his own life in the object; hence the independence of the object and the difference between it and the subject must not be too great. As a result of the unconscious act that precedes empathy, the sovereignty of the object is depotentiated, or rather it is overcompensated, because the subject immediately gains ascendancy over the object. This can only happen unconsciously, through an unconscious fantasy that either devalues and depotentiates the object or enhances the value and importance of the subject. Only in this way can that difference of potential arise which empathy needs in order to convey subjective contents into the object.[5]

Jung arrived at this formulation twenty-five years before Klein introduced her famous concept of projective identification. In the paper, "Notes on Some Schizoid Mechanisms" of 1946, she described for the first time how the infant splits off unwanted parts of the self, projects them into the object, identifies them in the object, and experiences them as belonging to the object, with a consequent depletion of the subject. Since then the concept has been enormously developed and has proved to be invaluable in the consulting room where the analyst can understand particular states of feeling in himself as a communication from the patient. With this concept in mind, I understood my reactions of embarrassment, anger, and resentment as a communication from Micha of aspects of his own emotional experience that he could not bear to know about in himself and defended against by projecting them onto me. In extending Klein's concept, the British psychoanalyst Wilfred Bion made a distinction between a) projective identification that functions as communication and b) projective identification that forces unwanted parts of the self into the object in an aggressive, sometimes violent way.[6] This distinction is helpful when thinking about the way a baby can communicate with his mother by wordlessly getting her to feel what he cannot bear to feel himself, so that she can be attentive to him and think about what it is like to be in his situation in a way that helps him to calm and get back inside himself. This kind of ordinary, everyday projective identification is very different from the intrusive means that Micha was using to get rid of unwanted parts of himself into me and to control me.

I began to think about whether Micha's way of pushing stories into my mind and feelings into my body might properly be called "intrusive identification." This is a term proposed by Donald Meltzer, a post-Kleinian psychoanalyst who has made a special study of Klein and Bion, and explored their thinking in relation to his clinical work in a particularly imaginative and original way.[7] Meltzer suggests that "intrusive identification" is a more accurate term for the aggressive type of projective identification. A parallel can be made with the battle of the hero with various monsters, reformulated by Jung in pre-oedipal terms "so that the monster can be understood as the mother whom the hero dismembers or enters into and destroys from within."[8] In extreme projective identification, the object is entered into and occupied in such a way that its separateness and individual qualities are destroyed in phantasy, much as in the process of empathy described by Jung in the passage above. According to Meltzer, what distinguishes intrusive identification is the omnipotence that pervades the unconscious phantasy of getting inside the object. Such an unconscious phantasy operates as a defense in the way that Micha was using it in his psychotherapy with me.

Meltzer suggests that we reserve the term projective identification for the unconscious phantasy that is aimed at communication rather than action.[9] In this way we can preserve the positive, teleological aspect of projective identification, and all that we mean when thinking about healthy infant development, maternal reverie, and the mother's capacity to be in tune with her baby (cf. Sidoli, "Oedipus as a Pre-Oedipal Hero" in this volume.)

Meltzer reflects that the object, or "container" of projective identification "has to have boundaries which, while they may be concretely represented, are fundamentally the boundaries drawn by selective attention."[10] This is a function of the analyst and part of my work with Micha, work in which I hoped that we could approach some understanding on his part of how he habitually used the defensive mode of "intrusive" identification. Meltzer writes that the term intrusive identification "catches the essential motive of invasion of an alien personality and body, as originally described by Melanie Klein."[11]

I am not quite sure why Meltzer uses the word "alien" here, except as it means not one's own; Micha was trying to prove that I was not alien at all, that I was familiar and he was utterly at home with me, able to invade my mind and push into it whatever he chose whenever he liked. Perhaps the word "alien" could refer to the malignant motive, which was revealed by Micha when he told me with glee about how, in role play, he entered the company of the evil Orks while he was in the guise of a good dwarf who resembled an Ork. The Orks were too stupid to spot him, and he was able to kill several of them before they realized that he was not one of them. I think this referred to his idea that he came to psychotherapy with the "good" motive of letting me treat him, and that I was too stupid to see the malignant, invasive motive that also underlay it. Here we can see the psychotic element in his personality, the part that got perverse pleasure out of destruction. Fantasies of sadistic battles, permeated with hatred and revenge, arose in response to encounters with authority figures who were experienced as deliberately humiliating him. He described the battle-encounters in terms of the fantasy novels that were his favorite reading, or in a narrative in which he played the hard guy, the hero-warrior who crushed his enemy. On the other hand, as hero-warrior he might magnanimously spare his enemy, secure in the knowledge of his own superior strength. What robbed the second scenario of any quality of real mercy or forgiveness was a sickening element of self-aggrandizement and self-deception that was part of his defense against extreme vulnerability.

Intrusion

Micha managed to pervade the clinic where I worked with his intrusiveness. When he arrived each week, he strode into the front office and elicited responses from all the secretaries. For a while he worked part-time in a bakery and pressed loaves of bread on them, and he always dropped in after his session to say good-bye. Once he got the part-time secretary to phone a shop and find out what time it closed and ask if they had his record for him. In this way I think he could dilute the transference and elicit the kind of everyday mothering that was missing from the psychotherapy where I was only available to think with him about his emotional life within a very limited time. At the same time he was able, in phantasy, to be the mother, the loaf-giver, and to deny his longing and need for my maternal preoccupation with him.

The most striking example of the infantile level at which this defensive intrusion operated involved the kitchen of the clinic: after one session he went straight into it and found the principal child psychotherapist making coffee. He declared that he had a sore throat that was as "dry as an elephant's backside," and, taken off guard, she instinctively gave him a glass of water.

The boy whom I saw before Micha was eleven, extremely obsessional and frightened and plagued by psychotic anxieties. I was told by this boy that Micha had greeted him and said, "What mood is she in today? I'm her next victim!" One of my outraged thoughts when I heard this was, "How dare he frighten my patient!"

And indeed, my response to all these incidents was to get annoyed and impatient and want to get rid of him, to push him out and rigidly control his access. I understood this as countertransference evidence—what Mara Sidoli calls "internal evidence"—of the split-off feelings that Micha was defending against in his omnipotent denial: "I'm not causing irritation; I'm not excluded: I'm loved and I'm right inside. I am not an elephant-sized, insatiable baby. I was not abandoned by Dad when I was four and my parents divorced; I had Mum all to myself. She was not erratic, eliciting intimate, excited responses and then suddenly pushing me off. She didn't betray me with boyfriends and perform the coup de grace when I was nine, by marrying my step-father and having a baby girl. This baby did not take my place in my mother's affections and occupy center stage in the family."

Exclusion

The counterpart to the intrusion was Micha's repeated experience of exclusion. He missed his first session because he mistook the name of the road and went to another clinic, thus finding himself unable to get into the therapy he had been eagerly awaiting for so long. He chatted nonstop at the end of the sessions, clinging to the time and my attention while he put on his jacket and slowly made his way to the door. He told me breezily that I was always in a hurry to get rid of him, but left absolutely no space for us to talk about this. In the early days of our work together, if I had not indicated clearly that he must go, sometimes interrupting the flow to say good-bye, we could have stood there endlessly suspended in a denial of separation. The material around this issue was about buses, how the stupid school gave him the wrong bus pass, with the result that the stupid conductor wouldn't let him on the bus, the dickhead. The longing for maternal containment and the pain of exclusion colored by oedipal jealousy was clear but only later became available for interpretation.

The acting out that he indulged in at the clinic meant that I found myself drawing the analytic boundaries extra firmly, especially around endings and gifts, and I felt that I was under severe psychological pressure to become a strict, super-ego parent. When he first offered me a loaf of bread, I took some time to explain the reason for my refusal and its meaning as part of the analytic frame, how in this work we would confine ourselves to the use of the time and to words for thinking about his feelings, dreams, fantasies, and thoughts. But he offered a loaf once or twice after that session, repeating in the transference the familiar experience of rejection. The technical difficulty lay in helping him to become aware of this, because he felt that all interventions of mine, whether interpretative or not, would be critical or rejecting, and he continually warded them off. When I tried to make a comment on his description of heroic battles, I felt that he experienced me as another sword-bearing enemy, posed to run him through with my penetrating words. I had only to draw breath and he launched into another paragraph of minutiae that prevented me from saying anything at all. It seemed there simply was not enough room for both of us in the available mental space. I managed to point this out to him, and gradually he was able to use me increasingly for the projection of mental pain in which the theme of rejection predominated.

At first it was focused on his girlfriend, Katy, who was barely thirteen at the time, and therefore halfway in age between him and his half-sister Natasha. Micha's feeling about Katy was romantic and chivalrous, and he scrutinized her every word and action for evidence that they were intuitively at one. In actuality she did not encourage his advances, and seemed a little afraid of him, but he played the role of her champion, threatening to knee any boy who brought her the least harm. He replayed to me scenes that must contain proof, as he construed it, that she loved him. He plotted to take her photograph when she was unaware and keep it secretly on his person. I linked this with fantasies, based on one of his favorite books, that he and Katy could slip into a fold in time where they could make love undiscovered. There was a disturbingly secretive, magic quality about these fantasies, as though he felt that he could steal her soul and identity, a secretiveness associated with incestuous fantasies about his mother and sister. During the period of his infatuation with Katy he was prone to primitive identifications; for example, although he was not a particularly fast runner, he did very well in a cross-country race at school by imagining that he was a deer. He claimed that he concentrated utterly, became the deer, and ran with a fleetness that was far beyond his normal capability. On another occasion he imagined that he was a wolf and fought another boy, as he felt, with superhuman strength. He was dominated by the archetype of the anima, and consequently by the Eros principle: restless, moody and sentimental, full of unconscious emotionality.

One day he arrived in great distress, because one of the teachers at school had taken him aside and told him that his attentions to Katy were unwanted and that he must leave her alone; Micha had been pestering her, the teacher said, and she did not want to see him any more. Micha was deeply hurt by this, and reacted by hating yet loving Katy, indulging in thoughts of suicide and relating these to me in minute detail, as well as inveighing against Katy's mother. Obviously she was behind it, and he wished for her the same suffering that he was going through. He would lock the mother in my consulting room with a plastic bomb between her knees. She would stare in horror at the timing device and then it would not go off after all, so that she would have his experience in reverse: fear and despair followed by relief and happiness. He had been happy and relieved that Katy continued to like him after the summer break, then suddenly rejection, despair and nothing to live for. If his dead body were found, it would be pretty obvious that the mother was responsible, since it must have been she who told the teacher what to say. Various themes emerge here, including his infantile rage at his own mother and her new girl baby, his deprivation in the transference and hatred of me because I did not give him enough time. More disturbing the element of rape can be seen in the bomb that will blow up the mother/therapist through the vagina. The need for containment is very real and desperate in this boy, but there is also the sadistic, destructive element in the thrust to get inside without any regard for the object; this was a cause of deep concern among his care-givers. However, the first thing to be done at this early stage of the therapy was to establish an atmosphere in which he knew that he could share and contain his pain.

Exclusion from the Family

His pain was expressed by recurring bouts of depression over Katy, sentimental poems about loneliness and rejection, and accounts of how he "knew" Katy's moods, even though they were apart. These immutably "true" experiences he verified by checking the evidence of time and place with her brother as proof of a participation mystique that was meant to deny the pain of loss and separation. It emerged that he had been repeatedly rejected by girlfriends since primary school. Before the Christmas break he was casting around for a new girl-friend, but felt that, if he lost her this time, it would be the end of him.

It is perhaps clear by now that anything approaching an experience of closeness in the transference contained a threat to his vulnerability that had to be rigidly defended against. It was difficult to interpret the transference, and I had to keep to myself most of the understanding of how the approaching Christmas break stirred up his fear of losing me and the therapy, and reactivated anxieties about a rejection by his family that had actually taken place some time before the therapy began. His mother learned from his diary that he had initiated some sexual play with his half-sister that involved his penetrating her vagina with his finger. His mother called the police, and he was removed from the house. He returned for a month, but after another incident with his sister he was removed permanently and put in the care of Social Services. Subsequently his visits to his family were strictly limited and controlled. He was given a foster placement, and young foster parents made a commitment to care for him for two years. They said that they were not planning a family and they understood that Micha had already suffered from feeling displaced. However, their baby was born after barely a year of fostering, thus repeating a history in which Micha felt displaced by a daughter who was more loved and valued than himself.

Discussion

All this seemed to me to express in a dramatic and concrete way the impact on Micha of his father's abandonment of him when he was four, his mother's second marriage, and the birth of his half-sister. Because he was unable to take in reconstructive interpretations at this stage in the therapy, I made an imaginative reconstruction for myself that he felt that his early oedipal wish to gain possession of his mother had come true when his father left the family. Then, having had her to himself for more than four years, he experienced his mother's preoccupation with her new husband and baby as totally excluding him, so that all his psychic energy became directed towards getting back in. I imagined that he was predisposed to experience it this way because of much earlier failures of projective identification with a mother whose interest in Micha as a baby came and went abruptly. From reading the social worker's notes I knew that the marriage with Micha's father had been unhappy, and that his mother was deeply disturbed by a miscarriage that she had had before Micha was born. I imagined that when Micha's unbearable baby feelings were projected into his mother, they found a container for short periods, but that when he became sexually excited, his projections were ejected by her, pushed back into the baby who was then left with unmodulated, persecutory feelings to manage by himself. It looks as though repeated arousal and then rejection of his wish to "penetrate" his mother, especially during the period after his father left, convinced him that he had a bad penis that had to be kept out. This I understood as the background to Micha's use of intrusive identification as a defense, a triumphant invasion of his object that brooks no refusal, but in its enactment is doomed to be rebuffed. I speculated that Micha's way of getting at his mother was through the little girl who was adored and very much admired by his mother and step-father: the way to punish mummy was to despoil mummy's beautiful little girl (malignant motive). There is the added motive of revenge on the step-father for taking Micha's place as his mother's partner.

Micha's exclusion from his family was traumatic, and when he was ejected from home he was hit by both his mother and his step-father, while his treatment in police custody verged on the brutal. It is striking that, a month after the first incident, he repeated the attempt on his sister, in spite of his first taste of the consequences; or was it because of them, proof positive that his attempts to get inside always met with summary rejection? This time his banishment from home was permanent. It would seem that the parents' response had a primitive, all-or-nothing quality that contained the archetypal elements of the incest taboo. It also looks as if the little girl was idealized, to Micha's detriment. When the kind of sexual intrusion that is the everyday fodder of infantile fantasy becomes concrete, then there is all hell to pay, and I think that Micha had to bear the projection of split-off infantile fantasies from others, such as parents, schoolfellows and policemen, in the collective way that Mara Sidoli describes in her paper, "Shame and the Shadow."[12]

Setting aside the malignant motive of revenge, I was struck by the unsuitability of the container that Micha chose for his intrusion, that is, the substitution of half-sister for mother. The sister was six-and-a-half at the time of the abuse, and there seemed to be a complete denial of his need for a breast-mother while he had domination over a helpless child-mother, as well gaining as a "proof positive" that the split-off affects that needed maternal containment could never be contained. It looked as if many of his mother's responses to him as a baby and young child were at an immature, young child level. Surely the tender vessel of Natasha's body and psyche could not possibly function as a container, or what Meltzer calls a "claustrum," that is, as I understand it, the vessel into which the urgent phantasy-impulses of intrusive identification are thrust. Meltzer suggests that, "for the sake of conceptual clarity, the term 'claustrum' should be used when talking of the object of projective and intrusive identification operating at the level of unconscious phantasy . . . while reserving the name 'container' for a more abstract level of discourse."[13] I worked hard to function at the level of container-contained in Micha's psychotherapy, holding within myself intensely powerful experiences of having extremely unpleasant voyeuristic or sadistic material forced into me, while struggling not to eject it, but to contain it and maintain the capacity to think about its meaning. I felt I was being treated like a claustrum while struggling to function as a container.

During sessions Micha sometimes came to sit right beside my chair to show me his computer drawings, his poems, and the medallion he engraved for Katy with elvan runes meaning love and fortune. He was "too close for comfort," and I felt as if he might fall into my lap. His uneasy sexuality was even more intense when he sat in his chair across from me and picked at his belt as if he might undo it, or slipped in a mention of his new red underpants, or described a medieval knight who only had the top part of his armor on as "being caught with his pants down." When he was particularly provocative with a sexy joke, I have to confess I lost patience and said, "Well Micha, you're making all kinds of innuendoes with this joke, but the couch is right here: we could get on it and have intercourse right now. We could do it but what would be the consequence?" He joked that I would lose my job, and there would be headlines in the local paper, but quickly sobered as he realized the parallel with what happened after the "incidents." From these experiences I understood that Micha's early relation with his mother had been highly eroticized, and this was substantiated by the social worker's notes.

I sorted out with Micha some good and bad aspects of his sword-penis, and he volunteered that the sword and the penis are neither good nor bad in themselves, but only in the use that they are put to, an insight that he had gained from a wise magician in one of his books. I was then able to point out the erotic atmosphere he was creating between us when he insisted on playing me his favorite tapes, and to describe his longing for my acceptance of his penis in a good inter-course.

Failure of Projective Identification

In the first session after the holiday break he told me that he had fallen in love with Mimi, a girl of his own age who was no longer going out with her boyfriend, Owen. No sooner had he taken her out than he found that Mimi and Owen were back together again, and he was the excluded one in the triangle. I saw that he had benefited from the experience of using me during the previous term for the projection of mental pain, particularly pain over the loss of Katy. We had been able, tentatively, to work on seeing a pattern in his relationships with girls that echoed his experience of exclusion by mother, step-father, and half-sister; he had not been included in the family celebration on Christmas day but had visited two days later. He was prepared to concede that I might have a point about there being a pattern linking his exclusion by mother on her second marriage, and his repeated disappointments with girls. Greatly encouraged, I suggested that he also felt left out by me during the holiday, and he said sadly that that was true, but my family needed me just as much as he did.

During this part of the session I was allowed to be in touch with Micha's feelings and to perform something like maternal reverie. But the experience of being understood, of having his pain taken in by me and accepted, made him too vulnerable to the fear of sudden expulsion, and so this state of things was short-lived. He went on to say that he had recently seen his own death in a kind of vision that he regarded as a prediction: in it he saw a car accident and a body on the road, then surgeons surrounding his own still figure on the operating table while he looked on from above from two vantage points simultaneously, and then one of the doctors spoke to his mother, and she was in tears. He was aged about twenty-two. I said that I thought we should take such a prediction very seriously as a counsel of despair from within about ever finding the love he was longing for. Micha's response left me completely at a loss, as he set out to refute and demolish what I had just said. I was baffled as to what point he was making and why he was so angry, since up to now he had not denied his pain and unhappiness. Under the onslaught I could hardly remember what I had said and felt deeply inadequate. He argued angrily that this had been a prediction, one of sixteen predictions that he had made in the last few months, and of those sixteen, about nine have come true, including his prediction that Katy would reject him, that Mimi and Owen would go through a test, and he had picked eight winners in the horseraces on television. "So weave something into that!" he exclaimed, leaning back challengingly in his seat. "Come on, let's see you weave some meaning into all sixteen of them! It's like saying that because ten metals burn with the same silver flame, they all have the same properties, but you would be very mistaken. See? I've just proved that you are completely wrong." After a good deal more haranguing along these lines he declared that predictions have nothing to do with feelings: I was trying to prove that he predicted a suicidal accident because he was feeling depressed. Sure he's depressed, but it has no connection with the prediction of his own death. "Nostradamus predicted the hour and place of his own death when he was happy and at the height of his powers. What has picking winners to do with feelings?" He left the session, still muttering and angry.

This kind of abrupt change from being in tune to being refuted in uncompromising terms was a common experience in the therapy and formed the basis of my reconstruction of Micha's early experiences of projective identifications that were abruptly cut short or ousted from their container, arousing rage, confusion, frustration, and a deep feeling of inadequacy. At the same time, the possibility of suicide was a serious threat in the therapy, partly because it was not possible for him to come more than once a week, so that the containment provided by the framework of the therapy itself was inadequate for this extremely uncontained boy.

At the time of writing this chapter, the therapy was at an early stage. Micha became increasingly able to calm down in the focus of my sympathetic attention and to tolerate and reflect on his depressed feelings. He was better able to tolerate and make some limited use of interpretations, his behavior with the secretaries modified, and he found it less difficult to leave each session. After the first summer break he went to a technical college and was enterprising about his part-time job and budgeting his expenses, as well as thinking about how to hold his life together in the face of his foster parents' move away from the area. But he continued to approach and be rejected by a long list of girlfriends, and was still quite unable to think about the defensive aspect of his long narratives about the girlfriends; that is, as a denial of his increasing reliance on his therapeutic relationship with me and my ability to contain him. It was also difficult for me to find a way that he could accept of talking about the infantile component of his feelings and his transference to me. But he came regularly and, from the beginning, was determined that his therapy would help him.

Conclusion

The flight into action, typical of adolescence, can be seen not only in Micha's role play games, actual fights with his peers, and confrontations with authority precipitated by his abuse of his half-sister, but most particularly in Micha's repetitive search for a girlfriend. This was most pressing at therapy breaks, when the loss of his therapist was not to be thought about and the burden of taking in all that he wished to thrust into me, both emotionally and physically, was to be borne by a young girl, who, naturally, was unable to fill this role and was repelled by his intrusiveness. Each time he was rejected, Micha capitalized on his feelings, playing the part of the heartbroken hero-lover and the solitary hero-poet. The regressive pull towards dependency on me and the containment provided by his therapy was fiercely denied.

In this chapter I have looked at the manic quality in Micha's attempts to assume a heroic stance, both in role play games and in the role he played in his own life dramas. Particular emphasis has been placed on his use of projective identification in a wholesale and violent way that Meltzer calls "intrusive identification." This was a function of his personality that had a psychotic tinge and was inadequately contained in the once-weekly psychotherapy that was available to him. Indeed I wished for him the kind of containment described by Gustav Bovensiepen in his paper, "The Clinic as Container."

Notes

1. M. Klein, "Notes on Some Schizoid Mechanisms," *The Writings of Melanie Klein* (London: Hogarth, 1961), v. 3, pp. 1–24.
2. M. Fordham, "Some Historical Reflections," *Journal of Analytical Psychology* 34 (1989) no. 3.
3. M. Fordham, *Jungian Psychotherapy* (London: Karnac, 1978) pp. 35–36.
4. M. Fordham, "Maturation of a Child Within the Family," *Journal of Analytical Psychology* 22 (1977) no. 2.
5. C. G. Jung, *Psychological Types, Collected Works* (London: Routledge and Kegan Paul) v. 6, para. 491.

6. W. Bion, *Learning From Experience,* (London: Heinemann, 1962).

7. D. Meltzer, et al., "The Conceptual Distinction Between Projective Identification (Klein) and Container-Contained (Bion)," *Journal of Child Psychology* 8 (1982) no. 2. Reprinted in *Studies in Extended Metapsychology* (London: Clunie, 1986).

8. M. Fordham, *Explorations into the Self* (London: Academic Press, 1985) p. 215.

9. Meltzer, et al. p. 202.

10. Ibid., p. 200.

11. Ibid.

12. M. Sidoli, "Shame and Shadow," *Journal of Analytical Psychology* 33 (1988), no. 2.

13. Meltzer, et al. p. 200.

SECTION 4

Defenses of the Self:
A Psychological Suicide

Introduction to Section 4

The way in which Jung uses the concept of the self differs fundamentally from the way this concept is used by other psychoanalytic schools. In Jung's view, the self contains both a person's potential and the unity of the personality as a whole. Jung states that the self is both the center and the circumference of the conscious and unconscious psychic system.[1] Whereas the self is seen as the center of the totality, the ego is seen as the center of consciousness. Jung has concentrated on the symbolic representations of the self (e.g., images of God, images of wholeness like mandalas, circles, etc.), but was not much interested in observing the activity of the self within the analytic process.

Michael Fordham extended Jung's theoretical concept as a developmental concept hypothesizing an original or primal self as existing from the beginning of life.[2] The primal self contains all the innate, archetypal potentials, and Fordham conceptualized it as a "steady state of integration" from which "the child's ego and bodily growth will unfold through the dynamic process he termed deintegration-reintegration."[3]

As in other separation phases of development (e.g. birth, the weaning process, etc.) puberty and adolescence form a development stage where the deintegration-reintegration processes are highly active. The psychosomatic, integrated state of the young person is threatened by physical, psychological, and social demands. These factors may create disturbances in the ego-self relationship in adolescence. Fordham states that the self has its own defensive organization that is different from the defense mechanisms of the ego. The theoretical as well as the clinical aspects of the defenses of the self are the subject of M. Davies' chapter.

Miranda Davies, in her chapter "Defenses of the Self in a Preadolescent Boy," discusses both the theoretical and the clinical aspects of these defenses. Her theoretical discussion clearly derives from Fordham's concept of defenses of the self, and from his model of the primal self as a psychosomatic unity, of which the ego is only one aspect. Defenses of the self as a total protective system are triggered in infancy when the survival of the infant is threatened. Such defenses protect the self, not only from a sense of outer attack and persecution, but also from the fear of implosion generated by uncontrollable anxiety and rage. This anxiety and rage derive from unmet needs and frustrated expectations. In Fordham's view, defenses of the self are a psychological immune response to extreme life-threatening situations in infancy; however, if they become habitual, autistic patterns develop.

Davies differentiates the defenses of the self from Anna Freud's mechanisms of ego defense, and relates them to the more primitive defense mechanisms that Melanie Klein has described. These are splitting, idealization, denial, and projective identification and are used against early infantile anxieties of a psychotic nature. The difference between Fordham's approach and Klein's approach to these primitive mechanisms is a matter of quantity: defenses of the self are more extreme, they are total. Klein's primitive defenses are understood to operate out of the unconscious in an infant's ego in the reverse schizoid-paranoid position, whereas Fordham's defenses of the self are seen as operating to protect the self as a totality and to prevent disintegration.

In the clinical section of her paper, Davies illustrates the unfolding of the defenses of the self during therapy of a prepuberty boy between ten and twelve years of age. The case material not only shows Davies' high degree of empathy and skill in treating a child in this difficult transitional stage, it is also a very good illustration of the total manner in which the defenses of the self operate. both psychically and physically. The child suffered from overwhelming pain of loss, rage, terror, and hate. And he expressed these feelings in physical symptoms such as drooling, letting his nose run, chewing his collar, and rubbing his nose, which operate as an autistic barrier. As an infant, this boy had experienced severe death anxieties, against which his defenses were directed. The self of this patient defends itself from any external input, in this case, the analyst's interpretations. Such defenses sometimes make the analytical process impossible. This was especially true in this case, where the boy destroyed interpretations. Additionally, anxieties arose from his fear of female identification.

It is interesting and helpful to see how Davies links the defenses of the self with the failure to symbolize. She makes a connection between Fordham's concept and Bion's concept of the transformation of beta elements into alpha elements by the alpha function, and the mother's/therapist's reverie, which in the transference is severely attacked by the defenses of the self.[4]

The biological changes of the body in puberty cause a great upsurge of confusion and anxieties in the child's inner world. This in turn activates defensive mechanisms that are reminiscent of the very early ones in infancy. Some adolescents experience the changes of their body as a catastrophe for their inner world and react with a psychotic breakdown. Because (as in infancy) the insides of their body and of the mother's body become the central focus of the adolescents' fantasies, brooding, and preoccupations, others experience their body as a "bad object" which has to be attacked, annihilated, or done away with by suicidal acting out. The body for such adolescents becomes a mother/claustrum/place full of bad parts inside which the adolescent feels stuck, and/or an object used to contain split-off, unbearable affects as well as aspects of the perverse infantile relationship to the inner parents. In a later phase of adolescence, defenses of the self may also operate as a total resistance to change both physically or psychologically.[5]

This state of affairs will be shown in Bovensiepen's chapter in a case of a seventeen-year-old boy (in the middle adolescence) who, to defend himself against disintegration, used his body as a robot-like shell which prevented him from coming into a loving and lively relationship with either his inner or outer world. In his mind the only way to break out of his constricting shell was to attack and destroy the body-robot in which he felt imprisoned, and he committed a serious suicidal attempt.

In experiencing his body, this boy showed two facets of the defenses of the self as described by Fordham: the more omnipotent and narcissistic perverse control of his body and mind by what he called the "system," a delusional-like control system that operated in the transference by projective/intrusive identification mechanisms and totally paralysed the analyst's capacity for reverie. The other aspect had a more autistic quality to it; he defended fiercely against any attempts on the analyst's part to reach him. He experienced these as intrusive penetrations threatening his survival. This more autistic mode of defense was represented by using his body as a cold, inanimate robot-shell or as a claustrum, in Meltzer's definition. One can understand the computerizing of his soul and body as an infantile grandiose solution for keeping in check his sexual excitement and the autonomous erections of his penis. These filled him with unbearable anxieties, as when they had occurred to him as a small child in bed with his mother, and he needed to defend himself against them.

Notes

1. C. G. Jung, *Psychology and Alchemy, Collected Works* (London: Routledge and Kegan Paul, 1953, rev. ed. 1967) p. 310. See also Glossary: Self.
2. M. Fordham, *Children as Individuals* (London: Hodder and Stroughton, 1969).
3. See M. Sidoli, *The Unfolding Self* (Boston: Sigo, 1989), p. 3.
4. W. Bion, *Learning From Experience* (London: Heinemann, 1962).
5. D. Meltzer, *The Claustrum* (London: Clunie, 1992).

7

Defenses of the Self in a Preadolescent Boy

Miranda Davies

This chapter examines the difficulties of a boy who was just enter-ing puberty. The material of his analysis illustrates one of the theses of this book: that the developmental surge of puberty and adolescence reactivates infantile conflicts. Such a reactivation is particularly clear in this case because the specific nature of his early infant experience can clearly be seen in its later manifestation as symptoms. The theo-retical argument of the paper arises from another of the themes of the book: Fordham's model of the primary self—deintegration and reintegration. In a model that sees the primary self arising at the begin-ning of life as psychosomatic unity, of which the ego is only one potentiality, it follows that there can be defenses to protect that unity, while defenses that protect the ego arise at a later stage of develop-ment. The chapter examines such "defenses of the self" in some detail, and follows Fordham in bringing in a formulation from the British object relations school, Bion's beta elements and alpha function, to aid our understanding.

Categories of Defense

In the development of a working model of the psyche, we have, broadly speaking, two main categories of defense: ego defenses, and the primitive, infantile defenses that underlie them. The ego defenses were delineated by Freud and further elaborated by Anna Freud in *The*

Ego and Mechanisms of Defence: they include regression, repression, reaction-formation, isolation, undoing, projection, introjection, turning against the self, and reversal.[1] Klein distinguished a subgroup of more primitive defense mechanisms used against early, infantile anxieties of a psychotic nature such as fear of death by falling to pieces (disintegration), or being crushed by annihilating forces. These are splitting, idealization, denial, and projective and introjective identification. It is these primitive defenses that Fordham explores in his paper, "Defences of the Self" where he writes that,

> in the case of part objects there is no unconsciousness, but rather more or less violent attempts to attack and do away with the bad object—they can reach a level at which one must speak in terms of annihilation. It is in this area that total defences are mobilized.[2]

Fordham has called these total defenses "defenses of the self." The difference between Klein's primitive, infantile defenses and Fordham's defenses of the self is quantitative: defenses of the self are more extreme; they are total. A definition by Lambert is helpful here.

> Although the distinction is by no means absolute, it is still possible to distinguish between a kind of half-blind defence against annihilation of the personality as such and defences that are involved in protecting the ego-consciousness from the experience of pain of all sorts.[3]

The difference between Fordham's defenses of the self and Klein's primitive, infantile defenses, is that Fordham's ideas are based on Jung's model of the psyche, in which the self is the central construct. Whereas in Klein's theory there is a rudimentary ego at birth that shows evidence of using projective and introjective mechanisms during the first months of life, Fordham proposes that there is a self at birth that is the total psychosomatic unity of the individual. This is a much more comprehensive model than that of the ego, one that is fundamental to Jung's idea of individuation.

The Self in Jungian Analysis

The self was one of Jung's most important concepts. He used the term in several ways that have been sorted out and delineated by

Fordham in his paper, "The Self in Jung's Works."[4] For our purposes a useful definition follows:

> Clearly, then, the personality as a total phenomenon does not coincide with the ego, that is, with the conscious personality, but forms an entity that has to be distinguished from the ego . . . I have suggested calling the total personality which, though present, cannot be fully known, the self.[5]

Carvalho, an analytical psychologist working in London, distinguishes clearly between ideas of the self in Freud and Jung's writings.

> Psychoanalysts tend to mean by the term an idea of the individual's identity. The concept in psychoanalysis therefore blurs with that of the ego, and this is particularly the case in Freud's writing. In Jung's writing, on the other hand, "self" designates the whole potential of the personality both conscious and unconscious. The ego is simply that part of the self which has become conscious. In Freud's psychology, the unconscious is derived almost exclusively from experiences that have been repudiated by the ego so that the work of analysis is to regain them. Jung's idea of the unconscious, however, though it includes aspects of experience which are unacceptable to the ego, is more importantly seen as the ground out of which consciousness and ego arise. The ego is not the dominant centre of the self but its facilitating executive.[6]

There is an important difference here: while Klein's primitive defenses are understood to operate out of the unconscious underlying an ego in the paranoid schizoid position, Fordham's defenses of the self are seen as operating to protect the self as totality, so that the defenses themselves are total. He writes,

> My work depends upon the view that the self in its ultimate sense is indestructible, since it does not belong to the realm of sensual experience. However, its deintegrates can become split up and distorted: these can then be expressed (experienced) in projective identification which forms the basis for the delusional transference.[7]

As a result of his work on infancy and childhood, Fordham postulated an original state of the self, which he called the primary self, "an original self integrate without phenomena," that exists from the onset of life.[8] The primary self contains all the potentiality of the individual, what might be called the blueprint of the individual's future development. This blueprint consists of "archetypal predispositions of potentiality, a potential for the emergence of bits of ego-consciousness, and certain potentialities connected with self-realization."[9] The primary self is an integrate, but in order that psychic structure may come into existence, it unfolds and moves outward towards the environment as a baby does in looking, touching, and feeding. Fordham called this capacity "deintegration" to describe how the integrate loosens and opens up, and to distinguish the process from disintegration. The deintegrate, the baby's looking, for example, meets the environment, the mother's eyes and all that is expressed through them, and the new experience is "integrated" to become part of the self in steady, quiet states and in sleep. This is a theory of process, often referred to as "primary self, deintegration and reintegration." The example most frequently given to illustrate the process is the baby's deintegration in breastfeeding and reintegration in sleep.

> After this matching has reliably taken place over a sufficient period of time, the self will be able to reintegrate something rather different from the original deintegrate. The infant now has the basis for a true internal object.[10]

More complex processes and the importance of the mother's containing capacity are beautifully illustrated in Sidoli's paper, "Deintegration and Reintegration in the First Two Weeks of Life."[11]

Fordham's paper, "Defences of the Self" describes the "total defense" exhibited by patients who are in a transference psychosis,

> where everything the analyst says is apparently done away with either by silence, ritualization of the interviews or by explicit verbal and other attacks directed to nullifying the analytic procedure.[12]

Case Illustration

I have gradually put together these theoretical reflections in the aftermath of the analysis of a boy whom I shall call Peter. I saw Peter for two years, when he was ten to twelve years old, and I consistently came up against his use of primitive defenses that seemed intractable, and presented a particular difficulty in the analytic work. While Peter did not have a full blown transference psychosis, I think that in what follows it is possible to see elements of a delusional transference to me as well as features that accord with Fordham's description, including silence, ritualization, and activities directed towards nullifying the analytic procedure.

History of Peter's Infancy

Peter's mother felt that he had had an unfortunate start in life, compared with his siblings. It was a long and difficult labor: he was born with a heavy bruise in a band around his head and across his forehead, because his head had been caught in a severe contraction. This is striking in the light of Fordham's speculations about when the earliest deintegrations of the primary self occur. He writes:

> In view of increasing knowledge about intrauterine life, we may think it happens before birth. The flood of stimuli provided by birth itself produces anxiety, the release of breathing and crying activities that must certainly suggest an early deintegrative state. It is assumed that the infant reintegrates again before he starts his first feed, in which further instinctual release (deintegration) occurs.[13]

This opens an area for speculation about the nature of deintegrative experience during life in the womb and its influence on the response of the mother's body to the fetal deintegrate that initiates the birth process. At the same time, we cannot know how Peter would have reintegrated this traumatic birth through repeated cycles of deintegration at the breast and reintegration in sleep, because it was succeeded by two life-threatening experiences.

Breastfeeding did become well established. Then at three weeks Peter's esophagus collapsed and he stopped breathing. He went blue and his rib cage protruded in a V-shape in front. An ambulance rushed mother and baby to the hospital where the collapsed cartilage was opened again, a feeding tube put down Peter's nose and he was put in an oxygen tent. When he recovered he was taken home, but a less severe collapse occurred again a few weeks later and was more easily dealt with. The condition was not operable and in time the cartilage strengthened naturally. At home he was kept in a sitting position in a little chair to aid his breathing. When he was in the pram in the garden or in bed at night, his mother listened to his rattling breathing through an intercom for babies, and the instant it was not audible she rushed to him. Within a few months, his parents noticed a way he had of opening his mouth wide and stretching his eyes open in an almost clownlike expression that made them laugh in spite of their feeling that their response was not appropriate. He did not like to be cuddled, and his mother felt that he kept her at a distance. She accepted this as his nature and did not press her attentions. As an older child he did not like tickling or rough-and-tumble and was particularly frightened when the duvet was thrown over him. He continued to fend off his mother's caresses, and she felt guilty about having to make an effort to provide them, especially as it was so easy to show affection to the other children.

Themes in the Material

In looking at my work with Peter, I hope to show that his defensive patterns were predominantly colored by defenses of the self, and for this reason, the gains that could be made in analysis were limited. I and my analytic attitude were identified by him at first as alien, as "not me" phenomena. As time went on, he became increasingly able to cooperate, although it was clear that he never really enjoyed his analysis, and his defenses of the self, by definition difficult to analyze, were not fundamentally changed during his short time with me.

Peter was referred because of his extreme timidity, and what he called his "habits." He was aware of these habits, but quite unable to control them. He was terrified of crossing the street or using a public telephone. From time to time he nodded convulsively, and he tried to stop it by putting his hand to his head. When he was preoccupied, his hand lifted the corner of his collar to his mouth and he chewed it, while saliva flowed copiously. Sometimes his saliva flowed and dripped to the floor when he was not chewing. He often sneezed violently into the air and the mucus, too, dripped to the floor.

Survival and Potency

Material early in the analysis showed his preoccupation with survival and his deep anxieties about making the transition from childhood to adulthood. These were vividly expressed by a comic book story that absorbed him called "Death Wish," in which a rope was strung across Grand Canyon and a daring motorcyclist had to ride across it. The sense of precariousness, of his life hanging by a thread, was played out in a series of fragile rescues. Usually these took place when he was curled up on a chair and his felt pen dropped to the floor. Then he had to bend down and "rescue" it by picking it up without any part of his body touching the floor. He went through many contortions to perform this apparently simple maneuver and in this way conveyed how dangerous and difficult it was. I understood the felt pen to be equated with his penis, and there was a long period when he was deeply preoccupied with anxieties about its potency and his fear that his floppy, little-boy penis would never develop into a man's penis that could maintain an erection. The capacity to stay erect was equated with spectacular accomplishments in sports and gaining world records, and he attributed these abilities to a father-like character called "Champion of the World" that he drew frequently. He was beset by a fear that he would have to do his growing up all at once in a way that made the risk of failure acute. The themes of survival, potency, and growing up were intertwined: he drew football players whom he wished to emulate, who had enormous fingers and feet. Play depicting a race against time showed how deeply pessimistic he was about having all his infantile needs met before adulthood overtook him. If he did manage to win the race, he always shortened the time in which it had to be run.

The Jankos and the Humans

A conflict emerged between his wish to be able to maintain an erection and his fear that his urge to penetrate was damaging and alien to human relations as he knew them. For months he drew a battle between the alien Janko men and the Humans. The Janko men were invading, one-eyed, penis-like creatures who came from Mars and were led by Thin Neck, while the Human defense was led by Super-Peter. This was an elaboration of the earlier themes of Death Wish and the rescues, a terrible battle against the invasion of alien forces (alien feeding tube, alien impulse to penetrate), that could only be represented when the invaders were projected into outer space. The outcome of the conflict was dangerously close: by the end of the war, the number of Jankos killed totaled 15,128, while the Humans won by a hair's breadth with a total of 15,119 dead. The battle ceased when he heard that he had passed the entrance exams and had been accepted by the school that his brother went to. Peter was entering puberty when he started his analysis, and his anxiety about leaving childhood, with both infantile and oedipal conflicts unresolved, intensified. He displayed anxieties about getting into secondary school, as well as anxieties about his body.

Constructing a Nipple and a Breast

When we consider Peter's infantile anxieties, it is clear from his symptom of collar chewing, that these centered around his mouth and its relation to the breast. He seemed to be unable to find a relationship to the nipple that could allow him to be fed from the breast, and this meant that the relationship between mouth and nipple could not be internalized as a container/contained experience or internal object. Here, the "object" is understood as having a function. Instead he constructed his own nipple-breast by means of the collar which was meant to fill the gap in his mouth, as he said, "like sweets."

It was becoming increasingly apparent with the onset of puberty that the collar could not replace the nipple and breast because the need for an internalized container/contained object that he could project was becoming more pressing. This pressure arose from the deintegration of puberty and adolescence, with its inexorable push towards a broadening of experience, adult sexuality, and parenthood. Instead, the nipple—that is, experiences felt to be nipple-like in their emotional impact—had to be attacked and eliminated at all costs. The nipple-like quality was to be found in any experience that Peter felt was intrusive, persecutory, and not familiar to his self. In the analysis, he experienced my interpretations in a concrete way as intrusive and persecutory, so he by-passed them by simply not hearing them. Sometimes he mimed crunching up my words in his "robot jaws," which he created by holding his arms out to the side and clamping them together in front of him while he made a noise like the garbage truck that made a weekly collection outside our window.

In the first section of this book, Sidoli describes the infant's proto-experience of maleness and femaleness at the breast through sensuous contact with the hard nipple and soft breast. In this way a symbolic equation is made between the nipple and the penis. In Peter's oedipal development, his unconscious experience that the nipple must always be attacked and damaged underlay his doubts about his penis. He was deeply unsure of its potency, and tried to compensate by waiting to pee until the last possible minute, building up maximum pressure. Yet he often entered the consulting room in what he called a "floppy" manner. As a consequence he was unable to feel that he could, in fantasy, get inside his mother in the way that his father could. He constructed a large but tightly enclosed spaceship that he could not get access to because he was quite unable to construct a door in it. Later in the analysis he began to feel he might approach his father's position when he acted the part of a character he called "Rich Man" who lived in a mansion and was thus symbolically able to get inside mother's rich body. He could not identify with a nipple/penis that was so badly attacked, so he struggled to make a masculine identification with the football players in his drawings. He was inclined to identify with the mouth, which was unconsciously equated with the vagina in the mouth-nipple intercourse. This made him anxious about his feminine identifications, and he warded them off by drawing his sister with erect, penis-like bunches of hair. For these reasons he strenuously resisted interpretations that drew attention to the feelings in his mouth.

The Obstacle Race

Peter was conducting a race against time at the onset of puberty to get these difficulties in his inner world resolved before childhood closed. It was enacted as an obstacle race and he instructed me to time him accurately by counting out the seconds while he rushed through a complex series of activities that included throwing up a plastic lid and catching it on his head and walking with his right foot in the bin with the lid balanced on his head. He was not skillful or dexterous, and his success was fragile. He was never satisfied with the score and continually reduced the number of seconds in which the race had to be run.

The Characters

I am concentrating mostly on the infantile components that came to light because defenses of the self are mobilized against infantile psychotic anxieties. But there was a period when Peter was more willing to cooperate because it was far less persecutory for him when we looked at his eleven-year-old self than when I interpreted his baby feelings. He started to draw figures while he had his eyes closed, so that the various parts of the body—head, torso, arms, legs—did not join, revealing his sense of not being all-of-a-piece. From this loosening up of his body image, there emerged four characters whom he drew and acted for months. They were Rich Man, who was superior and elegant, a composer and conductor who lived in a mansion; Champion of the World, who held the world record for everything, even eating breakfast; Yobbo, who was like a tramp, picked his nose, did not wash or brush his teeth, and just lay about; and Hitler. Peter often conducted an orchestra or a large choir (omnipotent defense) in the character of each of these in turn: Rich Man high-nosed, thin and elegant, with graceful gestures, Champion forthright and robust, Yobbo floppy and all over the place, and Hitler relentlessly four-square, beating his baton mercilessly. The baton, of course, was his ruler.

I felt that the orchestra conducting was a way of wooing me, a response to my love of music which I think he picked up from earlier play when I had to decipher which nursery rhyme he was tapping with a pencil on the table. I thought that Rich Man's elegance was a response to his perception of my clothes as elegant, and it was through Rich Man that we could get closest to his fantasy of being my husband, and thus to his oedipal rivalry with his father. At the same time, Champion of the World was an idealized version of his father, who actually did play sports well, while Peter felt defeated in his attempts to emulate his father and brother. Champion's feats were prodigious: he could build a mansion in one day and wallpaper it in .09 seconds, and, of course, he held the world record in all sports. As months went by, this defensive idealization lessened slightly and Champion began to lose records and be challenged by Champion Junior.

In the meantime, Peter was settling well into his new classes and enjoying extra cricket after school. Yobbo, however, was naturally not allowed to show his face at Peter's smart school, and had to be banned to outer space. His place was taken by Funny Man, who juggled and did clown-like falls to entertain people (manic defense). This was a side of Peter that his mother knew well, his tendency to take center stage, bow self-mockingly and send himself up, and she felt that it could become a distortion in his personality. Through Funny Man, we were able to look at how Peter got people to laugh at him so that they would not discern how much he feared that he was weird, that he was a Mindbloggs, brother of Sid Bloggs, with weird and shameful sensations in his penis that he was afraid would show on his face, the way they did in his drawings. He wanted to become a brain surgeon in order to operate and straighten out his own mind. (His analyst obviously was not going about it the right way, not giving him any medicine.) His speech impediment intervened here, and he said, "drain surgeon," betraying how quickly his hope of cure went down the drain. In time, interpretation of his masturbatory impulses brought relief, and Funny Man caught influenza and died; this did not mean that interpretation had penetrated to his more profound sense of being weird in his mouth, disabled by impulses that got enacted in relation to his mouth and caught him unawares.

Hitler did the goose step and beat his enemies into the ground. He obviously could not show his face at school and soon died, but another character called Fred Hurtman took his place. Fred Hurtman beat and hurt people and then felt so guilty that he pulled his own hair out. The characters battled in Peter's mind, and he received news in his earphones that Fred Hurtman was beating Sid Bloggs. At last the battle in outer space was coming down to earth and becoming humanized. I tried to show Peter how the exaggeration of the characters, particularly of Champion, illustrated how very much he needed to control and defend himself against his baby feelings of weakness and helplessness. It emerged that Champion had the same first name as Peter's father. He started to lose world records and was succeeded by his son who was about eleven years old. Not long after this, Peter heard in his earphones that the Janko-Human war had ceased for good.

Defenses against the Analytic Procedure

In spite of the greater humanization of this material, in the countertransference I felt that I was never fully human for Peter, that I was to some extent the object of a delusional transference. The result was that I had to contain a fairly fixed projective identification of bleakness, inaccessibility, impotence, and uselessness. My affective response can be likened to the attacked nipple that cannot make the feeding link. My interpretations were felt by him to be alien and needed to be fended off. For example, he told me, "Once when I was a baby, I could not breathe, and I would have died in another ten seconds." I linked his baby desperation to get air into his lungs with play he showed me in which he had to fold a paper fan and fan himself with it in ten seconds (also a race against time). He responded by redoubling his effort and folding the fan even quicker. While this activity had the appearance of confirming my interpretation, in reality it had the opposite effect: I knew that I had not reached him and rapport was not increased. The fan-folding became an endlessly repeated ritual of the kind outlined by Fordham, and its purpose was to nullify the analytic procedure, so that exploration of the feelings contained within the activity of fanning was not possible.

The way that most of my interpretations were experienced as attacks became clearer when he drew a computer game called "The Battle of the Squares and the Curlies." Square shapes and curly shapes were drawn up against each other on opposite sides of the page and attacked and blew each other up in space. It looked as if my interpretations were being broken up into word-shapes, attacked and dispersed so that any chance of their penetrating his mind in a nipple-like way and giving him food for thought was remote. While he concentrated on the game, his mouth dripped saliva; and while he drew with his right hand, his left gently lifted his collar to his mouth, and he chewed it, making it wet with a flow of saliva as copious as that of a baby mouthing his teething ring. Throughout our work together I talked about the longing of his mouth for the nipple and breast, and how he supplied his own collar-breast substitute, but very little change showed in his collar chewing.

Defenses of the Self

As Bovensiepen has outlined in the Introduction to this book, during the transition from latency to puberty, the defenses shift from a predominance of ego defenses to defenses that protect the self as a whole. These are described by Fordham in his Preface to *The Self and Autism,* where he puts forward "the concept of the self as a defense system designed to establish and maintain a child's individuality . . . ," a concept that resulted from his investigations into infantile autism.[14] The self as a defense system operates developmentally to preserve individuality, but it can become pathological, as in the case of autism when the defense system can serve to prevent development. We can see, in Peter's case, how a defense against deintegration was mobilized when the environment to be met, the feeding tube equated with the nipple, was experienced as too threatening. Peter's sense of his individual self was represented in one of his last drawings as an embryo-like shape, showing that it was so fragile and vulnerable that it had to be protected in a total way by a defense system that was self-contained and, to a considerable extent, inaccessible. Whereas interpretation of ego defenses against displaced genital impulses did enable Peter to stop his head-nodding, defenses of the self remained largely unaffected by interpretation, and his collar chewing and saliva dripping continued as before but happened rather less often. At the earliest, oral level, elements of the self stayed fixed and could not loosen and open out or deintegrate into a feeding experience, because of the very early trauma in Peter's life.

Beta Elements and Alpha Function[15]

It seemed likely to me that the feeding tube had been put down Peter's left nostril, because this was the one he constantly rubbed and worried while sneezing and blowing during his many colds and allergy attacks. These symptoms can be understood as proto-thoughts of the feeding tube, or, as Bion came to call them, beta elements. Beta elements are physical symptoms with emotional meaning—the sneezing and nose-rubbing—that have not been digested by alpha function. In other words, these elements had not come into an object relation with the mother who could take them in, understand them and return them to her baby in a way that had meaning and in a form that he could gradually digest. The performance of alpha function by the mother enables the baby gradually to bring beta experiences into a mental realm where he can begin to have fantasies about them and, as a child, to project them into dreams and fairy tales to symbolize them and begin to think about them.

Beta elements are defined by Bion as suited for use in projective identification and are influential in producing acting out; they are objects that can be evacuated or manipulated in a way that is a substitute for words or ideas.[16] In the absence of alpha function they are, like the suddenly unavailable breast, unavailable for conversion into thinkable form. Thus we can see in the insertion of the feeding tube after near death, the origins of the intrusive "nipple" that must be warded off at all costs, while the mouth is left as an empty gap, full of longing.

Fordham has adopted Bion's theory of beta elements and alpha function to help in understanding this area of experience. Peter's saliva dripping and collar chewing were beta elements, physical symptoms with emotional meaning that were not brought into an object relation with me in the analysis, and therefore not capable of being symbolized there. We never came to a stage in the analysis when my mind, or my words, could represent the breast his mouth sought, and he showed little attachment to me or sadness at leaving me. My attempts to perform alpha function and make the emotional meaning of his symptoms thinkable for him were a failure, and it is a characteristic of defenses of the self that these defenses have an inaccessible quality.

Early Deintegrates of the Self and Idealization

The breast created by Peter out of his collar can be understood as being very close to the primary self of Fordham's model, so that it was imbued with absolute, archetypal qualities and heavily idealized. He made his own nipple and breast from the collar, and he created milk from the flow of saliva as a defense against having to take in persecutory not-self. The persecutory not-self elements were depicted in the analysis as the attacks of the Janko men on the Humans or the Squares on the Curlies, and experienced as the penetrating, attacking qualities in my words. Intrinsic in an archetype is a pair of opposites: when idealization is turned inside out, there is an opposite experience of some external force that is mechanical and inhuman, trying to attack. As a three-week-old baby, Peter had not had enough experience, through deintegration and reintegration, of meeting the flesh-and-blood breast: he had not had time to internalize a good object, and so there was no internalized good breast to defend him against trauma, or, at puberty, to be projected into me. Instead the deintegrate had been arrested by trauma and remained in a position very close to the self. It was thus imbued with the extreme opposites of an ideally available breast and an inhuman attack that threatened annihilation. Peter's enactment of his robot jaws crunching up my interpretations was a beautiful depiction of Klein's concept of primitive annihilation of bad objects. While Peter experienced some aspects of the analysis as alien in the ways that we have seen, he experienced good aspects of the analysis as aspects of the collar-breast. These had been created out of his self through idealization.

Symbolization of the breast began late in the analysis when he drew a car full of sweet drinks and a bottomless glass of Coca-Cola beside his bed. It remains an open question whether, given more time, this could have provided the avenue to further deintegration, reintegration, internalization of the breast, projection, symbolization and reintrojection in the analytic process.

The Self and the Immune System

In outlining Fordham's defenses of the self, Samuels writes,

We are forced to posit a capacity of the self to form an absolute barrier between self and not-self when required or impelled through anxiety or threat. This is an important theoretical point: it is not simply trauma or disappointed expectation that destroys the capacity to symbolize. There are also defense systems which can react to insensitively presented not-self as if it were a vicious enemy which must be neutralized by any means.[17]

Samuels' definition sheds light on my understanding of the battle of the Squares and the Curlies, which represents the neutralization of a vicious enemy, particularly when I thought of it as a depiction of a biological defense system such as white corpuscles destroying an invading virus. When, in illness, the body fights to throw off infection, the biological defense system recognizes what is not-self and attacks and neutralizes it. An illuminating paper on this subject was written by L. Stein, an analytical psychologist in London who had a medical background. In his article, "Introducing Not-Self," he proposes the action of the immune system as an analogy to illustrate the actions of the self when it feels itself to be threatened with annihilation by elements that are not-self.[18] I did interpret this battle, as well as that of the Jankos and the Humans, as a depiction of Peter's early trauma. As a result, there was some modification of his extreme projection of the conflict into outer space, in that he eventually saw it as a punch-up between Fred Hurtman and Sid Bloggs. He dramatized himself as a single Robot Jaws crunching up and annihilating a single, talking Miss Davies, and I was seen to survive.

The Outcome

The analysis was ended at his mother's request. By this time Peter had found his feet at secondary school and gradually improved his marks. His mother told me that he enjoyed some modest success as a cross-country runner and was able to negotiate the ride on three buses to get home after school. He was more affectionate with his parents, his head-nodding had disappeared, and his collar chewing had lessened.

Summary

Some material from the analysis of a ten- to twelve-year-old boy has been described and discussed with particular emphasis on his defenses of the self. These defenses are seen as a total response, difficult to modify in analysis, and having the purpose of defending the whole personality from the experience of annihilation. Whereas ego defenses are available to a child who has obtained unit status, at around the age of two, an infant does not have the capacity to symbolize. When he is traumatized, defenses of an absolute kind spring spontaneously into being to cope with the miseries involved—what Lambert calls a "half-blind defense against annihilation of the personality as such."[19] In Peter's case the overwhelming pain of loss, rage, terror, hate, and compensatory idealization continued to be expressed in beta elements, physical symptoms with an affective content such as saliva dripping, collar chewing, nose rubbing, and mucus dripping. These beta elements were hardly accessible during the short analysis available to him and therefore, although a considerable amount was accomplished in other areas, little could be done to bring the psychosomatic symptoms into alpha function, the area of fantasy, dream, and myth, from where they could be brought into the analytic relationship and symbolized.

Notes

I should like to express my gratitude to Elizabeth Urban whose thinking about the self has contributed immeasurably to this paper.

1. A. Freud, *The Ego and Mechanisms of Defence* (London: Hogarth, 1937).
2. M. Fordham, "Defences of the Self," *Journal of Analytical Psychology* 19 (1974):153.
3. K. Lambert, *Analysis, Repair and Individuation* (London: Hogarth, 1981), p. 211.
4. M. Fordham, *Explorations into the Self* (London: Academic Press, 1985)
5. C. G. Jung, *Aion, Collected Works* (London: Routledge and Kegan Paul, 1959) v. 9:2.
6. R. Carvalho, "Therapy and Analysis as Activities of the Self," *British Association of Psychotherapists* 18 (1987): 21–31.

7. M. Fordham, *Explorations of the Self,* pp. 159–160.

8. Ibid., p. 109.

9. K. Lambert, p. 193.

10. A. Samuels, *Jung and the Post-Jungians* (London: Routledge and Kegan Paul, 1985) p. 158.

11. M. Sidoli, "Deintegration and Reintegration in the First Two Weeks of Life." *Journal of Analytical Psychology* 28 (1983): 201–212.

12. M. Fordham, "Defences of the Self." p. 153.

13. M. Fordham, "Explorations into the Self," p. 108.

14. M. Fordham, *The Self and Autism* (London: Heinemann, 1976) p. xiv.

15. See Glossary.

16. W. Bion, *Learning From Experience.* (London: Heinemann, 1962) p. 6.

17. A. Samuels, p. 121.

18. L. Stein, "Introducing Not-Self," *Journal of Analytical Psychology* 12 (1967): 97–113.

19. K. Lambert, p. 211.

8

Suicide and Attacks on the Body as a Containing Object

Gustav Bovensiepen

Suicide, suicide attempts, and self-inflicted injuries are widespread phenomena that may accompany either a temporary developmental crisis or outbreaks of serious psychic disturbances in adolescence. A variety of conflicts can lead to such behaviour. Even when there is no dramatic crisis, either fantasied or acted out, self-mutilations or suicidal wishes play an important role in almost each psychotherapy with adolescents at one time or another.

The cult film of the 1950s *Rebel Without a Cause,* depicts the psychological cliché of the weak, mother-bound youngster whose father is a "henpecked husband," not a strong man with whom the boy can identify in order to separate from the mother. The son, Jim (played by James Dean), seeks refuge in a delinquent juvenile gang where he has to submit to a test of courage to become initiated into the gang. In a game of "chicken," he has to race against the gang leader, Buzz, straight towards the edge of a cliff and throw himself out of the car at the last possible minute before it plunges into the abyss. Whoever jumps last wins the race, but Buzz waits too long and plunges to his death. Here the delinquent peer group serves as a container for the youngsters' conflicts with their parents. Thus Jim projects into Buzz, the strong gang leader, an older male with whom he can fight as an oedipal rival. It is vital for the boy to be able to identify with a strong oedipal rival, and he could not do this with his own weak father with whom he did not have a sufficiently strong bond. The confrontation with the rival, the risk of his own life and his subsequent victory, makes him a hero. Unfortunately, the conflict is concretely acted out in the film, and one of the two males is killed.

Any attacks on the body are aspects of the same problem, especially when fighting or confrontation cannot take place for fear of the inadequacy of the rival: hence the attacks are turned inwards against oneself. By attacking and attempting to destroy one's own body, the youth feels powerful, and has the illusion of surviving, at least psychically, and thus maintaining his identity. Perhaps this was one reason why James Dean became a hero of a generation of young people, for Dean himself raced to his death in a fast car, thereby enacting the fantasy.

The premature death of the hero guarantees his immortality; this is a widespread societal pattern. A classic example is the impact that Goethe's novel *The Sorrows of Young Werther* (1772) had on an earlier generation of young people. It caused an epidemic of suicides in the "Werther style" among his young contemporaries, who dressed like Werther in blue jackets with brass buttons, yellow waistcoats, high brown boots and round felt hats with unpowdered hair.[1] The inflation of the Werther cult is comparable to the mass adolescent adoration of numerous cult figures today. The importance of the outfit indicates that these heroic figures who die young lend themselves as models for self-identification.

Young people split the ego between the good and the bad object. The hero, because of his strength and courage, becomes the "good object," while the body, experienced as vulnerable, imperfect, a source of inevitable turmoil and dependency, is equated with weakness and becomes a "bad object" to be disposed of. In extreme cases of splitting, the good internal object and the idealization connected to it can only be maintained when the bad object, which the young person projects into his or her body, is done away with.

The Transformation of the Body in Adolescence

The difficulty for the young person is to bring the transformation of the body and bodily experiences into harmony with the rapidly developing psychic world in order to achieve what we call identity. There are adolescents who experience the bodily changes in puberty as an almost catastrophic change of their inner world or their total personality. To express it metaphorically, the changes affect the body in its symbolic function as "container of the soul," its inner capacity for containment. Containment means the capacity to hold within oneself anxiety-provoking inner and outer stimuli and to transform bodily instinctual perceptions into psychic experiences. This transformation is what the Kleinian analyst Bion calls transformation of beta elements (e.g. sensations) into alpha elements (fantasies, symbols).[2] In Jung's view, this transformation from the physical to the psychic brings about the operation of the transcendent function; that is, the mental capacity to symbolize.[3]

The capacity for containment can be permanently impaired by schizoid processes set in motion by bodily changes in the course of puberty. In such extreme cases, the youngster experiences himself or herself, consciously or unconsciously, totally filled with destructiveness. There is no inner space available either for the unfolding fantasies of "good" internal object relations, or the prerequisite for love relationships in the internal family, the actual family, the peer group, and the larger world.

This state of affairs can be seen in the case of a psychotic boy who, with the onset of sexuality, experiences his whole body as filled with pornographic ideas. As he expressed it, "Porno has taken the place of my soul," and "The evil in me eats up the good stuff." His sexual obsessions in the course of his compulsive masturbatory activities had a mechanical, brutal, and soulless quality. This boy repeatedly felt the impulse to kill himself and exhibited self-destructive behaviour in sessions, such as banging his head against the wall or scratching his skin until it was bloody.

In this dramatic situation, one can interpret this behaviour as stemming from an early experience where there had not been a "good enough" fit with the breast/mother. If the ego of a child has become rigidly defended and full of bad feelings, it is because the baby has not been able to experience the mother as a container for unbearable and overwhelming affects in infant states of panic and disintegration. The defense against the failure of containment becomes even more rigid during latency. In puberty, the instinctual drives threaten the ego complex with fragmentation once again, and thus unintegrated infantile experiences will come to the fore and infantile unconscious fantasies will begin to emerge, producing high levels of anxiety. These infantile unconscious fantasies are part object fantasies connected to the adolescent's own body and his or her mother's body, especially her skin, breasts, orifices, and insides. When adolescents feel threatened by disintegration once again, they try to avoid it by fantasizing about their own body as a containing object. The specific difficulty at this age is that the shape of the body as a containing object keeps changing. An added complication for adolescents is that part-object relations become increasingly sexualized and projected into sexualized genital objects.

The Body as Container in Adolescent Girls

When schizoid mechanisms are activated by puberty, there is a great upsurge of anxieties in the young person. The body, which is equated in a nonsymbolic way with the body of the mother, is rejected, ignored, denatured, or experienced as alien, so that it has no containing function. With this formulation in mind, it may be helpful to look at typical adolescent disturbances that can be understood as attacks on the body or as dysfunction of the body as a containing object. These attacks include anorexia nervosa, self-mutilating behaviour, and actual suicide. Self-mutilating behavior is seen frequently, predominantly in adolescent girls. It varies from ritualized ear piercing and tattoos to severe injuries. Girls who injure themselves with knives, needles, or other sharp objects do not have a clear intention to commit suicide. They describe themselves as having been in a state of psychic absence, an emotional and sensory anesthesia. Some of them act impulsively and compulsively and then wonder how this possibly could have happened. They seem to have temporarily lost the capacity to feel and experience themselves. Through painful mutilation they reenter their body and consciousness. Because of the sexualization of the early part object, the fantasy of the "bad breast/nipple" has developed into the "bad penis" fantasy. The penis is equated with sharp hard destructive objects that cut, kill, or shoot—like knives, needles, and pieces of glass—rather than soft, flexible, nourishing, satisfying, and loving objects. In the course of their self-mutilating attacks, they fantasize about violent penetration by the bad object into the containing object.

The Body as a Robot in an Adolescent Boy

The following case illustrates the way in which the body as a containing object takes the shape of a rigid, hard, robot-like shell which can only function in a controlling and constricting way. Thinking about this patient, the legend of the Golem and its modern equivalent, the computer, comes to mind. In 1965 in Israel, the first big computer system was installed. Gershom Scholem baptized it the "Golem I" in his inauguration speech. He pointed out the underlying idea that connected the computer with the Golem—a man made of clay—of medieval Jewish mysticism:

> The idea was to create another Adam, a being who was under the control of his creator, and who carried out the tasks assigned to him, but who could also develop a dangerous tendency to escape this control and display destructive capacities just like human beings.[4]

Both the modern and the ancient Golem lack spontaneity, feeling, and, most of all, language. In other words. they lack a human soul and the capacity for symbolization.

In the case of the patient, Martin, his schizoid defense was to experience his body becoming a robot-like shell that prevented him from coming into a loving and lively relationship with either his inner or outer world. In his mind, the only way to break out of his constricting shell was to attack and destroy the body-robot in which he was imprisoned. In fact he attempted suicide by ingesting sodium hydroxide, commonly known as lye or caustic soda. As a result of this episode, he was referred for treatment.

Martin was a pale, tall, lanky sixteen-year-old with obsessional symptoms, and whose academic performance had been deteriorating. With the onset of puberty, he withdrew from his peer group and lived in total isolation. His only playmate was his sister who was eight years younger than he. Together they played a game he called Tournament. He had a whole army of play soldiers, medieval knights, and cannons which he arranged according to a set of his own rules. He made his sister commander of the rebellious troops whose revolt he always managed to wipe out. He was the most powerful emperor, unbeatable, and his idol was Julius Caesar. When his sister eventually grew tired of playing his games, his parents became increasingly concerned because he withdrew to his room and spent most of the time brooding, drawing battle plans, or sleeping. Occasionally he participated in family games; regularly he watched sports programs on television with his father.

When his therapy began, he justified his retreats to his room as "fits of tiredness," which he wanted me to treat him for. His mother complained that he was nothing but aggressive, extremely oppositional, and as such he resembled his father in his attitude towards her. Martin described his father, who was an administrative judge, as a cool, silent man who could he seized by "sudden, uncontrollable good or bad mood swings." Martin complained that his mother had too many visits from girlfriends, and she went into his room too often to ask him how he was.

The parents reported that when he was two and a half and started nursery school, Martin suffered severe separation anxieties. Between the ages of six and twelve he was on antiepileptic drugs for grand mal epileptic seizures which took place during his sleep. These seizures had since disappeared. Martin's version was, "I must have been a bit agitated." Thus Martin experienced his body as out of his control; an autonomous, powerful, and overwhelming entity took him over and then collapsed over him. The situation brought to mind the Golem who, in one of the old legends, became alive and then collapsed over his creator and killed him.

As is often the case in treating adolescents, Martin stuck to the here-and-now in sessions and made it impossible for me to make reconstructions. This went on for a long time, and only much later did any transference fantasy emerge, so it was very difficult to enter his inner world. I had to observe his behaviour in the session and draw on my countertransference experience. At the outset of therapy Martin never bothered to greet me; he went straight into my room, passed my chair, moved like a very rigid and controlled puppet. He then sat across from me with an impassive, somber expression and slowly scanned me with cold eyes. I often felt myself becoming stiff and thinking to myself. "Don't make a false move, don't show any expression, don't let him guess that you have feelings!" It was almost impossible for me to have fantasies, images, or thoughts about what was going on inside him.

Initially he told me in passing that he had a system in his brain that could switch his feelings on and off according to the situation. I understood this as a manifestation of his compulsive defense structure in which he felt utterly omnipotent in relation to me. Any attempt to talk to him about his present life situation evoked little response. Instead, he took four pfennig coins out of his pocket, gave two to me, and insisted on playing "table soccer" with them. He declared that the sessions with me were training periods for improving his skills for a soccer match with his father whom he planned to beat. This coin soccer seemed to be the only link with his father, as it was with me. He was much more expert in this boring and repetitive game than I was, and regularly beat me but concealed any feelings of triumph. The sessions followed one another in similar monotony, interrupted occasionally by short reports about his school or the soccer league. Occasionally he wondered ironically when I was ever going to learn this game. At this point, the therapy appeared to be completely unproductive. Before his sessions, I began to feel physically uncomfortable and experienced a vague anxiety. My symptoms started to disappear when I allowed myself to fantasize that he would not turn up, that he had forgotten his session or had fallen ill. Alas, he came with merciless regularity and seemed to enjoy it, even though he would not let it show. I had not yet been able to let a reverie develop for working through and digesting the stiffness and anxiety that he was projecting into me. I had no fantasies, and I could not find a language in which to formulate what he was trying to communicate to me through his behavior since no symbolic process had yet been set in motion. At this time it seemed to me, through his soccer game and assiduous attendance, he was transferring onto me a positive homoerotic relationship with his "good" father/analyst in order to experience me as an ally against his "bad" mother. I sensed that our relationship had grown closer, but I still felt uncomfortable. This was a sign that he was controlling me with massive projective identification. The medium of his projective identification was the beta elements that affected my body, and my fantasies between sessions indicated that he had got inside me, leaving me anxious and without the capacity to make sense of them.[5]

About six months later he came in one day and said, without betraying the least emotion, "I have something to tell you that depresses me: tomorrow I am going to kill myself. I have messed everything up." He then told me that the joy he had felt during the previous session, when he had beaten me at table soccer, represented a serious violation of "his system" of guidelines and laws. The three basic tasks of the system were to protect him from getting interested in girls, to prevent him from feeling, and to shelter him from unexpected, unforeseeable, and unpredictable new events. He defined his system as a "non-human personality" that functioned like a computer and had the "soul of a robot." When the system felt attacked, it could become as hard as granite and burn whoever dared come close to it with its laser energy.

I sat quietly with this but was inwardly very worried. While he described how he planned to commit suicide. I felt a strong impulse to hospitalize him, but I did not share these thoughts with him. Then I concerned myself with his "system." Had I missed something? Had I not been aware of the delusional quality of his system? I then asked him, "Could you negotiate with your system, to postpone the date of the suicide? If it agrees, then come to your next session in two days time and tell me the results of your negotiation." He looked at me for quite a long time, as if he wanted to test me, but he was also open, as if he was ready to accept me. This was a moment of unspoken recognition. Then he agreed on condition that I guarantee not to reveal his suicide plan to his parents. I agreed, he left, and I had a very anxious two days.

I was very relieved two days later when he reappeared and coolly stated, "Reason and feeling have fought: reason has won." He added, "You took me seriously last time." He meant that he worried about me: he had been concerned that I would be professionally ruined if one of my patients had committed suicide. For the rest of the session he told me about a film that dealt with two ruffians. He didn't like the ending because one of the heroes, a self-declared women-hater, had been seduced by a woman. This was the first reference to myself as a potential maternal container in the transference, and after this breakthrough the treatment proceeded with greater ease. He related more and more fantasies about the system, which no longer stood as a separating element between us. At this point another fantasy began to appear, and he talked at length about his fascination with outer space. He felt that outer space was infinitely wide, and, most important, pure and clean, unpopulated by living creatures, human bodies, or "sea serpents and other such animals" of the kind that pursued him in his dreams and fantasies. One can understand the computerizing of his soul and body as an infantile, grandiose solution for keeping in check his sexual excitement and the autonomous erections of his penis, which filled him with unbearable anxieties. When the system inflated his ego, it escaped his control and allowed his murderous masturbatory unconscious fantasies and his incestuous impulses towards his mother and sister to come through.

In later sessions he described the system as a kind of hierarchically organized military caste. It seemed to be related to his childhood war games with his sister through which he channeled his aggressive and incestuous fantasies about her. His earlier fantasies about control were now transformed and structured in the system. He stressed that the system was his own creation, but it had become autonomous, like his epileptic seizures, making him its victim and slave. The system was omniscient, had absolute power, and was ruthless. It operated his thoughts, and had autonomously programmed his brain for self-destruction. During the initial phase of analysis, he believed that the only way to escape from the power of the system was to kill himself: "No power in this world can prevent me from applying the universal solution!", his expression for suicide.

By sharing his suicidal wish, Martin had brought me into emotional connection with him, and I could therefore develop genuine concern for his life. Before this occurred, it had been very difficult for me to experience caring feelings for him due to his massive attack on feelings. That is, I could not develop a reverie, or symbolic attitude: instead I felt paralyzed, bored, and cut off. But what did he reenact in his suicidal intention? When he experienced too much joy about the victories over me. I think that he was overwhelmed by an uncontainable upsurge of physical excitement, probably an erection, which his system could not tolerate. The triumph over the father/therapist brought powerful, sexual feelings into his penis which reconnected him to his erotic wishes for his mother and terrified him. Until the age of eight he had slept with his parents. In my view, it is possible to make a reconstruction that this aroused him to the extent that he developed epileptic fits. For this reason, the physical and emotional excitement would have been uncontainable without the defensive protection of his robot fantasy. It is interesting that the robot lacked feelings and was missing a penis too. This adds force to the idea that the erect penis and the absolute need to control it had generated in him the system/robot split. It is clear that his father was weak and ineffective in performing his function of oedipal guardian (protecting him against his incestuous wishes to possess mother). On the other hand the warm feelings that he experienced during our emotional exchange reactivated his loving feelings for the early mother and his genital desire to possess her. This was intolerable to his ego/system, so the system sentenced him to death. The way Martin had managed to protect himself from his erotic wish for his mother had transformed his body as a containing object into the robot. His fantasy of the earth/mother being populated by snakes and sea serpents as well as his fantasy of escape into the "purity" of outer space were other means of protection in fantasy from the danger of acting out incestuous wishes towards his mother and sister.

The aggressive and sexual impulses, which are intensified by the onset of puberty and the homoerotic element in the transference, brought about in Martin an anxiety-ridden deintegration of the self. During reintegrative phases of the therapy, these states of mind could be worked through because of the containment experienced by the boy in the session brought about by the analyst's reverie and symbolic attitude, a reverie that his mother had failed to perform for him during his earliest infancy. In addition, both the analyst and the patient had withstood and survived murderous attacks, and, thanks to the analytic work, Martin could now reintroject both the penis as a loving, flexible and nourishing object and the nipple of the good breast of the early mother that had been lost. He no longer needed to attack his body to do away with nameless, overwhelming anxieties and affects.

The survival and nonretaliatory stance of the analyst is of the utmost importance for the boy to be able to experience him as a strong mother-body-container. The hope is that this experience can then become integrated in his psyche. Martin was able to feel that the going in and out of the mother's body, represented by the analyst's consulting room and the analytic framework, could take place without damage to either partner. He could then begin to experience the potential for a "good intercourse" without fear of violence or destruction, or of being trapped, dropped, or contaminated. The fact that I experienced concern and loving feeling for him provided him with the experience of a loving parental couple united in a creative intercourse, where the mother could perform the reverie and the father could sustain her.

Notes

1. W. Jens, *Kindlers Neues Literatur Lexicon* (Munich: Kindler Verlag, 1989) v. 6, p. 486.
2. W. Bion, *Learning From Experience* (London: Heinemann, 1962).
3. C. G. Jung, *The Transcendent Function, Collected Works* (London: Routledge and Kegan Paul, 1960) v.8.
4. G. Scholem, "Der Golem von Prag und der Golem von Rehovot," in *Judaica* 2 (Frankfurt/M.: Surkamp Verlag, 1970), p. 86.
5. See note 2.

SECTION 5

Heterosexual and Homosexual Elements in the Search for Identity

Introduction to Section 5

In her chapter, "What to Do about Mother?" Jane Bunster writes that one very important development for a girl seems to rest upon how well she relates to the mother, and whether she has been able to introject a good enough "mother breast." If the identification in early infancy with the maternal breast has been good enough, the girl will be able to proceed in her feminine development and freely identify with her mother. But when the maternal introject has negative connotations, the girl has to fight the fulfillment of her own feminine identity. Diana's case is one of a severe identity problem within a mother-daughter conflict. Her narcissistic pathology was severe; Diana attempted to destroy herself by demanding a hysterectomy at the age of eighteen with the aim of suppressing menstruation and any possibility of becoming like mother.

The course of Diana's therapy was fraught with resistance and heavy negative transference projections. Her conflict between remaining attached to her mother, with the danger of merger, and attempting to separate by doing away drastically with her female parts came clearly to the fore. The concreteness of the situation made it very difficult for the analytic work to proceed because Diana tended to displace the conflict using the defense of reality. She used sociopolitical arguments to keep the therapist at bay, and more often than not her sessions had the quality of political harangue.

Bunster kept working with the negative transference, which she understood in the light of severe early mother-infant disturbance. In her conceptualization she uses both Fordham's primal self concept and Bion's model of the mind. Diana feared dependency and helplessness;

both these emotions she split off and fiercely projected in an intrusive way onto the world around her and onto the analyst. In turn she projected the victimized aspects of her baby self into nature and animals whose rights she fought for. She expressed the wish to kill all humans who killed and tortured animals. In the analysis, she was gradually made to see how her hostility to the world of humans had really to do with her own feelings of neglect and hunger as a baby. Her toddler's rage at the birth of a sister, followed by her mother's depression, seems to have triggered the severe pathology of this girl. Her envy of her mother and her severe jealousy of the mother's relationship with her sisters, made her conclude that only by attacking herself could she protect her mother and sisters from her destructiveness.

Bunster again stresses that adolescence offers a second chance to work through early infantile conflicts with the internal mother/breast. Diana tried to tackle this task in a particularly perverse and sadistic way because she was apparently stuck in a primitive stage of projective identification with the mother. Thanks to the extreme capacity of the analyst to tolerate her vicious and spiteful attacks, Diana was helped to make use of her omnipotence to try to develop her own independence.

In the "Search for Identity in Late Adolescence," Brian Feldman presents the same theme of gender identity from the perspective of a late adolescent boy trapped in an internal conflict with a negative father identification. The interesting aspect of this case of Feldman's is that the boy entered analysis on his own volition and attended treatment four times a week with commitment and considerable capacity for insight. He seemed to have a strong need and desire for an intimate relationship with an older male to experience a positive homosexual relationship with a father figure whom he could admire and idealize.

However, the difficulty arose from his splitting the good and bad aspects of the father imago, projecting the good one onto the analyst and the bad one onto his real father. The interpretative work around this splitting brought his early relationship to the pre-oedipal father to the fore. He was made to reflect on how his hatred and rage against his father was caused by his unconscious wish for strong affirmation and support from his father and by his unsatisfied attachment needs from early infancy. He had felt betrayed by his father. He had experienced the paternal phallus as inanimate and inert, disgusting and ugly, and therefore could not identify with his own masculinity. He too, like Diana, wanted to do away with his masculine parts by surgery because he perceived the penis as a damaged object. On the other hand his early relationship with the maternal object was also fraught with negative feelings deriving from prolonged abandonment and premature separation. These stemmed from his toddler stage, when his mother had been ill with cancer and therefore unavailable to him.

Once again, we see in the case of Ed that his difficulties in evolving a core male identity were related to psychological conflicts with both parental figures in the early stages of development. The analytic work enabled Ed to gradually make sense of his confusing psychological states. He became able to think about himself with greater clarity.

9

What to Do about Mother?
An Adolescent Girl's Dilemma

Jane Bunster

This chapter describes my work with an adolescent girl whose conflicted state of mind stemmed from conflicts around the archetypal constellation of the Demeter/Kore and Cybele/Attis, mother/daughter pairs. She was torn between remaining attached to her mother with attendant dangers of merger and too close an identification, and attempting to separate from her mother by means of rather omnipotent and grandiose destructive fantasies. The latter fantasies were a defense against her various anxieties linked to oedipal and pre-oedipal impulses and wishes. She attempted to deal with these extreme difficulties by demanding a hysterectomy, with the stated aim of suppressing menstruation. Hence her referral to me at the age of fourteen.

Adolescence is, of course, an important phase in development towards adulthood, but it is also something more in that it gives the young person a second chance to work through some conflicts that may not have been resolved at an earlier stage.

One very important part of maturational development for a girl seems to rest upon how well she relates to the mother and whether she has been able to introject a good enough "mother breast." This relationship is based on her earliest feeding experience and the extent to which she has been able to negotiate the transition from part-object relations to whole-object relations. On this foundation rests her development and her ability to negotiate such normal, yet traumatic, events as weaning and the birth of a sibling. If the girl remains fixed in a part-object position, for whatever reason, the normal introjective, projective processes become distorted. Thus extreme splitting may take place, and rigid omnipotent defense systems aimed at controlling anxiety may develop.

On the foundation of the "good-enough" relationship with the breast rests the girl's possibility of negotiating her envy of her mother and of managing her incestuous wishes for her father. If these psychic conflicts are not resolved, the girl may be totally at the mercy of frightening introjective and projective identifications and unconscious impulses.

The psychic unconscious conflicts have their roots in infantile states of mind. In the concept of the primary self, the baby's self is a psychomatic unity, a unity that includes archetypal elements and inherited dispositions and all his potential for growth and development. This primary self differentiates by putting out feelers, analogous to an amoeba's pseudopods, by the process of deintegration, then reintegration, unfolding and folding back in a long-term process similar to breathing in and out. This process enables the self to allow some of its archetypal elements to separate out and be ready to meet the outside world.[1] Thus the predisposition to expect a nipple unfolds at birth, through the instincts, and if a good enough fit occurs, reintegration takes place and the experience is digested. If the deintegrative move is not sufficiently well met in the external world, there is a feeling of disintegration and catastrophe, of emptiness and frustration.[2]

A way of trying to deal with this frustration is to fantasize sadistic attacks on the breast, and to destroy the object that causes so much pain and anger. Furthermore, the envy of the baby is aroused because the mother possesses and has the control of full, nourishing breasts, and has the power to withhold or give them to the baby. If she withholds them, it must mean that she is giving them to a rival, either the father or another baby. Therefore they have to be attacked.

But danger may lurk in the very act of attacking these breasts, if there is not a good-enough container for the attacks, that can provide an alpha-function and understanding. In the fantasy of the infant, the breasts may retaliate and powerfully exact their revenge; if this fear is consistently experienced, there may be a cut-off from the relationship to the mother/breast, which can result in autistic states of mind where the self protects itself at all costs.[3] This "protection" can sometimes manifest itself in nihilistic and self-destructive acts, and invariably limits relationships and functioning in the adult world.

Case History

Diana was the middle child of a family of three, who was referred to me from a local hospital because of severe depression, nonattendance at school since the age of eleven, and menstrual difficulties. She had not cooperated in the hospital setting, nor did she agree to family therapy. But she agreed to come into treatment with me on condition that I did not see her parents. She thought it would be the first step towards achieving what she really wanted, namely a hysterectomy at age eighteen. Her main ambition was to champion animal rights and promote conservation, and she hoped to gain university qualifications for this. She had ideas about being a politician, but was cynical because she thought that when politicians came into power, they lost their ideals and only became interested in their own gains. However, she was herself quite a soap-box politician in the sessions, and harangued me about animal rights. She tried to persuade me to follow her vegan way of life.

Relationships with Family

Her family life was difficult: her mother had suffered from depression all Diana's life. Diana could remember her mother being in bed a lot, and somebody else looking after them as children. Diana was very scathing and contemptuous of her mother, and feared that being a woman meant being like her: "lazy and a good-for-nothing." Her father led a long-houred self-employed business life, and was not as much involved in the family as Diana would have liked. She criticized him for not organizing his business properly and for being overweight. Diana claimed that he never spoke much to anyone but could lose his temper ferociously on occasion, which she found frightening.

Her relationship with her older sister was bad. Diana thought her bossy, and, when her mother was unwell, resented her taking over household responsibilities. Diana admitted to me that she felt jealous of the close relationship between her mother and sister, and told me they spent time together talking in the bedroom, gossiping and enjoying a sisterly intimacy. They both had menstrual and back problems, and were often confined to bed. Hence Diana's feminine "model" was a poor and damaged one. The sister had left home for a short time to share a house with a boyfriend, but during Diana's treatment with me, she was at home without a job, evidently looking after her mother and helping her run the home. Diana considered them both to be worthless parasites, feeding off the father who himself did not have the strength to stand up to them. In particular, Diana wanted him to tell the sister to leave the house.

Diana's relationship with her younger sister seemed better. Occasionally they went out together, and although Diana refused to join in with her sister's more age-appropriate, teen-age lifestyle, she admitted that she was envious of her sister's ability to go out and socialize. At the time I first knew her, Diana hardly went out at all. By not going to school, she had cut off all contact with contemporaries. On starting school again at age fourteen-and-a-half, she took no part in social activities, ate her packed lunch in the classroom on her own, and remained very isolated for at least two years. As treatment finally drew to a close just before Diana went to university, this situation had eased a little. But she still had few friends, felt bored with her contemporaries' interests—chiefly boyfriends and parties—and so stayed at home most of the time.

I saw Diana for four years altogether, with sessions arranged regularly on a weekly basis during the first two years, and thereafter intermittently until she went to university. We made contact once or twice after that. During this time she attended school regularly, did well in her exams, and followed the course of study she had chosen. Her menstrual problems were suppressed and controlled, and eventually she relinquished her wish to have radical surgery. But she said that she would like to have her breasts made smaller, and my last contact with her was over this matter. She was told by the consultant psychiatrist that she could make her own decision about this when she turned twenty-one.

Therapeutic Work

Although Diana would like to have denied it, she was in many ways typically adolescent in the therapeutic situation. At her request, I had minimal dealings with her parents (I never met her father) and she, alone, decided whether she would come or not. She rarely let me know if she was not coming, and during sessions she was often silent, saying she had nothing to say. She would say that she saw no point in coming, since she had no intention of changing in order to please me.

Very early on she told me that she wanted to keep her "inner part to herself." This I tried to respect. I tried not to ask questions, and did my best to tolerate her wish to be omnipotent. I was helped in this because from the beginning, she elicited in me positive countertransference feelings.

In our work together I came to understand that Diana was trying to deal with powerful unconscious fears. These fears were all interrelated, but I see them as fear of dependency and helplessness, fear of greed and demandingness, fear of flooding and loss of control, and fear of destructive envy. It seemed that Diana was acting out a defense system against experiencing these fears, splitting them off so that she did not have to suffer them. It seemed to be my therapeutic role to help her be more in touch with them, understand them, and tolerate them better: that is, to provide a container for the violent affects she was experiencing.

Fear of Dependency and Helplessness

As previously stated, Diana equated dependency and helplessness with being parasitic and weak. She had ambivalent feelings about coming to see me: on the one hand, she knew it was essential, or she would not be considered for a hysterectomy; on the other hand, she saw the need for therapy as a sign of weakness. She felt trapped, but the trap was of her own making, albeit unconsciously. By refusing to go to school and by insisting on the suppression of her periods, she was maintaining her dependency and delaying her entry into the adult female world. What seemed to be allied to fear of dependency was her fear of separation. While it was impossible for her to acknowledge her own infantile dependency, she projected her feelings into protecting the rights of animals, such as campaigning against vivisection and the eating of animal products. Later on in treatment she maintained a strict vegan diet; she managed to spend her holidays on a wildlife preserve, looking after the young of a rare small cat species. But about human infants and their care-givers, she was extremely scathing. She felt her mother should have never had children; she felt it wrong for people to want to have babies and bring them into a world that was over populated, polluted, and potentially dangerous with the threat of warlike, quarreling nations and a nuclear arsenal. In one extreme session she expressed the view that there would be no peace until all humans had been killed, although she did not include herself in this. She would survive in order to look after the animals.

At the same time she was puzzled about some aspects of her own behavior and feelings and admitted to me that she thought she was hypocritical. For example, she was aware that when the family cat wished to jump up on her knee, or rubbed on her legs, or demanded to be fed, she wanted to kick it away. On visits from a neighbor's dog, which she thought was neglected, she felt indifferent and grumpy to such an extent that her siblings accused her of not really having any interest in animals at all. This gave us the opportunity to explore together her denial of her wish to be as demanding as a helpless animal—and its corollary, a small baby—and that her hostility to the world had really to do with her own feelings of neglect and hunger. But as dependency for Diana was equated with being parasitic and weak, hunger and neediness meant greed.

Fear of Demandingness and Greed

When discussing the neighbor's dog, Diana said that it was pointless giving the dog a treat now and again because that missed getting to the root of the problem. To her, the solution to the dog's problem was that the owner should give the animal a way to somebody who would care for it properly. The dog, which was large, was cooped up in a flat, and came to visit Diana's family in order to enjoy the garden. Diana felt that this treatment was unfair. This gave me the opportunity to wonder with her whether she had a close identification with the dog and felt that she was being treated unfairly by me because I only saw her once a week. She admitted that she thought there was not much point in coming just once a week and wished she could come every day.

As time went on she was able to admit to being cross about holidays, and jealous of the other people I saw. She told me that she only wanted to have one-to-one relationships, and that the few she had experienced very quickly broke up when the "other" did not agree with her view or would not adhere to vegetarianism. Thus relating to a separate "other", who might have separate views from hers, made her feel valueless and unloved.

I think her strict veganism was due to anxiety about her greed and oral aggression. In the sessions with me, her oral aggression was particularly apparent in the long silences and the reiterations that she was bored. She repeatedly said that there was no point in saying anything. Nothing would change, since the problem lay with her problems at home. This sentiment seemed to relate to her omnipotent wish to control the all-providing mother/breast all the time. Cheated of this by other demanding members of the family, she projected all her rage into cruel meat-eaters who had no interest in the rights of helpless animals. But this rage seemed to be displacement of her wish to attack the mother's breast for not providing her fully with what she wanted. It was as if Diana were still in a very early, deluded state of mind, where the mother's attention would be at her command.

In her inner world she had not been weaned. By adhering to veganism, and trying to get all the family to agree with her views, she was trying to achieve a closeness with her mother and get special attention. In some way she succeeded, since her mother did her utmost to accommodate Diana's dietary needs. But whatever she did was never enough, and at the same time Diana despised her mother for being easily swayed and incapable of limiting or containing Diana's omnipotent demands.

In the sessions with me, Diana often said that people thought she was too radical and that they were frightened of her. Once she told me about a book she had been reading that involved the destruction of the world. She admitted she would like to do this, and the first people she would destroy would be politicians. She was able to link this with her parents, and admitted to me that she had feelings of wanting to kill her mother. She also indulged in fantasies of other aggressive acts, such as breaking windows. She told me she had an enormous appetite and was worried that I would think her greedy. When we linked this with her talking, she said she remained silent in the sessions because she feared that she would talk too much and I would get bored, or she feared that she would flood and drown me with her "verbal" attacks. To be a soap-box politician was a positive way of dealing with this, but she would brook no opposition.

Fear of Flooding and Loss of Control

The fear of flooding was manifest most obviously in her trying to suppress her menstrual flow, at first by remaining static in a chair in the hope that the flow would be blocked and later by persuading the family doctor to prescribe medication. As previously stated, Diana openly expressed murderous hatred and contempt of babies. This hatred was caused by a ruthless, terrible jealousy of the mother's potential babies and resulted in the wish to kill them. Similarly her fear about "boring" me was perhaps related to her unconscious wish to "bore" into my body and mind and so destroy the creative thoughts/babies there by her silent withholdingness or by her "floods" of words, both of which were an attack on my thinking capacity. Furthermore, to compound Diana's internal conflict about flooding and destructive fantasies, there were at least two traumatic events in her history. The first was her mother's depressive illness when Diana was a toddler, presumably around the birth of her younger sister, and also her mother's subsequent menstrual difficulties, with which she was fully conversant. These fed into Diana's fantasies that perhaps it was her murderous wish to get rid of the baby sister that had caused damage to her mother's inside. The second traumatic event related to a difficult tonsillectomy operation when she was nine years old. Diana was in hospital with her younger sister who was also undergoing the same operation and whom she was told to protect and look after. Diana hemorraged badly and became ill. She remembered her predominant emotion at this time was shame and anger that she was the weak, vulnerable one while the baby sister was strong. One might hypothesize here that Diana's destructive, cannabalistic wish to attack the rival inside the mother's body was turned back onto her throat. Only by attacking herself could she protect her sister and mother, but in so doing she lost her status and felt humiliated, frightened, and helpless.

Diana's traumatic surgery serves as a poignant example of how she felt totally ousted and replaced by the baby sister, with her birthright stolen away.[4] Her fantasized wish to destroy the rival could not be carried out, so she turned the aggressive attacks upon herself. Perhaps more specifically, the pair of tonsils could stand for the pair of breasts that Diana felt she had lost to her rival. By the process of introjective and projective identification, these breasts became hostile and poisonous. They felt lodged in her throat, so they had to be cut out.

In addition, the new infant had been created in the womb as a result of the mother and father mutually giving their attention to each other to the exclusion of Diana. So the humiliation was compounded by the oedipal conflict. Thus she not only wished to attack the mother's top half/breasts but her bottom half/womb. As her pubertal development began, the onset of menstruation and the possibility of making new babies herself made Diana feel that the only way of managing and controlling such intense and catastrophic intrapsychic conflicts was to suppress her own capacity for childbearing.

By denying the function of her womb, she was trying to make a very strong identification with her father on a homosexual level. Only by castrating herself could she couple with him safely. The alternative, of wishing to heterosexually couple with him, was too dangerous, because she so much feared her destructive impulses against her mother and her wish to break up the marriage. The fear of the mother's retaliatory attacks added to Diana's anxieties. If she suppressed her periods and completely employed her mind, she was safe from sexual coupling, hence her determined efforts to do well at this university and not to have any "romantic" involvement. When I saw her once or twice during college holidays, she told me that she had a good male friend, but that they had decided not to have any physical contact, as that would spoil the relationship. By denying her sexuality, Diana did not have to confront or suffer any primal scene fantasies either.

These conflicts were based upon very early infantile impulses and fantasies. At this stage in the infant's mind, the nipple in the baby's mouth can be equated with the penis in the mother's vagina; orifices are confused, and parts of the mother's and father's body become concretized and take on a life of their own, separate from the whole person; hence the term part objects.

Because of Diana's projected hostility onto the nipple, stolen from her by the rival father and/or baby, the breast became a dangerous object to be controlled at all costs. The traumatic experience of the tonsillectomy operation, when a confusion took place between the fantasy and reality, might have exacerbated this defense so that when puberty developed and the menstrual flow began, similar feelings were activated, and the bleeding had to be stopped. There was anger that her vagina might be attacked as her throat had been; and in order to control this destructive fantasy, she wished to have her womb removed, thus effecting a kind of self-castration. The hostile penis/nipple could not penetrate her then.

Fear of Destructive Envy

Diana's fear of destructive envy was perhaps at the root of all her other fears and related to the envy she felt towards her mother, who had within her womb the other children and her father's penis. It was impossible for Diana to think of her parents as a couple. She would often say that the father longed to leave home and travel. I was particularly aware of the archetypal forces in this area, and in some sessions felt pulled into what I imagined was the full force of the negative mother archetype and its destructive power.

It was difficult to work with Diana on such a primitive level because the archetypal forces were so powerful. At times I felt overwhelmed by the forces out of my control, especially in the long silences. I felt wiped out and annihilated, at the receiving end of ruthless negative projections. Depressive and objectless empty states of mind often gripped the sessions, and I felt compelled to fill up the gaps of silence by talking too much, in the same way that Diana did when she harangued me and her family about animal rights, and her need to have a hysterectomy. This was her way of controlling the powerful destructive forces of the negative mother archetype, and protecting herself from being trapped and overwhelmed by them.

Adolescence as a Second Chance

Adolescence gave Diana a second chance to work through her internalized conflicts with her mother. Because she seemed to be stuck at a primitive stage of introjective identification with her mother, she tried to tackle this task in a particularly omnipotent and perverse way. The only way that Diana could separate from her internalized mother-object was to evacuate and destroy her. If she allowed herself to have a functioning womb with a potential for babies, she would have to acknowledge that it was all right for her mother to have had them too, however inadequately. This Diana could not allow to happen because it would have involved forgiveness and gratitude, and her envy was too rampant to allow for any modification.

Diana's extreme and self-mutilating demand was a cry for help; answering that cry gave her a second chance to work through these psychic conflicts. If she had remained closely identified with her mother, there would have been no further growth. Diana would have replicated her mother's relationship and the cycle would have been repeated, as had happened with the older daughter. Diana made use of her adolescence to try to break this cycle and develop her own independence.

But the only way she felt she could deal with the hostile envious mother/womb inside her was to try and destroy it and thus neutralize its power, thereby attempting to mutilate her own feminine potential. Perhaps this was the only means she had at the time to separate from her mother?

Diana's behavior was rigid and inhibiting, but at the same time I felt her rigid menstrual and dietary control and her passion for animal rights issues had as its purpose separation from the mother and an attempt to find her own identity. It was sad that Diana had to resort to such extreme measures in her attempt to do this. But by holding this paradoxical understanding of omnipotence in my mind, I think I was better able to withstand and survive her ruthless attacks on me and the therapy, and thus help her survive her conflicted struggle with her mother on all its levels, conscious and unconscious.

Notes

1. M. Fordham, *The Self and Autism* (London: Heinemann, 1976).
2. See M. Sidoli, "Deintegration and Reintegration in the First Two Weeks of Life," in *Jungian Child Psychotherapy,* eds. M. Sidoli and M. Davies (London: Karnac, 1988).
3. M. Fordham.
4. See M. Sidoli, "The Myth of Cain and Abel and Its Roots in Infancy," in *The British Journal of Psychotherapy* 3, no.4 (1987).

10

The Search for Identity in Late Adolescence

Brian Feldman

Introduction

The concept of identity formation in late adolescence has been a prominent theme in clinical analytic literature from the first studies by the pioneer adolescent analyst August Aichhorn (1925), through the work of Erikson (1968), Blos (1985), and Laufer and Laufer (1984).[1] There is considerable theoretical agreement that the most prominent task of late adolescence is the establishment of a sense of identity. When a sense of identity is achieved, the adolescent feels a more authentic sense of self: there emerges a feeling that a meaningful synthesis of the various parts of the personality can be consolidated into a meaningful whole. As the development of a coherent identity evolves in analysis, the adolescent often begins to feel more sure about sexuality, life's goals, and desired life-style. A sense of inner confidence begins to emerge, which makes possible attempts to establish and maintain interpersonal intimacy.

Jung has elaborated on the theme of adolescence in his book *Symbols of Transformation* where he comments on the problem of incestuous desire between mother and son. Jung states that "the basis of the 'incestuous desire' is not cohabitation, but the strange idea of becoming a child again, of returning to the parental shelter, and of entering into the mother in order to be reborn through her."[2] Jung's symbolic approach to the problem of incest implies that the adolescent needs to understand symbolically the tension between the desire to regress and remain a child and the desire to assert his individuality and autonomy. The separation from the parental figures is fraught with conflict, but becomes resolvable as the adolescent is able to engage in what Jung would term a "heroic" conflict to assert autonomy and independence by utilizing his creative symbolic capacity to forge a coherent identity. Jung focuses on the parallels between the myth of the hero and the development of adolescent identity. He sees the evolution of identity as taking place through the struggle for self-definition arising out of a confrontation with the creative matrix of the unconscious.

In the following case discussion, the focus is on how the theme of identity in late adolescence emerged in the course of an analysis. The adolescent, referred to as Ed, was able to utilize the analytic relationship and the analytic process to help him to reflect upon and creatively transform significant emotional difficulties and eventually form a more coherent identity and integrated view of himself.

The Beginning Phase of Analytic Work

I was somewhat surprised when I was contacted by phone by an eighteen-year-old young man asking for an analysis. At the time, I found this an unusual request, since it is uncommon for an adolescent to request an analysis outright. Usually I have seen adolescents in once or twice-weekly psychotherapy before starting analytic work on a more intensive basis, so I was naturally intrigued and curious about this request. I told Ed that I would be able to see him for one session to give him a chance to meet me, and for me to find out more about his situation and his desire to be analyzed. At that point he told me that he had been given the names of two analysts by a child psychiatrist who had had several interviews with him and had determined that it would be helpful for Ed to have an analysis.

When I first met Ed, he was hesitant yet articulate about his current situation. He told me that he was eager to have an analysis because of his current predicament. He had been at a residential treatment center specializing in adolescents for two years, and during the last few months he had enrolled as a freshman in a college several hundred miles from his family home. Although he had done well at the residential facility and felt he had made a good deal of progress, his adjustment to college had been filled with stress and anxiety. He was having difficulty focusing and concentrating and maintaining interpersonal relationships. He was not doing well academically, and he had failed several courses. He felt like a failure as he was not able to succeed. During the first interview, I decided not to elicit a detailed history as Ed was so tentative and anxious about seeing an analyst or embarking on treatment. Instead we focused a good deal on his current situation. He was living with his parents, no longer using drugs, and trying to find a job. He said that he had used drugs extensively, mostly marijuana and hallucinogens, and that they had gotten him into trouble emotionally and academically. As a child he was not able to attend the local public schools due to truancy and oppositional behavior, and had had to attend special private schools starting in sixth grade.

I found Ed likable and approachable. I did not feel that he was either closed off emotionally or overly anxious about starting treatment. His openness and eagerness to begin seemed to indicate to me the level of consciousness about his current concerns and distress. He felt stuck in his ongoing psychological development, and he had no idea what direction his life would move in. He appeared uncertain about his goals, his choice of a career and work, and his friendships and intimate relationships. While he appeared to be in the midst of an identity crisis, I felt a rapport that made me feel that I would be able to help him analytically if he chose to continue working with me.

During our next interviews, Ed began to tell me about his life. He was upset about his parents' marital situation. There was much arguing in the house, and Ed thought that his parents were headed for a divorce. Ed stated that he always remembered a difficult and strained relationship with his father, who was a recovered alcoholic, yet a highly successful professional in the community. He felt closer to his mother, yet also more conflicted. He had uncomfortable sexual feelings in her presence, and he felt that perhaps she also had these feelings towards him. She had recently told him that she had been sexually molested as a child. Ed wondered how that had effected her sexually. He did not feel that his parents had a satisfying sexual relationship and thought that this was another area that was leading them to divorce. Ed also mentioned that he had been sexually molested by a woman teacher several years ago. The consequences of the molestation were devastating for him: he had reported the incidents to his parents, and they had proceeded to have the teacher decertified. Ed seemed to hold a great deal of guilt about this, yet he also felt a sense of betrayal and sexual confusion, especially since he mostly felt sexually attracted to older women. He was confused as to why he was not more involved with women who were his own age. He felt that this could be related to feelings of inadequacy about his body. He felt that both his nose and his penis were too small, and that his lips were too large. He felt skinny and ugly and feared that age-appropriate women would not be attracted to him.

After the initial evaluation sessions were completed, we decided to embark upon a four-times-weekly analysis. I told Ed that I would have to have one session with his parents to both explain to them the parameters of the analysis and to understand from their point of view Ed's desire to be analyzed. I told Ed that if he wanted, he could attend the session I would be having with his parents. Ed decided not to attend.

When I met Ed's parents they were cognizant yet confused about the conflicts Ed was experiencing. Ed's father spoke openly about his alcoholism and the impact that must have had upon Ed growing up. His mother spoke about the trauma of the sexual molestation issue she had recently begun to work on in her own therapy. They were eager for Ed to see me in analysis. While the parents were able to talk in depth about Ed's current predicament, they had few recollections of his infancy and early childhood. Ed's birth and delivery were uneventful, as was his life up until age six. Something felt amiss to me. Finally, Ed's mother spoke of surgery for skin cancer when Ed was two years old. The skin cancer occurred after the birth of Ed's only sibling, a sister. Ed had not yet told me about her. From what his mother said, she had been separated from the children for several weeks, and had been severely anxious after that for some time. I thought that the prolonged separation and the mother's subsequent anxiety could be one explanation for Ed's feeling that his mother of infancy was unavailable and detached. I found out that his sister also had profound problems. She too had been seriously involved in drugs, and was attending the same residential treatment center that Ed had gone to. Ed's parents seemed to understand the severe nature of Ed's conflicts and his blocked emotional development. They were fearful that his pattern of failure could become a life-long problem.

This meeting was the only face to face contact that I had with Ed's parents during the course of his analysis. There were several phone contacts during the three year period of our work, but these were always conducted with Ed's consent and the content of the calls was not hidden from him. I wanted Ed to have a sense of a contained analytic environment where he would be able to explore and investigate his psychological and emotional conflicts with as great freedom as possible.

The Initial Dream

The first reported dream in an analysis often helps to elucidate the course of the analytic work.[3] The initial dream can offer useful information about the analysand's most critical areas of psychological conflict as well as the conceptions and expectations that the analysand has about embarking upon analytic work. Jung (1934) has mentioned that the first dream in an analysis often has an important significance, as it can delineate the psychological material that will emerge as the analysis progresses. Ed's first dream delineated many of his psychological conflicts, and pointed to issues in the transference/countertransference relationship that would be important in our work. During the first week of analysis Ed reported his dream as follows:

> I pulled up in front of a house in my dad's jeep. I was lost and shaking. I said to myself in a questioning manner: "what town is this?" A man was in the house and he invited me inside. I was wary of being diverted. I insisted on knowing what town it was that I was in. I went into the house. The man was talking to me. There was a large table in the room. There was a big sex toy near the ceiling which was lowered on a chain. It was made out of a soft material. In the front there was a penis, and in the back there were two legs. Later in the dream I did not have clothes on. I was thinking that I was horny, and that this guy wants me to suck his penis. I'll do it. I don't care. When I went out of the house there was a truck that was backed into the driveway. Somebody was in the front of the truck and I asked again what town was this. They looked at me like I was pregnant.

When I asked Ed to make associations about this dream he made the following remarks: "The older man was short, dark with straight hair and about fortyish, and he reminded me of you. I felt that the man wanted to seduce me and this brought up my fear about what had happened when I had sex with my teacher."

In this dream, Ed's transference relationship with me is expressed with great clarity. He had fears that I could seduce him, as he was seduced by a teacher he admired and respected, a situation in which he was used to satisfy the desires and demands of another. This is only a partial explanation of the sexual/erotic content of the dream, since he says that he became sexually charged before a sexual enactment took place. In this sense, Ed's more suppressed sexual desires were expressed.

Ed's emotional state in the beginning of the dream indicates how difficult it has been for Ed to identify with his father. In his dream he is not sure where he is or where he is going: he does not have his bearings and is anxious about his predicament. This I think reflects his conflicts over finding an adequate identity. When associated with his father internally. Ed does not know were he is going; thus his father cannot help him find the right direction in his life. The invitation to come inside, I believe, is related to the analysis. He perceived me, and rightly so, inviting him to be analyzed. His wariness of being diverted represents his fear and anxiety about the analytic work. Will it be helpful to him? Will it enable him to get where he feels he needs to go in the future? His anxiety about place may describe the urgency of his plea for analytic help. He is saying that he needs to know where he is going, and where the analysis is going to take him. Then in the dream, the man is talking to him and Ed goes into the house. In a parallel way he has entered into the analytic consulting room and embarked upon analysis to determine "where he is" psychologically.

As the dream progresses, the atmosphere becomes more murky and more sexualized. When Ed made further associations based on the dream, he related the sex toy to his childhood masturbatory activity and sexual play. When he was four years old, he engaged in sexual play with a male playmate. He allowed the small boy to urinate into his mouth, and this led him to feel humiliated. He spoke about this incident with an intense amount of shame. In addition, there were soft objects that he utilized to masturbate by rubbing them against his penis so that he would become excited. His own sense of phallic excitement is contained in the image of the large phallic sex toy. It appears that he was first conscious of this when he was four years old and entering into the oedipal period of child development. Then in the dream he reports that he does not have clothes on, becomes sexually excited, and thinks that the man wants Ed to perform fellatio on him. Ed does this in the dream. The desire to engage in oral intercourse represents symbolically Ed's need for a close and physically intimate relationship with an older male. Ed had not discussed homosexual relationships with me at this point. I did not want to inquire into them, since I felt that the dream was more related to suppressed sexual desire for his father that arose in the oedipal period and that was being transferred onto me in the present. The need for close sexual contact with an older man seemed to indicate both what had been suppressed as well as the desire for a close and intimate relationship with an older male in the present. While the molestation by the female teacher was in the background of our discussion about the dream, I think that both Ed and I felt that the dream seemed to be more related to his emotional state and his desire for male influence, symbolized in the dream as fellatio.

The maternal aspects of the dream are symbolized by the truck backed into the driveway, an image that could represent his mother's body. His primary envy of his mother's body and her reproductive capacity is here dealt with by his becoming pregnant through oral intercourse. In addition, the fellatio could be a symbolic representation of his negative oedipal strivings; that is, his desire to be in close sexual contact with his father and his jealousy of his mother's ongoing sexual relationship with his father. Children in the oedipal phase often conceptualize impregnation and the conception of babies as taking place through oral intercourse. Often children describe fantasies of the father placing a seed inside of the mother's mouth, which then grows into a baby in her stomach. The baby is often thought to emerge out of the mother's anus, and the birth-giving process is then associated with defecation. The pregnancy in the dream could also be related to his desire to conceive an analytic baby with me. The analytic baby would then be symbolically related to the birth of a new sense of self.

As we worked on the psychological implications of the dream over the next weeks, Ed appeared to be able to engage me increasingly in an analytic relationship where we could reflect together on his internal psychological states and try together to generate their psychological meanings.

The Idealizing Transference and the Absent Father

During the first months of analysis, Ed and I focused on our relationship. The meanings that we were able to derive from it helped us to understand his earlier relationships and the impact they had on his present circumstances. Ed seemed to have a strong need and desire for an intimate and secure relationship with an older father figure whom he could admire and idealize. He needed to have a sense of being able to idealize someone he could look up to, since he felt his own father was unable to contain because of his alcoholism. He had felt betrayed and alienated from his father in childhood, and he was trying to repair his unsatisfied desires for a close father/son relationship in his analysis with me. I felt encouraged that we were able to evolve a sense of intimacy and depth in our relationship. I felt at this point as if he were an analytical son, and I enjoyed the depth and intimacy of our ongoing contact. It appeared that he was able to begin to have some good feelings about himself as a result of holding onto some of the good feelings that were generated by our relationship. However, I was somewhat wary of the intensity of his idealization of me and the subsequent devaluation of his father. I felt that it was difficult for him to integrate both the good and bad aspects of the father imago. The split was being perpetuated through his deflection of anger and "badness" onto his father, and that he was preserving me for his good feelings and idealizations. I interpreted the splitting that was occurring in the transference, and this led Ed to reflect on his early pre-oedipal relationship with his father.

We discussed in depth both the actual historical relationship as he remembered it, as well as the internal representations of that relationship as they emerged in his dreams and fantasies. The transference/countertransference relationship also gave us a deeper understanding of much that was unconscious in his relationship with his father, in particular his strong need for affirmation, support, and approval and his unsatisfied attachment needs from earliest infancy. He yearned to be more connected to his father, yet he felt his father had betrayed him by not being able to form a more emotionally connected relationship with him. I felt the paternal homosexual aspect of his transference relationship represented an unsatisfied yearning stemming from the pre-oedipal infantile period. In his own mind I became a desired and desirable man, someone whom he wanted to be like and with whom he wanted to psychologically merge, as he had desired in his earlier childhood. He felt calmed and soothed by the analytic ambiance, much as an infant would feel soothed and calmed by a father who was able to hold him securely in his arms and in his mind. I had the distinct feeling in these sessions that Ed was both experiencing and satisfying a deep hunger for masculine/paternal contact at the most developmentally primitive level.

During this period of the analysis, Ed decided to become a poet/ musician, and he began again his music studies, which had provided him with some sense of positive affirmation when he was younger. He started to write poetry, and began to date a woman who was close to his own age. He described needing to feel satisfied in his father hunger before he could feel comfortable with women, before he could experience and affirm a sense of his core maleness. Ed needed to experience this core sense of maleness before he could experience his own body image as being intact and male. As we began to explore this bodily aspect of his development, he had the following dream:

I am sleeping in my parents bedroom. I see a casting of my father's genitals, his penis and his testicles. The penis is ugly, a blimp shape, elongated and bulbous. The head of the penis is large, and it has an ugly vein in it. I woke up with a feeling of disgust.

I think that this dream represents the feeling that Ed had towards the realm of the father, the paternal phallus, and his masculine body image in relationship to the primal scene. For him, the paternal phallus is something inanimate, lifeless and inert, as well as something disgusting and ugly. Ed had difficulty conceptualizing parental intercourse as something loving and involving mutual caring. Rather he fantasized his parents' sexual relationship as something violent and impersonal. He had difficulty identifying with his father's penis as a connecting and generative organ. He saw his own penis as deficient, and he had ongoing difficulties in his sexual encounters with women because of this. It was difficult for him to consolidate a coherent sense of his body image, since his tendency was to view his body and his genitals as being malformed.

In addition, Ed had a morbid fear that he looked like his father. He loathed those body parts that were similar to his father's. He felt that his lips and nose were like those of his father's, and he expressed a desire to have them altered through plastic surgery. In part, his view of the ugly paternal phallus was a fear that his own penis was not attractive enough. He feared that he would have difficulty performing intercourse because of his "damaged" penis, which could be so much like his father's. These fears seemed to represent Ed's anxiety about women's bodies and their sexual functioning. He experienced a dread of the vagina that caused erection difficulties accompanied by deep anxiety. As the analysis progressed, Ed was able to see how his own image of himself was enmeshed and confused with his image of his father. The gradual differentiation of his image of self from that of his father was an important aspect of the analytic work at this time.

Ed's attempt to feel more secure with his heterosexuality went through a beginning transitional period, where same sex emotional attachments were a significant feature of his interpersonal relationships. He was more conscious of his homosexual impulses and desires as well as his need to idealize men. At this time he formed a close relationship with a male artist, Fred, whom he wished to emulate. This relationship was not sexualized, and it appeared to offer him a sense of support for his own artistic strivings. Fred became an admired friend. His feelings about this relationship were expressed well in the following dream:

> There is a guy like Fred with really big muscles. They are not so accentuated, but they are big and round, and the arm had a full-bodied feeling. Fred was lying naked next to me. He was talking about all the girls he had intercourse with.

His relationship with Fred helped him to feel that he could experience male intimacy outside of the analytic relationship. As the friendship grew, he became increasingly free of the fear that he would be "caught" in our relationship. I think Ed felt entangled in his relationship with me, and this made him feel dependent and lacking in autonomy. In addition, he began to feel different from his friends because he was in analysis, and he feared they would find out about it and think that he was "weird." The emergence of negative feelings toward me, and his need to isolate himself and me from strong hostile affects, may have pushed him into finding another positive male role model.

Ed's rage first emerged in projected form. He had dreams of his father and other male figures who were hurting him. In one dream he had broken something in the roof of his mouth, and his father insensitively stuck his fingers in his mouth and hurt him. In another, a man was pulling at his groin, and he was writhing in pain. These dreams seemed to signal the emergence of primal rage and murderous feelings directed towards his father of infancy and early childhood. He felt profoundly guilty because of his murderous feelings towards his father, since he feared that he could be overwhelmed by these affects and act them out in some violent manner. The emergence of these feelings made him feel disorganized, and he was fearful that they would come into the analytic relationship and disrupt or destroy it. He now understood that his analysis was important to help him counteract his feelings that he could become insane and act out his dreaded impulses.

Dealing with Mother

Ed's relationship with his mother did not offer him a viable alternative: his memories of his mother of infancy were filled with feelings of abandonment and prolonged separateness. He did not appear to have evolved a secure attachment with her, and this made him feel psychologically vulnerable. There were prolonged separations when he was a toddler and his mother was sick with cancer. Related to his experience of his mother as being unavailable, and not offering the soothing and care that he so desired, were Ed's difficulties with self-regulation resulting in addictive behaviors. Ed was able to find solace and soothing in substance abuse, but he could not depend on human relationships to offer him comfort.

Compounding the complexities of their relationship was the fact that his mother, as a result of her molestation, viewed men as sexually violent and out of control. She expressed in our initial parent interview a fear that Ed might become a rapist. I felt that this was a distorted projection, based on her own childhood experience. At the same time I think that Ed was influenced by his mother's negative view of male sexuality, and that his own psychosexual development was complicated by this. At a more unconscious level, there appeared to be a mutually seductive relationship between mother and son. In the analysis, this emerged in the form of incestuous fantasies and desires.

While Ed experienced shame in regard to his sexual preoccupations concerning older women, his most satisfying sexual experiences had been with older women. His molestation by an older female teacher seemed to be linked in a clear way with his relationship to his mother. His relationship to his teacher was a complicated one. There were significant role confusions. The teacher was also a therapist for Ed, and later he moved into her home so that she could have a greater impact on him. It was during this period that an explicitly sexual relationship evolved. The teacher made him feel special, unique, and lovable, even though he realized that he was being controlled, manipulate, and exploited by her. His need for admiration was so great that he allowed himself to become victimized in this way.

Ed's incestuous feelings towards his mother also emerged in masturbatory fantasies and dreams. While masturbating, his central and most prominent fantasy involved his mother rubbing his testicles and arousing him. His image of his mother was of her being powerful and controlling. He wanted to give over his body to her so that she could manipulate him while he was passive. This image of his mother alternated with a more assertive fantasy where he attacks his mother and rapes her. The alternating images of passive molestation and active raping seemed to point to the extreme split in his view of the maternal/feminine.

Ed's difficulties in achieving an experience of a core male identity was related to his psychological conflicts with both parents. He experienced disruptions in bonding and attachment with both parents, and this severely affected the development of his self and body images. The reparative aspect of the analysis could only be realized as he carefully worked through his painful and intensely experienced affects and attempted to give them symbolic expression. As he reflected with me on his experiences, he was able to give shape to experiences that had been confusing and overwhelming. Slowly, he was able to form concepts about his psychological state, and he became able to think about himself with greater clarity.

Concluding the Analysis

As we entered into the third and final year of his analysis, Ed began to mourn the passing of his childhood. He began to realize that his infantile and childhood desires would never be fulfilled by his parents, and that he would have to rely upon himself to generate a sense of purpose and meaning. His sense of the tragic, as well as hopeful aspects of his life could be better understood as his psychological development and internal world were given shape and dimensionality. Ed's sense of having an identity that could exist with some coherence over time was strengthened as a result of the analysis. Ed decided to stop his analysis after three years, since he felt that he had gained the insights that he had desired, insights that resulted in more stable relationships. I told him that while I did not think that we had completed our work, it seemed a good place to stop. I told him that I would appreciate hearing how things went for him over time. I had a strong feeling that he needed to separate from me as he had, psychologically, from his own parents, and I did not want to thwart that development. We both felt satisfied that we had done a significant amount of good work together and that we both had been deeply affected by what had transpired.

During our last session Ed gave me the following poem which he said expressed some of his experience of where he had arrived as a result of his analysis.

> God is love and evil,
> and everything that's real,
> and nothing yet to come for us,
> is too extreme to feel.
> It doesn't take a miracle
> to catch the truth alive,
> God is love and evil
> and willing to survive.
>
> God is love and evil
> and all that lies between,
> in colors from a world of light
> that eyes have never seen.
> But any fool can recognize
> that up and down the stairs
> God is love and evil
> beyond their wildest prayers.
>
> God is love and evil
> whatever you believe.
> The gifts of imperfection
> are yours to go receive.
> And I hope you're not afraid to love
> when you have love to give,
> 'cause God is love and evil
> and not afraid to live.

Notes

1. C. G. Jung, *Symbols of Transformation,* (Princeton, N.J.: Princeton University Press, 1956), p. 223.
2. See E. Erickson, *Identity: Youth and Crisis.* (New York: W. W. Norton, 1968); P. Blos, *Son and Father: Before and Beyond the Oedipus Complex* (New York: Macmillan, 1985); M. Laufer and M. E. Laufer, *Adolescence and Developmental Breakdown* (New Haven, CT:1984).
3. R. Maduro, "The Initial Dream and Analyzability in Beginning Analysis," *Journal of Analytical Psychology* 32 (1984):3.

SECTION 6

Attacks on the Body

Introduction to Section 6

The two chapters in this section deal with severe psychosomatic disorders that are self-destructive attacks on the body. Although Brian Feldman and Francesco Bisagni have different approaches, both papers provide impressive examples of how in adolescence the body can represent inner objects.

Brian Feldman's chapter deals with bulimia. Typically, the first manifestations of bulimia occur in adolescence. It is a disorder that has a high rate of occurrence in industrialized societies. Feldman's general thesis follows Fordham's concept of deintegration/reintegration of the self. He states that bulimia represents a disorder of the self in which the deitegrative/reitegrative process is basically disturbed and the bulimia can be understood as a "desperate attempt to forestall psychological breakdown." Following the general approach of the authors presented in this book, Feldman assumes that bulimia has its roots in the pre-oedipal disturbances of the mother infant relationship. When the infant does not gradually introject a maternal function that "involves the capacity for self-soothing and self-calming," a disconnection between infant and environment occurs that inhibits the development of symbolic functioning.

It is often noted—and not only by psychoanalytic researchers—that bulimic women lack a basic capacity for symbolizing. Feldman states: "This function involves utilizing internal psychological experiences and creating meaning out of them in order to further emotional growth and development . . . " and thus the bulimic behavior and the atypical use of food as an addictive substance are used as defenses of the self against further impingements. (See M. Davies' paper "Defenses of the Self" included here.) The bulimia can, therefore, represent basic difficulties in the introjection and assimilation of psychological experience.

The bulimic attack on the body is a form of defense of the self. In the patient's unconscious fantasy, the body represents a relationship to the mother as a "part object level" (Klein): "Through binging and purging the fantasy of ejecting the bad parts of the self, including negative thoughts or taboo feelings, emerges. These feelings and fantasies are often related to murderous impulses that have been initially directed toward the mother. In her absence as a containing and detoxifying agent, they are redirected against the self."

Feldman illustrates his theoretical assumptions in the case of nineteen-year-old Diana. Diana's binges and purges became the mechanisms by which she could control states of disorganization, confusion, depression, and anxiety. As a child she had the fantasy of having worms inside her body, and in an autistic manner she encapsulated herself in a sensation-dominated universe where food and bodily sensations were her sole preoccupation. This form of defense of the self is similar to those autistic barriers that Tustin has observed in neurotic patients.

Diana's envious attacks upon her internal mother of infancy colored the transference/countertransference relationship. The rage that stemmed from infancy was transformed into attacks on all internal goodness, as well as the potential goodness she could receive from the therapist. Thus she could not let psychic space develop between her and the therapist, because she feared that any connection in the analytic relationship would unleash her rage.

But in the course of therapy, and thanks to the stable containing capacity of the therapist, Diana slowly developed a capacity to symbolize. This was first seen in separation situations, during weekend breaks and the therapist's holidays, to which she reacted with severe anxiety. Diana's discovery of her longing for dependency was the beginning of a reparative process. Gradually she was able to overcome her autistic withdrawal. In the course of therapy Diana began to study art. She developed a deep interest in the work of the Mexican painter Frida Kahlo, whose paintings symbolized for her her own psychic pains and injured body.

Francesco Bisagni's chapter deals with a young patient who suffers from severe attacks on her body. Bisagni's especially interesting theoretical approach focuses on both Jung's concept of the self as a wholeness of personality and Fordham's ideas on the disturbances in the early deintegration/reintegration process and their connection with difficulties in the developmental movement from the paranoid-schizoid position to the depressive position as described by W.R. Bion. Bisagni illustrates this with the psychodynamic of hysteria in a case of severe psychogenic paralysis. He goes along with Brenman, who describes hysterical patterns as a combination of denial and catastrophic dread. The manipulatory tendency of hysterical patients is rooted in a particular aspect of relating to objects, which he assumes are not whole objects (Klein) but pseudo-whole objects that undergo a splitting. The hysterical part of the personality defends against depressive schizoid anxieties and therefore Bisagni distinguishes between two components of defenses: "One appears on the surface, in the way the hysterical part of the personality uses anxiety, and has to do with falsification and narcissistic omnipotent manipulation of the object; whereas the second and real underlying anxiety, is split off and defended against."

Bisagni's case is of a patient in late adolescence, twenty-year-old Anna. Anna had been affected three years before starting therapy by a pseudoparalysis of the lower body that had also affected both hands to a lesser degree. The core image needed to understand the psychodynamic of Anna's disorder occurs in a dream. In her dream, Anna is in a tunnel dug deep into a mountain, surrounded by rocks. Outside the opening is a waterfall. In the dream Anna does not want to get out of the mountain, because outside is "only wasteland and the water might be dangerous." The image can be considered as a symbol of a mountain-stone-womb. The dream describes an experience of containment without transformative potential, and Anna experiences the "omnipotence of immobility." The mountain can also represent the breast, but without the nipple as a mediating factor between mouth and breast, a form of a petrified, death breast. Bisagni describes Anna's experience and state of mind as "the death of her mind and the devitalization of her body. The "lapis philosophorum" (according to Jung a symbol of the self) is lost, and a self-mother-breast experienced as a "lapis vilis" (coarse stone) is substituted." In this state of mind Anna often manifested violent attacks upon her own thinking and upon the analytic function. This is again a form of Fordham's defenses of the self or in Bion's terms, an "attack on linking." In the countertransference, Bisagni experienced Anna's attack on her body as a sensation of paralysis and total immobility of his own body. Interpretations were negated even before they could be formulated. The therapist felt used by Anna in the same way that Anna used her mother: "like a hard, lifeless, petrified autistic object, not a soft, lively, and warm but hard separate object by which she might be penetrated." Although there was a gradual but significant progress in Anna's development and she began to walk again, she stopped therapy when the therapist once came late to a session. Anna perceived this as a repetition of her experience when she was sixteen and her father had died in a car accident.

Bisagni writes: "Anna's case also shows how the use of the body can be distinguished in two ways: a barrier use, as an attack upon linking, and a psychosomatic use, partly more evolved and connected to a wider possibility of communication through projective identification. The psychosomatic use tends to stimulate an activity in another person in a similar way to the infant who activates the breast response through crying."

The chapters of both Feldman and Bisagni confirm our experience that the successful decisive factor in the adolescent's ability to cope with the transformation of his or her body during puberty is a sufficiently satisfactory psychosomatic infantile experience. When the infantile experience is not good enough, the adolescent's body cannot function as a containing object and the "second chance" for reorganizing personality in adolescence fails.

11

Bulimia in Adolescent Women: An Exploration of Personal and Archetypal Dynamics in Analysis

Brian Feldman

Introduction

The inner world of the bulimic woman is fraught with anxiety, dread, and terror. She comes to analysis in a state of confusion and hopelessness. Typically, she has tried to stop the repetitive bouts of binging and vomiting but has been unable to reduce their length and frequency. During the initial evaluation interviews, she often talks of being unable to cope with depression, internal chaos, and feelings of self-hatred, which are often related to the bulimia itself. Often the level of psychic pain has become so intense that bulimic episodes involving binging and purging are the only form of emotional relief. They take on the quality of magical rituals, the purpose of which is to calm, soothe, and reinstate some semblance of psychic balance following periods of disintegrated mental states.

The disorder, primarily associated with women, appears in early adolescence with the beginning of the major psychosexual and physical changes at puberty. The young women I have treated analytically often experience confusion about their sexual identity as well as fears of intimacy. They are fearful of changes in their bodies, particularly of their menstruation, which they often try to stop by lowering their body weight. They also fear that they will gain weight and become fat, which would lower their self-esteem and make them feel undesirable to others.

Based on research and analytic experience, I believe bulimia represents a disorder of the self in which the deintegrative-reintegrative processes of the self are damaged. Thus bulimia can be conceptualized as a desperate attempt to forestall psychological breakdown. Fordham's concept of deintegrative processes has been important in helping me to understand the clinical material presented in the analyses of bulimic women.[1] The infant is conceptualized by Fordham as having a primary self from which psychic structure evolves through the process of deintegration and reintegration. One of the first deintegrative-reintegrative processes occurs during the first breast feeding experience. If the infant experiences the breast and the maternal care associated with it in a reliable manner, an empathically attuned relationship develops between the mother and baby. The baby then begins slowly to introject an image of a good breast that comforts, soothes, calms, and provides important nutrients. When the breast is absent for tolerable lengths of time, the infant begins to form mental representations out of its remembered experiences in time, symbolic thinking begins to evolve.

Judging from my work in infant observation, it appears that the way the mother is able to hold onto the baby in her mind is most important for the psychological development of the infant. If she is able to allow the baby to exist inside of herself in a mindful manner, she is attuned to the baby and the baby is affirmed in having an individual self separate from the mother. When the mother and baby connect, the infant slowly introjects a maternal function that involves the capacity for self-soothing and self-calming. When the two do not connect, Fordham postulates that defense systems can arise spontaneously out of the primal self.[2] These defenses of the self are designed to preserve a sense of individual safety and intactness, but they also create an impermeable barrier between the infant's self and the environment at a time when the infant is beginning to develop a symbolic function. When the defenses of the self are operative, the processes of deintegration-reintegration are blocked and the unfolding of archetypal and symbolic experience is thwarted.

In the analytic treatment of young bulimic women, the symbolic function has been either poorly developed or severely damaged. This function involves utilizing internal psychological experience and creates meaning out of it in order to further emotional growth and development. In most cases, there has been a basic and early failure of the deintegrative-reintegrative processes of the self, and thus the bulimic behavior and the atypical use of food as an addictive substance are used as defenses of the self against further impingements. The bulimia can, therefore, represent basic difficulties in the introjection and assimilation of psychological experience.

During the beginning phases of analysis, bulimic women have great difficulty using the analytic space and the analytic relationship. They have a hard time both accepting and digesting what transpires in analysis. The efficacy of the analytic process can be both rejected and denied. In addition, they often describe difficulties that arise from an the inability to create meaning out of internal experiences. Experiences of hollowness and deadness are felt to be pervasive. These women seem unable to rely upon their own internal resources for self-care and self-soothing, and as a result self-calming functions are poorly developed. These internal functions usually develop out of the normal deintegration-reintegration processes of early childhood, but with the young bulimic women these processes have failed to unfold. As analysis progresses, few memories are reported of good feeds or good early empathic interactions with parenting figures; rather experiences of feeling mistreated, misunderstood, or neglected are articulated. These women have encapsulated themselves in their bulimia as a response to the dysfunctional infant/mother relationship. Fears and suspicions stemming from the original mother/infant interaction first predominate in the transference relationship, as these women are often exquisitely sensitive to failures of empathy or potential misinterpretations of their psychological experience. They are fearful of becoming dependent on the analyst and want to give the impression that they can care for themselves. Fantasies of doing away with the parent/analyst and taking care of themselves are accompanied by a great need for support, care, and involvement.

In the treatment of adolescents with bulimia, these defenses of the self are a major focus of the analytical process. As the early developmental roots of the conflict become clearer, the meaning and function of the bulimia begins to unfold. The bulimia is used to stabilize a fragile sense of self. Through binging and purging the fantasy of ejecting the bad parts of the self, including negative thoughts or taboo feelings, emerges. These feelings and fantasies are often related to murderous impulses that have been initially directed towards the mother. In her absence as a containing and detoxifying agent, they are redirected against the self. Binging and purging help to get rid of the anger and rage, thereby creating the illusion that internal emotional states are manageable.

There are some striking similarities in both the personal origins and the archetypal patterns that emerge during the course of analysis with bulimic women. On a personal level, these women describe feeling abandoned in childhood by self-absorbed, absent, or immature mothers. As these feelings are carried over in the transference/countertransference process, deep feelings of wanting to be held and cared for emerge, accompanied by fears of merging resulting in loss of a sense of self. These feelings represent the unresolved, infantile root of the disorder. At the archetypal level the image of the all-giving and nurturing breast-feeding mother alternates with the image of the devouring and negating mother.[3] The archetypal image of the bliss-giving mother is yearned for with intense desire. It is this archetypal image that the biological mother has not been able to incarnate during infancy. Thus this image remains in the mind of the adolescent as an unattainable object of desire. Instead, the archetypal image of the castrating, devouring, withholding, and abandoning witch-mother predominates. For the bulimic, this image is primarily associated with the biological mother.

In the transference, the desire to restore a feeling of lost union with the good aspects of the breast-feeding mother/analyst clashes with a fear of being caught in the clutches of a devouring, negating mother/analyst. The analyst needs to monitor and be sensitive to countertransference responses in order to make sense out of the analytical material at both the archetypal and personal levels, since the adolescent often has difficulty articulating internal experiences. This difficulty with verbal expression is related to the failure in the development of the symbolic function. Due to this failure, the expression of fantasies and affects remains stuck in body processes. Offering a safe and containing analytical environment is essential in order for the unfolding of the personal and archetypal unconscious to take place. The analyst needs to be able to contain and help the adolescent to integrate the affect that threatens to be overwhelming.

Analysis of a Case of Bulimia

When I began to see Diana in analytical therapy for the treatment of bulimia nervosa, she was nineteen years old and in her second year of university. Diana was seen in analysis for four and a half years and attended five times a week until the ending phases, when she reduced her visits to four and then three times weekly.

Attractive, athletic, and slender, Diana came to my consulting room dressed in neat, "preppy" clothes. She appeared nervous and began to talk about her difficulties in a detached and muted manner. She spoke as if she were talking about someone else, and it was difficult to form any emotional connection with her. During my first sessions with Diana, she described feeling empty and hopeless about her bulimia. At the university Diana had tried to maintain the outward appearance of social normalcy, but this pose was difficult to sustain since it made her feel unreal and false. She was a member of a sorority but did not like it. Because she felt alienated and separate from the others because of her bulimia, Diana found it difficult to go to the social meetings and to participate. None of her friends knew about her bulimia, and she wanted to keep it a secret because she feared rejection.

Diana felt tentative about entering analysis. While she was pessimistic about embarking upon therapy, she also felt that she had little alternative since her bulimia was controlling her life. She felt enslaved and imprisoned by an addiction she could not control and which she did not understand.

The Initial Phase of Analysis

Diana knew little about her birth history. She had been told by her mother that she was a planned baby and born at full term. There were, as far as she knew, no problems at the birth, and she was a healthy baby. Diana's parents divorced when she was seven years old. They had been married for ten years. After the divorce she lived with her mother and spent weekends with her father. She did not like the visitation arrangements and often felt that she was being controlled and manipulated by her father. Her mother worked full-time, and Diana remembered being left with two younger siblings and baby-sitters on numerous occasions when her mother was away on business. Diana felt inadequately cared for by both parents and unable to establish a stable emotional bond with either of them.

In her first sessions, Diana said that she became withdrawn and suspicious during her bulimic episodes. She felt profoundly guilty about her bulimia and often had self-destructive thoughts, but she saw no other way to control her chaotic states of mind. Excessive anxiety and depression often triggered the binging episodes, which, at the beginning of treatment, often occurred up to six hours a day. Diana also described her intense anxiety. She felt profoundly isolated from others, her disconnection compounded by her own withdrawn, disconnected mental state. She felt that the bulimia was like an impermeable wall around herself which kept her encapsulated in a world of food preoccupations. The marked schizoid trends in her personality were indicated by her feelings of emptiness and fear of not being able to make meaningful contact with others.

It became clearer during the initial sessions that Diana used her binging as a form of escape from difficult, anxiety-evoking internal and external situations. She described her behavior as an "escape from the pressures in my mind." Binging and purging became the mechanism by which she could control states of disorganization, confusion, depression, and anxiety. At the same time, she had punitive thoughts and feelings after the binge/purge episodes, so the system was never completely effective. She described looking for calmness through her bulimia, but she often found it difficult to soothe herself. During the binge/purge episodes she got into and out of control in frenzied states that ended with a feeling of momentary calm. She said, "I escape from the feeling of hardness by binging, and after a binge I feel dead and drained out." Her bulimic behavior seemed to take place while she was in an altered state of consciousness where there was minimal ego control. Diana spoke of the bulimia as helping to provide her with an intense focus to keep away some highly intrusive and painful thoughts. It served as a means of exerting profound control over her states of mind and affect.

Diana described an experience of having a disordered appetite in her childhood. When she was seven years old, she had a fantasy of having worms inside her body. This fantasy, she thought, was the only possible explanation for her enormous and insatiable appetite. She felt at the time that something was eating her up from within, and if she did not feed the worms they could eat up her insides and eventually her whole body. Her own consuming need to be emotionally fed was being turned against herself and filling her with terror. Feeding herself became a way of fending off this terror and creating a boundary so that she could experience safety; vomiting became a way of trying get rid of the worm and its potentially devouring presence.

The Therapeutic Alliance and the Transference Relationship

During the first stage of treatment, Diana began to talk more openly about her binging and purging episodes, and I tried to help her to elucidate the meaning of her experience. I attempted to help her gain some understanding of what meaning the bulimia had in her current life. Diana stated that before the episodes began, a depressed empty feeling consistently emerged. She felt depersonalized and robot-like, yearning for a close interpersonal contact she could not have, trapped and imprisoned in a world she did not understand, a world of racing, uncontrollable thoughts and emotions that could only be contained through binging and vomiting. I felt she was defending herself against a fear of paralyzing depression and psychological breakdown. Her experience of disconnection from others was complete during these periods. In an autistic manner, she encapsulated herself in a sensation-dominated universe where food and bodily sensations were her sole preoccupation. Her binge/purge episodes often lasted several hours and could be repeated several times a day.

In early sessions, Diana was often secluded in her own thoughts, difficult to reach, and I often felt helpless and ineffective, as if my own capacity for thought and reflection had been attacked and destroyed. I described the impact that her emotional states had upon my thought processes, and she slowly began to realize the power of her destructive and rageful feelings. She was attempting to make me understand through my own inner experience the potency of her feelings and the devastating impact they had upon her own psychological functioning. Because of her difficulty in articulating her emotional experiences, she needed to have me experience the nature and intensity of her destructive affects through my countertransference response. At times I felt possessed by her, filled with toxic emotions I needed to expel. Frequently I felt enormously hungry after our sessions. At one point after a session my hands were trembling and I felt filled with Diana's presence, a state of possession that I could only abate by actually leaving the consulting room and making space for reflection.

Between these sessions I felt anxious and concerned about Diana, a preoccupation that made me feel that something was happening at a deeper emotional level, and that I was the one who was experiencing, via projective identification, my own warded-off emotional needs. I experienced rage and anger towards her as well as a preoccupation with her fragmented emotional states. I felt she was too much to handle, that she needed too much of my care, that perhaps some of my other patients would suffer because I was too preoccupied with her, and that eventually I would become emotionally depleted and not want to see her anymore. I reflected on my own desire to reject her and get rid of her. At the same time I feared she could have a breakdown as her affective states became more labile.

Therapeutic Regression within the Transference/ Countertransference Relationship

As the issues in the transference/countertransference relationship began to revolve more around the maternal-infant relationship, the development of a sense of security, trust, and the containment of Diana's rage and destructiveness became paramount. Memories of the early mother-infant relationship came to the fore with ever-increasing intensity. Her memories were of a mother during infancy and childhood who denied the appearance of negative emotions in their relationship. Diana felt that she was made to feel guilty, strange, and wrong for feeling depressed. She did not think that her mother could understand her, and because of this past pattern, she felt hopeless about the possibility of finding solace or union in the therapeutic relationship.

She felt at this point that her binging was something that she needed because it was the only thing that had been consistent for her during the past years. It served a self-mothering function, since she could nurture herself by binging and give herself the illusion of being fed by a mothering figure. She described having the image in her mind of a breast that would nourish her, but she had strong ambivalent feelings toward this internal breast because it also aroused feelings of frustration, anger, and despair.

Diana's envious attacks upon her internal mother of infancy continued relentlessly. The rage that stemmed from infancy was transformed into attacks on all internal goodness, as well as the potential goodness she could receive from me. She was determined to gain complete control of the internal mother and obliterate any experience of dependency. Her gradual recognition of something positive in her mother only came about through her commitment to the analysis and her search to find something in it of value for herself, namely the development of her creativity.

Although she yearned for a close relationship to her mother and all that her mother represented to her, Diana believed she could not turn successfully to a real maternal relationship. Instead, she turned to the inanimate world for a sense of security. She yearned to be close to the sea, to "mother nature," and to recreate in a sensory manner the soothing and contained feeling of her early childhood when she spent holidays near the ocean. She experienced a need for a connection to an archetypal "earth mother" that was difficult to quell. It was as if she were attempting to hold herself together by adhering to sensory images and experiences of a time long ago, to an experience of an impersonal force of mother nature. This pointed to the severe deprivation of maternal care suffered in her early development. Only through her ongoing contact with me in the transference relationship could her contact with the mother archetype be humanized.

The anger and rage Diana felt towards her internal mother of infancy became more pronounced as the infantile memories continued to emerge. In the transference she needed to have my total attention, and she was acutely sensitive to the times when my attention veered away from her. I, then, became the rejecting, inattentive mother who did not have the patience to hold her securely in my mind. What became clearer as the analysis delved more deeply into the period of infancy was that she did not experience her mother as being able either to think about her or hold her emotionally in mind in a stable, ongoing manner. In therapy, she was attempting to recreate this experience with me. This infantile relationship needed to be reenacted within the transference before she could feel its significance. While she experienced a strong need to be admired and acknowledged, Diana kept feeling that her mother was largely unavailable or needed Diana to mirror her own largely unfulfilled, narcissistic needs. A safe place inside my mind was intensely desired. Despite her yearning for care, annihilating attacks on the mother of infancy and on me in the transference erupted whenever she began to feel close. Under the surface there was seething conflict focused around feelings of rage and despair and a hopeless feeling that no relationship could possibly take care of her insatiable emotional needs. She feared that any connection in the analytic relationship would unleash her rage and fury. As a result of her strong, contradictory impulses, she felt suspended between the Scylla of withdrawn isolation and the Charybdis of an interactional intimacy that would unleash the destructive fury aroused by helpless dependency.

As more space was given to reflection on her emotional responses stemming from the infantile and early childhood periods, murderous impulses towards her mother and me emerged in violent fantasies. She described wanting to rip us apart and tear us to pieces. In these fantasies, we were to be made to feel worthless and helpless, disarmed so that she would not feel that anyone could have any power or influence over her. As her violent fantasies were explored and as she began to tolerate their presence in the analysis, she started to report dreams and fantasies of a highly symbolic nature. It seemed as if her internal symbolic development had been thwarted by the suppression of her murderous, aggressive impulses. Once these were freed she could begin to use symbols and imagery as an expression of her internal states.

Diana's capacity to symbolize and become further involved in the analytical relationship increased as she began to generate more thoughts about the meaning of her condition. She realized how much she needed her bulimia to stabilize her fragile sense of self. She began to acknowledge that through binging and purging she was attempting to eject bad parts of herself, especially rage, anger, and self-destructive thoughts. These feelings and thoughts were difficult to bear, and binging helped give her the illusion of coping. Yet the most difficult feeling to bear was that of no feeling at all, a kind of inner deadness, a black hole that was cold, vast, empty and devouring. It was a hole into which she could fall and become lost in an ominous void of nonbeing. She felt that if she did not binge she would "either burst and go crazy, or else fall into the black hole." These fears were related to infantile anxieties of an overwhelming nature. Winnicott relates this anxiety of annihilation to the infant's experience of impingements in the early mother-infant relationship, especially as a result of the mother's inability to be empathically attuned to the infant's needs.[4] At times, Diana felt completely incapacitated like a baby who was dropped down a cold, dark well. Her experience of disconnection was total. She spoke of her mother as being a snake inside her that she could not get rid of. The snake was related to the childhood fantasy of having worms eating up her insides. Her hatred, murderousness, and rage were consuming her emotionally.

It was at this time that Diana had a dream of being with her mother in a boat that capsized. In the dream her mother was steering the boat and apparently had made a terrible mistake. We explored the meaning of the dream as it related to her infantile emotional reaction to the inconsistency of maternal care. She felt like an infant who had awoken from a bad dream and was left in her crib to cry. Her experience of the catastrophe of her early infancy filled her with all unbearable pain.

Emergence of a Capacity to Symbolize

As emotions from infancy continued to emerge, Diana experienced an increased need for emotional holding in the transference. She felt anxious about the weekend breaks and feared becoming self-destructive and suicidal. I also found the breaks stressful and became filled with a sense of helplessness and fear about her condition. The fear that I would not be able to hold her securely in mind during the separations made her panic. She longed for a close, soothing relationship yet feared the dependency and intimacy engendered by the analytic process. Her emerging needs terrorized her, especially when she realized how unsatisfied they were. At this point in the therapeutic process, Diana began to understand her deep suspicion of relationships, her fear of intimacy, and the strain she felt in recognizing her needs for support and dependence as having their roots in infancy. She described a relentless search for a lost breast that, if found, could restore a feeling of wholeness. But what she found was only a substitute, food, which could not satisfy her deeper emotional needs.

Her experience of herself during this time was erratic, and she had a ravenous emotional appetite, which she could not satisfy. She imagined envious attacks upon her internal mother and myself who in her mind contained some inner goodness which she was entirely deprived of. Her fear of breakdown intensified and she began to feel that I was crazy to continue analysis with her. She was convinced that I was angry at her because she sometimes did not want to listen to my interpretations. While she felt rejected, misunderstood, isolated, separated, and detached from me, she also thought that I was too much inside her, that I knew too much about her. In order to create some boundaries between us, she binged before and after the sessions. She would not allow herself to "feed" on my interpretations and she needed to eject them before they could be "digested."

Her desire for closeness in the analytical relationship was mixed with the fear of fusion and loss of personal identity. The binging magically held her together and blocked the feeling that she was falling apart. Although she never missed a session and was consistently prompt, she spoke of hating having an internal analyst and being controlled by the analysis. She felt that it was the analysis which was exacerbating her problems and contaminating her life, yet she yearned for a closeness to me that would enable her to feel safe. Recurring dreams and waking images of falling down dark holes and being inside empty caves pointed to her terror of disconnection from a supportive maternal/analytic milieu. The daily ritual of analysis and the consistency of the analytic frame were essential features that "held" her together.

It was at this time that Diana started to study studio art and art history. She developed a deep interest in the work of Frida Kahlo and Jackson Pollack. She was drawn to Kahlo's self-portraits, which were depictions of her deep physical and psychic pain. Kahlo, a Mexican painter, had been severely injured in a bus accident as an adolescent. During the bus accident Kahlo had been impaled by a pole that had penetrated her vagina and damaged both her uterus and spine. She was unable to bear children and had numerous operations throughout her life. She spent much of her adult life painting self-portraits that expressed her anguish over her physical injury. Thus her body became the symbol of both her anguish and her art. Diana felt a kinship to Kahlo's focus on the body as the arena for the expression of deep psychic pain. Similarly, Pollack's abstract and expressionistic work seemed to echo Diana's own chaotic internal states. She began to paint self-portraits and abstract paintings with large quantities of paint layered on the canvas. It seemed that in her self-portraits she was attempting to define her body image while in her abstract paintings she was attempting to create a sensation of having a skin that could contain her tortured self-experiences. Her artistic interests eventually became an important nucleus around which her sense of self evolved. Her art provided her with a way of digesting, assimilating, and giving shape to her inner experiences, a means of giving expression to her self in a direct way. During this period her art began to take on more meaning for her, and she utilized it to contain, give shape to, and clarify her emotional states. While painting, her desire to be bulimic decreased, and she felt more in control of herself. In her paintings an important dialogue with the self was conducted, one which gave Diana the feeling that something worthwhile was taking place inside her. This process helped to consolidate her own identity.

During the last phases of the analysis, Diana and I focused on the meaning of her art, her desires for the future, and her eventual separation from the analysis as she was about to graduate from the university and enter art school in another locale. While we both realized that the analytic work had not been completed, she felt strongly a need to be autonomous and independent. I encouraged her in making her own decision about art school. The decision was a difficult one for her, but once made, she was able to deal with its repercussions. The separation was a painful one, yet filled with hope and a sense of accomplishment for us both.

Conclusion

The course of Diana's analysis indicates the depth of emotional pain and despair that resides beneath bulimic symptomatology. As I think the course of Diana's analysis indicates, bulimia is utilized defensively to evacuate unbearable anxieties stemming from the infantile period, specifically from a lack of attunement in the mother/infant relationship. It is only by working through the defensive nature of the bulimic symptomatology and the emotional reactions to early mother/infant deprivation that the relationship to the self can be repaired and a more functional dialogue with the self can evolve.

Diana utilized defenses of the self when she attempted to nullify the analytic process by rejecting me. It was during these times that she appeared to be emotionally encapsulated, completely withdrawn and impossible to reach. She experienced me during these moments as a threat to her very sense of psychological intactness. As the analysis progressed Diana utilized projective identification increasingly as a primitive means of communication of her emotional states and was slowly able to give up the total use of encapsulating self defenses. It was through Diana's use of projective identification that I slowly began to gain an understanding of her internal life and help her articulate her often chaotic emotional experiences.

Diana's analysis uncovered and clarified the severe and early damage to her symbolic function and her capacity for thought and reflection. During the initial stages of her analysis, she had virtually no ability to symbolize and primarily utilized her bodily functions via her bulimia to expel her psychological conflicts. The bulimia represented a basic difficulty in the introjection and assimilation of psychological experience. Diana's struggle to forge psychological meaning through analytic reflection and through her creative expression was at the core of the reparative process that unfolded during her analysis. Diana suffered from what Ogden has termed a disorder of the recognition of desire. According to Ogden, in eating disorders (such as bulimia) food is utilized ritualistically to ward off the feeling of emotional deadness and to deny the core problem of a deficit in the ability to create meaning out of psychological experience.[5]

For Diana, creating a safe space, where the emotional reactions to the early infant/mother relationship could be reexperienced and worked through in the analytical interaction, was critical. Allowing space in my mind for the experience of her rage and murderous fantasies and helping her to link these experiences to her infantile past in a deeply emotional way enabled her to be able to work through the defensive nature of her bulimia and created a possibility for her to gain a viable connection with a more creative and intact sense of self.

Notes

1. M. Fordham, *The Self and Autism* (London: Heinemann, 1976). See also B. Feldman, "Infant Observation: Its Significance for Training and Research in Analytical Psychology," *Proceedings of the National Conference of Jungian Analysts.* (San Francisco, 1988).

2. M. Fordham, "Defences of the Self," *Explorations into the Self* (London: Academic Press, 1985).

3. E. Neumann, *The Great Mother: An Analysis of the Archetype.* (Princeton, N.J.: Princeton University Press, 1963).

4. D. W. Winnicott, "The Theory of the Parent-Infant Relationship," in *The Maturational Processes and the Facilitating Environment* (New York: International University Press, 1965).

5. T. Ogden, *The Primitive Edge of Experience* (Northvale, N.J.: Jason Aronson, 1989).

12

The Stone Womb: A Case of
Psychogenic Paralysis

Francesco Bisagni

In recent years it has been incredibly difficult to give a clear definition and categorization of hysteria. As reported in psychiatric literature, even from a purely descriptive point of view, the term is regarded as obsolete and considered by many to belong to the history of psychiatry. A similar process has taken place in the psychoanalytic field. However, in many analytic situations so-called hysterical traits can be commonly observed. For social and cultural reasons, the hysterical symptom has no doubt lost the "Viennese enamel" of the last century, but the hysterical character is not so rare.

If, instead of speaking of character or of personality structure, we speak of hysterical parts, or, even better, of a mode of mental functioning and of typical object relations, then we can supply more frequent and complex examples. For instance, E. Brenman writes: "hysteria is so plastic, and presents itself in any and every possible disease, and is such an umbrella term that it covers a multitude of sins.[1] Brenman goes on to describe the typical hysterical pattern as a combination of denial and catastrophic dread, the latter mainly concerning persecutory fantasies in phobic hysteria and paralysing, crippling symptoms in conversion hysteria. The catastrophic dread is usually split off from the rest of the personality, which tends to appear ostensibly healthy and well-functioning. In *belle indifference* such a splitting process is carried to the extreme. Catastrophic dread is the shadow side of the hero/heroine psychology; the phenomenology of these opposites is a typical problem in adolescence, where the inner confusion is brought to a climax and the task of deep reorganization of the personality is fundamental.

The part of the personality that functions according to the hysterical mode continues to relate to live and whole external objects. However, this kind of object relation quite often reveals itself as a narcissistic one, where the whole object, even if perceived as such, is used at a part-object level. This can be understood as a defense against a schizophrenic or depressive breakdown. The other, equated to a part object (breast and/or penis) is used by the patient's self with the expectation of receiving love, gratification, and even adoration, but not for a relationship based on reciprocity and exchange. Parallel to this attitude runs the wish to either triumph over the object or despise it and annihilate it when it does not conform to the narcissistic ideal.

The multiple identifications that derive from the part of the personality with a hysterical functioning mode are based on this kind of object relation. We are not dealing with truly introjective identifications, but rather with partly adhesive and partly projective, primitive, and unstable identifications. According to Brenman, projective identifications, usually of whole objects having idealized fantasy features, tend to occur. The external object then represents characteristics of a whole object "loaded" with projected elements of an idealized kind, "whole live-cum-fantasy objects."[2]

Strictly speaking, in hysteria one may talk of pseudo-whole objects that undergo a splitting. The manipulatory tendency, which is typical of hysteria, is rooted in this particular aspect of relating to the object. Here one may refer to the tendency to seduction (meaning bringing towards oneself), to use the other as a representative, or alternatively, agent of the idealized or destructive part of the self. The hysterical part of the personality is therefore on a quest for love and gratification mainly in an infantile and omnipotent way. The possibility of receiving authentic love and understanding is attacked, as is the help from the analyst, together with any possibility of making sense out of an emotional experience. What the hysterical part of the personality avoids is both the movement Ps<>D, as described by W. R. Bion, which represents the movement from chaos to order and back, and at the same time, the pain, which is linked to that movement.[3] Michael Fordham has also pointed out a correlation between both paranoid-schizoid states and deintegration, and depressive states and reintegration.[4]

The Ps<>D movement involves getting in touch with overwhelming anxieties (which Brenman describes as depressive and schizoid) against which the hysterical part of the personality operates as a defensive structure. Therefore, when we refer to catastrophic fantasies in the psychology of hysteria, we have to distinguish between two components. One appears on the surface, in the way the hysterical part of the personality uses anxiety, and has to do with falsification and narcissistic omnipotent manipulation of the object; whereas the second, the real underlying anxiety, is split off and defended against.

These anxieties derive from a deteriorated image of the early mother, due to fantasized sadistic attacks by the infant on her inside. These fantasies result in a faulty image of the whole breast/mandala primal object. The wholeness and integrity of this primary object is the precondition for a subsequent adequate development of the paranoid-schizoid and depressive position as described by Bion. Here, I am referring to a nonstatic experience of the primal object, which continuously includes a balanced intercourse between closeness and separation, chaos and order, relatedness and isolation. The attacks can manifest themselves in a more or less primitive manner, more or less pregenital in style or with more evolved triadic genital traits.

In other situations, like the one described further on, a very early and dramatic break from the breast is apparent. These cases show an inadequacy of the original container and a fault in the processes of deintegration and reintegration of the self as described by Fordham. The potential for a positive or negative outcome of the analysis is related to the intensity of primitive anxieties, hence to the hardness or flexibility of the hysterical defensive structure.

In this context, the connection between autistic-like and hysterical functioning modes is of special concern. These modes have a dual purpose: first to defend against anxieties of nuclear disintegration and second to represent this same anxiety through symptoms. When speaking of autism I am not referring to a syndrome but I intend to consider, following Tustin's theory, those personality traits and defense mechanisms that could be defined as "autistic" and which coexist in a more or less marked way with other, nonautistic defensive mechanisms.[5]

These traits are close to those which Meltzer has defined as failure of postnatal adaptation or as failure of primary mental developments.[6] This concept relates to Fordham's concept of autism as a disturbance of the deintegrative-reintegrative sequence of the primal self of the neonate.[7] The features have relevance during adolescence, where a reorganization of the inner world is at a crucial point and the development of relatively healthy or deeply pathological modes of functioning has fundamental consequences.

Case Material

In the case of Anna, a twenty-year-old young woman, she had been affected three years previously by a pseudo-paralysis of the lower body that also affected both hands to a lesser degree. These symptoms appeared at the age of seventeen after a failed attempt to separate from her mother by means of a sexual relationship with a partner of her own age. Paralysis occurred following a seizure of Grand Mal, epilepsy being a datum clinically ascertained, although its typology and the development and severity of the crises were never clearly specified. The patient was being treated with antiepileptic drugs in heavy doses.

The paralysis had been interpreted as due to a rather late appearance of epilepsy and as a possible manifestation of multiple sclerosis. This diagnosis was later dismissed, but as a result of this misdiagnosis, the patient was classified as totally handicapped and had been on social security since then. The paralysis, as in the case of the great hysteria of Charcot, did not follow the anatomic distribution of the nervous system, though it had appeared very massive and stable at first and used to change according to the circumstances. When the diagnosis of hysteria was at last established, the patient had already managed to rally a whole court of relatives, friends, social workers, neurologists, psychiatrists, and physiotherapists who had all become fascinated and involved with this supposed rare and extraordinary case. The analysis, three sessions per week, lasted twenty-three months and was terminated by a sudden irrevocable decision on the part of the patient. Thus, it was a "failed" analysis.

A dream, which occurred about three months into the treatment, seems to me to illustrate with accuracy the internal situation of the patient:

> I am in a tunnel dug deeply in the inside of a mountain. I am sitting on the floor, immobile, surrounded by rocks. I do not want to move even though I can perceive a light far away at the end of the tunnel. Outside the opening I see some water running, like a waterfall. I stay put.

Among the associations the patient made with the dream were the following lines that further clarify the dream:

> I do not want to get out, because I think that there is only a wasteland outside there. I would be very scared. I would not find anybody, and the water might be dangerous.

It is interesting to note that the immobility of the patient in the dream has nothing to do with physical impediments, but it appears to be a "choice" derived from the need to avoid the anxiety of coming out.

The first consideration is the mountain-stone-womb. The image describes an experience of containment without transformative potential, where the immobility of the container mirrors that of the contained. In Anna's dream, the stone womb is compact, huge, and apparently indestructible. She experiences the omnipotence of immobility.

The scene is situated in the realm of "pre-deintegration:" there is no possibility for a human dialogue because the only other element is the stone. In this image, any drive whatsoever towards action, dialogue, or interaction seems to be lacking. One might consider the image of the mountain cave not just as a womb-container but also as a representation of the breast, thus evaluating other features of the primal mother-infant dyad. In this regard, Anna's experience concerns a water-like milk, which runs outwards in the guise of a waterfall. The dyad nipple-mouth is turned inside out, formally it presupposes a state of having been outside before the hallucinatory experience of fusion. The experience of separation is required for the infant to need the experience of getting back into and being at one with the nourishing breast, because the state of need is linked with having felt pushed out by the mother. This state of affairs creates a deintegration in the infant and activates the drive towards reconnecting. Striving towards an eternal imagined state of fusion is short-lived and represents a temporary stage. In this way the dynamics of psychic movement and development may evolve.

The inside-out position and the stone breast implies the absence of the nipple as a mediating factor between mouth and breast. Without the nipple, contact fantasies of fusion and interchange are all impossible. In fact, one may hypothesize that it is just this inside-out position that is the cause of the stone breast image. The milk pours outside as a waterfall; it is an outburst, thus unavailable and therefore not nourishing, which might overwhelm the baby as there is no possibility of latching onto a nipple to suck. The external world is therefore a waste-land. This image seems to depict a deprived nature. It is the absence of any human beings, together with the fear of isolation and loneliness, that appears to me to be persecutory in nature. The dream underlines the experience of the milk-waterfall, due to the inverted mouth-nipple relationship. We are dealing with a vicious circle, where it is difficult to sort out what comes first: the petrification of the breast seems to be the alpha and omega of what happens here.

In my view, this image of the stone breast represents what Fordham defines as a system of defenses of the self. This defensive system is activated in situations of extreme danger, where the actual survival of the infant is felt to be endangered.[8] In the case of my patient, the para-lyzed immobile body constitutes a concrete somatic representation of this defense. In a certain way, the experience of the self in Anna's case is the exact opposite of the process described by Jung in the image of the philosophical tree. In this image, Jung depicts a process continu-ously moving upwards and from within outwards, and then back in-wards, thus allowing for growth to take place through progression and regression.[9] In Anna, this process appears to be completely perverted. Therefore the patient cannot build an experience of her own self and of her own mental parts in the sense of the "subtle body" mentioned by Jung.[10] She does not manage to reach the perception of the stage of intercourse between mind and matter, which involves the idea of a mentalized body and an embodied mind whose corollaries are move-ment, development, and interpersonal relationships. Instead my patient experienced both the death of her mind and the devitalization of her body. The "lapis philosophorum" is lost, and a self-mother-breast ex-perienced as a "lapis vilis" (coarse stone) is substituted. As a conse-quence of this state of affairs, Anna often manifested violent attacks upon thinking and upon the analytic function of the kind Bion refers to when he deals with the concept of "attacks on linking" and of "inver-sion of alpha functioning."[11]

In the countertransference I experienced a sensation of paralysis. Every now and then I realized I had been holding my breath for too long, or I experienced pins and needles in one of my legs or arms because I had been totally immobile in an uncomfortable position. My interpretations seemed to lose vitality even before formulation. When-ever I did manage to express them, I had the feeling of enduring a difficult pregnancy. However, Anna managed to kill off my interpretations by voiding them of life and transforming them into empty shells. The dream that follows clarifies further the sort of anxiety the dreamer is trying to defend herself from by using the device of petrifaction:

> My young nephew, my sister's son, is in the garden with his paternal grandmother, my brother-in-law's mother. At a certain moment, the grandmother is distracted and the child falls down and dies.

While associating, Anna made a significant slip: she says "my brother-in-law's mother-in-law," meaning her own mother. She then speaks of a one-year old child who had been abused and battered by his parents, whose story had been told by the media during the past few days. She then adds; "I have dreamt about what I shouldn't have," and she goes on to say that the child in the dream falls off four steps. At the time of this dream, Anna used to step off her wheel-chair in the hall, stand up and walk, clinging heavily to her mother up the four steps to my office. The same ritual repeated itself when Anna left. Throughout this process, Anna's facial expression was hard: she seemed disgusted. Whenever I observed them together, I could never tell just who was supporting whom. They looked like two paraplegics who had to support each other in order not to separate or fall apart. They seemed to be clinging to each other for life.

At the time of Anna's dream, her nephew, who is an adopted child, was beginning to walk. My patient had experienced a strong ambivalence about the arrival of this child. She seemed jealous because she was dethroned from the "little child" role in the family. There was also a strong component of envy in her relationship with her older sister, whom she considered to be another maternal figure. The dream presents various levels of representations. The most primitive one, closer to the autistic sphere, is the one equating the fall with death. The image of the distractible mother is connected to the experience of the lack of a stable containment in the mother's mind. The slipping away from the maternal mind is equated with death. It conveys a maternal image that is felt present only when providing a concrete kind of care and where a mental and emotional care is felt to be lacking or inadequate. If a mental representation of the child is absent from the mother's mind, the child can exist only in a sensory dimension. The physical separation is experienced as total separation. In this type of situation, the fall represents an abortion or weaning. The walking stage, which is an essential step in the separation-individuation process, is experienced by the baby as a fall from the mother's mind into the void. The support provided by the maternal mind, which allows for a regressive step when needed, is unavailable. For the baby, the mother's absent-mindedness is experienced as the death of the mother. If relationship cannot develop because it is replaced by maternal distraction, the alternative for the dyad is to stay paralyzed and fused in a symbiotic relationship where a system of reciprocal omnipotent control prevails with the elimination of all others experienced as intrusive.[12]

Other transferential aspects are also conveyed by this dream; now the child who falls is a boy. This is the first reference to the patient's young brother. These two children had always been close, both in age, as playmates, and as rivals for the possession of an older mother who was obviously busy and involved with the other siblings. The unconscious wish that the rival sibling might die, killed by the mother's absentmindedness, was confirmed by an intense anxiety about this brother's departure for military service. In one session, Anna expressed the fear that he might die due to an accident, or forget about his family.

The theme of slipping away from the mind appears again in this fantasy where Anna creates an equation between forgetting/killing and being forgotten/dying. The fight to keep a place in the mother's mind, a mother easily distracted, involves the fantasy of weeding out all rivals, with its inevitable consequences, the fear of being done away with by them. Therefore, the problem of death/survival becomes the pathology of the internal family system, as well as the basic assumption of the actual family. Each component of the group survives or succumbs in so far as he/she is projectively identified with the other members of the group; thus a separation-individuation proper cannot take place.

There is another important aspect in the dream of the dead child. Anna's father died in an automobile accident when she was five years old. He had a heart attack while driving back from taking Anna and her brother to school. On their way, they had stopped at a cafe and had had a pleasant breakfast together. When Anna returned from school she was shocked: she could not believe that her father had disappeared so suddenly.

This was the only memory, or screen memory, that Anna had of her father. She never spoke of him in analysis and appeared not to remember anything, except some generic comments that he was a good man. However, once she said, "My mother has told me to inform you that daddy used to drink a lot." Then she added that her father never used to beat the children but told her mother to do it on his behalf. She stopped suddenly in the midst of this report, changed the subject, and when I pointed this out to her, she stated that she could not remember what she had been saying.

A few days later in the course of one session, I had a fleeting fantasy of sexually abusing Anna. Anna was a pretty girl who did not look sick; nevertheless she evoked in me sexual feelings in the countertransference. Her body looked well built and was tightly modeled by the fashionable clothes she wore, but her seductiveness was like a thin film on the surface of her body. Her appearance mirrored her way of thinking about life in general. She wanted to have only good opinions accompanied by a superficial joyfulness and amusements. Her pleasantness of appearance greatly contrasted with her gloomy expression. This pseudoadaptation appeared to be an adhesive identification. Rarely was she able to evoke deep, modulated feelings in me.

It is well known that the fantasy of adhering to the surface of the external object, as described by Ester Bick, produces an identification with the most superficial and socially perceivable qualities of the object, rather than with its deep qualities and its psychic states.[13] It is, therefore, a mimesis, a negative imitation, whose characteristics can be compared to some of the negative aspects of the persona, split off from the anima.[14] As presented by autistic children, this type of defensive adhesive identification has been described by Meltzer et al.[15] The adhesive identification seems to be a mode of "holding the personality together" when the internal object represents a precarious and inadequate container.

I was able to link my fantasy of sexual abuse towards the patient with a vague report about her father's alcoholism. That communication had been experienced by me as a sudden cracking in the stone, as if the defenses had momentarily given way to let an episode of violent and dramatic intensity emerge in the session, almost a potential for a disintegrative anxiety. The suddenness of the communication seemed to exclude the possibility that the patient's consciousness could integrate it, due to its nondigestibility and to the catastrophic anxieties connected with it. The psychic element related to rape and sexual abuse thus remained excluded, at that moment, from the deintegrative-reintegrative process as described by Fordham. Furthermore, the sudden disappearance of the fantasy described the falling-dying problem and signals the rebuilding of a defensive evacuation system. The father's death replays a primal sequence of events in Anna's dream: both the father and the child fall and do not survive. In addition, the father is the more dangerous rival in the fight for possession of the mother. As such, he needs to be eliminated.

As a hypothesis that I was not able to verify in the course of treatment, I would suggest that sexual abuse may have been an actual experience that occurred in early childhood. Such an event could have become the deep and unspeakable secret of the family group. In any case, either real or fantasized abuse represents a sadistic primal scene. This was evident when thinking about Anna's typical modes of communication during the analytic session. I am now referring to her attacks upon the analyst's attempts to link the different, split-off parts of her self and, above all, the attacks upon the transference/countertransference relationship, the analytic "coitus."

In fact, I was used by the patient as she used her mother: like a hard, lifeless, petrified autistic object and not as a warm, lively, and soft but hard separate object by which she might be penetrated. The patient experienced the penis as violent, raping, and breaking-up symbiosis. Therefore, it must be avoided and eliminated. But the mother herself becomes a "hard body" that Anna can realize in an autistic fusion and can use in order to stand up or walk. In this way, an "erection" is possible; together with her mother, Anna can become a penis. By killing the father, this "stone penis" is substituted for the paternal erected phallus.

This petrified, "autistic" penis can prevent the personality from being overwhelmed by persecutory anxieties and disintegrative dreads and can also become an instrument for an omnipotent control of reality. However, it has no inner life—no warmth, no fertility. Its hardness has no human traits and so no nourishing exchange can take place. In this patient, the identification with the penis, and consequently the functioning of the hysterical part of the personality, is based on a parricide, where the raping paternal penis is eliminated and then recreated through the petrified mother-daughter relationship. In that way, any development of the personality is arrested.

In her everyday life, Anna had a remarkable capacity for the manipulation and omnipotent control of reality. Even in the course of the sessions, she tried to establish confusion by involving me in manipulatory games; for instance, by reporting telephone calls she had with doctors to whom she voiced her complaints about me. I kept telling her the truth in the most simple way, without accusing her but without being manipulated. Anna looked astonished, especially since she had always been successful in using that kind of communication. My response seemed to make her feel less omnipotent and thus more relaxed within the analytic relationship.

What also seemed to reassure her was the fact that I continued to give her interpretations in spite of her denials and silence. The representational level of her language was very primitive; she used language as trickery to provoke a response or to keep her distance. Meaninglessness and sterility in the communication was aimed at destroying my attempts to exchange emotions and thoughts. By working through the mother-child relationship in the transference/countertransference and using interpretation as a container, one that seeks for the truth, Anna and I partly succeeded in turning her rigid stone capsule into a solid but penetrable possibility for containment in the analysis. Unfortunately, this process could not be completed, and the positive effects on the patient's condition could not last long because of a premature break up of the analysis.

After one year of treatment, Anna had another dream in which she was in a tunnel dug inside the mountain. This dream was completely identical to the previous one, except now Anna was desperately crying, asking for somebody to come and help her. Her crying indicated that deintegration had started. I thought of this as a possible break up of autistic barriers, since the emergence from autism is characterized by pain and death anxieties that were previously encapsulated. Anna's crying can be regarded as a painful linking of the death anxieties to the ego. An elaboration can therefore take place through the function of crying in activating the "breast response" in the countertransference, a response in which the analyst uses verbal communicating as a means of getting in touch with the patient. The activation of a maternal response in the countertransference meant that there was a possibility for Anna to use projective identification as an evacuation defense and as a mode of developing, step by step, a relation with an external object. This time the dream was reexperienced, linking Anna to her infantile self and to my ego and maternal objects as an observer.

In the following sessions, Anna was more accessible, seeming to listen and cooperate more with me. Apparently she could now build up an emotional memory of the analytic work, though it was still weak and discontinuous. Denial was less massive. I felt that she was scared of me and yet reassured by my presence and by the continuity of our meetings. Such transferential contents induced a fundamental change. At this time, Anna decided she would no longer let her mother take her to my consulting room. She asked another relative or a friend to accompany her, but then she asked for a change of time in order to come on her own, which she did. She reached my office by private coach, got some assistance with the door, and navigated her way by using another wheel chair inside. Watching her contortions made me think of a baby who cannot or does not dare to stand up and walk. When Anna finally reached the analytic couch, she climbed onto it like a baby searching for her mother's arms, not like a paralytic.

During the following period and in the last months of her analysis, Anna often fantasized that she would find her own house to live in. When talking to me about it, she mostly spoke about the quarrels she had with her mother and her older sister. According to Anna, her mother felt betrayed because of the link established between her daughter and me, one which obviously excluded her. Apparently, her mother used to say, "If you want to go away, go at once, but don't come back again. We shall be dead for you; you won't have any help from us anymore." Although the authenticity of these words may be suspect, the entire family group seemed to have taken a stand against Anna's centrifugal throws. Of course, the fantasy was that I wanted to substitute myself for the mother and the paralyzed family group in order to capture baby-Anna and take her away. Evidently, this projection activated deep death anxieties related to separation. Anna's denial of the dread of killing or being killed by her mother during the separation process activated a strong centripetal countermovement aimed at reinforcing the symbiotic petrifying mother-daughter relationship. This happened through "killing" and separating from me, an act accompanied by fear of revenge. This movement and its transferential aspect was also denied: Anna rejected any interpretation aimed at working through this matter. Here the countertransference was characterized by an intense feeling, rather physical and in some ways rhythmical, of our coming close to one another and then being thrown apart. Furthermore, it was difficult to work through a variety of puzzling communications dealing with partly actual and partly projective transferential elements belonging to the patient and her environment. Indeed I felt as if I had an entire family group in analysis with me, not just an internal family but, via projective identification, a concrete, actual one.

This family apparently had a mode of learning through projective identification, according to Meltzer's classification, where the group members were pushed to acquire the qualities of an object, quite immediately, by penetrating and ravaging it, thus mechanically gaining its qualities.[16] As Meltzer states, these modes of learning are peculiar to the kind of family that functions as a "basic assumption or pairing" which aims at preserving a myth of self-sufficiency and impenetrability. This kind of group also presents itself as a "monad with neither door nor windows" notwithstanding an apparently conventional and consistent style in social and interpersonal relationships.

Thus Anna's communications were focused on her mother and family's opposition to her autonomy. Any attempt whatsoever to work through the other aspects of this matter, particularly those related to the positive and negative transference, resulted in complete failure. Anna resembled a typical adolescent, whose goal is the strengthening of the purposive and active aspects of the ego, yet she refused any awareness of the shadow. In this way, Anna was trying to appear as a more grown-up, desirable woman, the one she imagined I would like to appreciate and love. Being more active and self-confident, she could become both a partner and a daughter, thus enabling herself to become identified with me, an "erected" self-determined man. Through imitation, this was an attempt to reach a genitalized oedipal position, where her feelings of rivalry towards her mother and her older sister could find an adequate space. Her denial of the pregenital components, as expressed in the transference, reinforced frail and unstable adult-like attitudes, ones rooted in stereotyped, unrealistic patterns of behavior and based on adhesive identifications.

All these contents might have been worked through, if not for an unfortunate accident. I arrived late for one of Anna's sessions when my car broke down. I met her in the street, apologized, and rescheduled. During the next session, Anna strongly denied that she had been touched by the event. However, she adopted an attitude of deep isolation. I tried to interpret her having felt threatened by the fact that I was not invulnerable, that I could have an accident like her father's, but my interpretations were dismissed as "not-self" objects.[17] A few weeks later, just as Anna began to communicate with me again, she slipped from her chair and broke her collar bone. She missed a session and was uncomfortable during subsequent sessions because of the pain.

After the accident, she avoided eye contact and seemed nervous. When I interpreted her falling as a representation of the inner baby's anxieties about my being unreliable and as a concrete show of how badly I had hurt her, Anna seemed to relax. I was struck by her responsiveness. In comparison with the autistic barriers, the psychosomatic response apparently represented a higher level of development as a mode of communication. The psychosomatic response was emotionally more intense, which the patient herself could partly perceive. The possibility of communicating was enhanced rather than destroyed.

A few days later another accident occurred. Anna did not come to her session. Instead of waiting until the last minute, as is my policy, I left five minutes before her time was up. In the next session, Anna reproached me for my infringement. Apparently she had arrived late because of the traffic and saw me leaving. She appeared more triumphant than disappointed. I admitted to my mistake, adding that I thought she viewed my actions as further betrayals. In addition, I said that she seemed to enjoy what appeared to be my complete unreliability. She denied my interpretations, saying "You may have had other things to do!" I commented that she seemed troubled by the thought that I could use some of her time for my private affairs. Perhaps she felt the need to control me in order to feel that I belonged to her, as a way of thinking of me as useful rather than dead and useless. Again she denied this.

In the following session, Anna was depressed, saying she had experienced a very severe epileptic seizure, the first one after quite some time. The seizure started when she slipped from a chair, which she described as a slow but headlong flight to the ground and unconsciousness. Her mother told her that she was lucky someone else was there to take care of her. I commented that the epilepsy seemed to represent, on an emotional level, what occurred during the previous session. I felt that something had broken: Anna had reactivated an actual organic illness, not just a psychosomatic response. Thus she seemed to decree my impotence as an analyst and the impossibility of substituting myself for the symbiotic mother through the therapeutic relationship.

Although epilepsy could indirectly express a transferential reality, it also showed the victory of the petrified body, of the "lapis vilis."

Anna had felt betrayed, and the therapeutic attempt at developing a positive alliance was now seriously in danger. The omnipotence of autism and of the identification with a stone penis, rooted in the symbiotic fusion with her mother, was seen again as more desirable. As a consequence of the epileptic seizure, it seemed as if I were about to disappear like her father. When I attempted to interpret this angry and disappointed part of herself that was trying to undo the progress we had made in analysis, Anna looked distant and annoyed. Once she said, after returning from a trip to the country, "After being away for a while, it's necessary to stay close to mummy again." In Anna's fantasy, the male was now being excluded and made to feel jealous of the relationship between the two females. In other words, my destiny was bound to be the same as her father's.

In her second to last session, Anna spoke to me of a boyfriend she had had when she was sixteen, just before the first epileptic seizure. They had had sexual intercourse, but he had later left her, and she felt sad and angry. She took out her revenge by treating roughly a friend of her former boyfriend's who was in love with her. She exploited him, yet he gave her presents, which made her angry. This scenario represents the problem of omnipotent expectations that involve the low capacity to tolerate frustration and disappointment and the impossibility of being nourished by good objects. Instead, the object had to be sadistically controlled and devalued. My interpretation was rejected by Anna, who, in the following session, informed me without accepting further discussion that she had decided to terminate her analysis. Although she did not know just what she needed, she said the sessions were useless to her.

Conclusion

Theoretical conclusions regarding pregenital components in hysteria can be drawn from the case of Anna. The part of the personality that functions in a hysterical mode presents a typical pattern of relation with a pseudo-whole object. This kind of object lacks those features we usually define in Jungian terms as the "shadows." The attempt to obtain an omnipotent gratification fails in the case described because of a deep devitalization of the mother-object, who dies as container and is replaced by stone. This situation can arise when a mother is experienced as incapable of thinking about the baby, thus preventing the baby from feeling held in her mind. The physical, actual, but rigid closeness takes the place of an emotional and adaptable closeness, able to allow for separation. As a consequence, the development of a symbolic activity is severely damaged. More specifically, hysterical paralysis as a symptom seems to have a dual meaning: first it expresses an identification of the infantile self with the stone womb-mind; second, it represents a defensive structure, of an autistic kind, against the death anxieties activated by the risk of slipping out of the mother's mind. Therefore, the patient's *belle indifference* can be defined as a result of the splitting and evacuation of beta elements. In Bion's terms, these are physical contents with emotional meaning that cannot undergo a psychic process leading to a mental representation of the elements themselves: they can only be eliminated. In Anna's case, such an evacuation is linked to deep anxieties about the dissolution of the primal self.

The original catastrophic dread is what one must evacuate from the perceptive structure of the self. I think I can state that this mechanism can also be related to very peculiar modes of functioning, like adhesive identification. These latter modes can support a variety of behaviors usually regarded as hysterical and caused by both a severe fault in the structure of the personality and internal objects that are too weak. The meaning of paralysis, especially Anna's, lends itself to a general description of primary features of hysteria with regard to penetrating attitudes, manipulation, control, and omnipotence. The "hysterical penis" does not seem to be a positive parental penis in situations I have observed. As heir to the nipple, the good paternal penis is experienced, both at a part-object level and later on at a whole-object level, as a soft, hard object with human characteristics, actively penetrating but not damaging, the sperm of which is as nourishing as milk. In such a vital framework, the penis is associated to a positive primal scene, and its introjection leads to the development of a symbolic capacity and abstract thinking, and to an active and penetrating attitude toward reality and toward affective relationships.

The "hysterical penis" appears to be rigid and petrified, often linked to images of a sadistic primal scene. The more deteriorated the primary maternal container, the more intense the sadistic primal scene. In Anna's case, the father's penis is experienced as sadistic, not only because it could kill the mother but also for its fantasized ability to break up the mother-daughter symbiotic relationship and the baby's omnipotent control of the maternal body. Therefore, the father is dismissed. By using the mother as an autistic object, through invading and taking possession of the maternal body, a penis is "recreated." In some ways, the dyad itself functions as a penis, used for manipulation and seduction of the external object but not, of course, for an authentically nurturing relationship or to develop a true receptivity and a positive, creative, penetrating attitude.

In my view, the "hysterical penis" usually appears as intrusively controlling but absolutely barren. This, too, comes out of a sadistic primal scene, which prevents any good mental intercourse from taking place. These features may be more or less hidden, and therefore difficult to recognize in analysis due to the triadic oedipal components that are always present. These elements may express themselves through "rationalistic" or "intellectual" modes, possibly related to a surface idealized father figure. This use of the mind does not correspond to a true creative activity: it could be defined as "negative animus," an animal that breaks up the *coniunctio* by controlling and devouring the object.

Anna's case also shows how the use of the body can be distinguished in two ways: a barrier use, as an attack upon linking (*belle indifference*), and a psychosomatic use partly more evolved and connected to a wider possibility of communication through projective identification. The psychosomatic use tends to stimulate an activity in another person in a similar way to that of the infant who activates the breast response through crying.

Notes

1. E. Brenman, "Hysteria," *International Journal of Psycho-Analysis* 66 (1985):423.
2. Ibid., p.426.
3. W. Bion, *Learning From Experience* (London: Heinemann, 1962).
4. M. Fordham, *Explorations into the Self* (London: Heinemann, 1985).
5. F. Tustin, *Autistic Barriers in Neurotic Patients* (London: Karnac, 1986).
6. D. Meltzer, "Family Patterns and Cultural Educability," *Studies in Extended Metapsychology* (London: Clunie, 1986), chap. xiv.
7. M. Fordham, *The Self and Autism* (London: Heinemann, 1976).
8. Ibid.
9. C.G. Jung, *The Philosophical Tree. Collected Works* (London: Routledge and Kegan Paul, 1967) v.13.
10. C.G. Jung, *Psychology and Alchemy, Collected Works* (London: Routledge and Kegan Paul, 1953, rev. ed. 1967) v. 12.

11. W. Bion, *Learning From Experience* and W. Bion, "Attacks on Linking," *Second Thoughts* (London: Heinemann, 1967).
12. F. Tustin, pp. 193–4.
13. E. Bick, "The Experience of Skin in Early Object Relations," *International Journal of Psycho-Analysis* 49:484-6.
14. See C. G. Jung, *Psychological Types, Collected Works* (London: Routledge and Kegan Paul, 1957) v.6.
15. Meltzer, "Family Patterns."
16. Ibid.
17. Fordham, *The Self and Autism.*

SECTION 7

Attacks on the Mind

Introduction to Section 7

The chapters in this section deal with a group of young people who are so emotionally bound to their mothers that, although they have physiologically reached adolescence, they are no way near it in a psychological sense.

These youngsters have great difficulty functioning at an age-appropriate level, both in their schoolwork and in their peer group relationships. In school, they are either failing or are school refusers; in their peer group, they are either too withdrawn, or behave too aggressively. These psychologically mother-bound adolescents, boys and girls alike, appear to be caught in a subtle web of ambivalence. They use regressive behaviour in order to avoid facing separation or working through separation anxieties. The seduction of the breast mother lures them into a "Garden of Eden," and leaves them in a state of mindless doldrums.

As one group of adolescents may attack their own bodies in an attempt to break away from their pre-oedipal infantile cravings for the mother's body, the adolescents described in this section attack their minds by refusing, in an omnipotent way, to accept any restrictions on acting out their "Garden of Eden" fantasies. They wish to be taken care of by the breast mother forever. In most cases their fathers in real life have been physically or emotionally absent and this has allowed incestuous fantasies to prevail and damage an age-appropriate sense of reality. To be caught up in these fantasies is very destructive since the more healthy part of the young person feels stuck in an unreal and isolating delusional system.

The mother-child incestuous relationship is not so obviously and outwardly physically violent as the father-child one, but is just as destructive. In a very insidious way it attacks the child's thinking and differentiating capacities. In the classical oedipal sense, the intervention of the father is required to cut the umbilical cord. In the absence of the real father, as in the cases of these young people, the school or state authorities have to take up the paternal role and force the separation to take place. Thus this group of children (with few exceptions) is not brought to therapy by the parents, but is sent mainly by the school or by the courts.

This motif is very well illustrated in the chapter by Helga Anderssen, "First Steps Toward Independence," where she describes the painful struggle of fifteen-year-old Stephan who was referred to her by the school. Anderssen points out that the lack of initiation rituals in Western culture today is an added element that increases difficulties in the separation from mother in adolescence. Jungian analysts have traditionally valued rites of passage as cultural reenforcements to stages of psychological change in life.

Anderssen describes Stephan as a boy who, because of his parents' divorce, had to play the part of the husband in relation to his mother with whom he lived. He became too compliant with his mother. Because of the father's unreliable presence, Stephan had not managed to work through his oedipal conflicts. The internal father, due to the intensity of his emotional connection to the mother, had a wrathful archetypal quality to him. This terrifying paternal image inside the boy had not allowed him to make a healthy move towards father in latency. With the onset of adolescence and the intensifications of his sexual drives (and consequently of his unconscious sexual fantasies in relation to his mother) he needed to work through his relationship to his father to get away from the oedipal entanglement. Anderssen describes how she was able to function as a firm, caring father container for him and at the same time allow him to project onto her and work through the oedipal fantasies about the mother until the boy eventually was able to relate to his peer group, improve his performance in school, and find an age-appropriate girlfriend. Anderssen's sensitive, nonimpinging approach, respectful of the young man's space and boundaries, allowed Stephan to trust her and get close to her without fear of acting out the dreaded incest. She created for Stephan a mental/emotional space where the boy could begin to reflect on and re-own his mental capacity that he had sacrificed to the "incestuous mother" relationship.

In the "Fight Against Big Nose," Mara Sidoli presents the same theme of a young adolescent boy's struggle to separate from his mother. At age eleven and a half at the start of therapy, Bill is at the very onset of adolescence.

Sidoli begins her chapter with a description of some of the specific technical problems that arise working with this age group. An approach is required that is centered on working with the patient's ego defenses, as is done in the latency stage. The difficulty consists, according to Sidoli, in a strong resistance on the part of the young person to play imaginatively or communicate verbally with the therapist. This situation tends to create a sense of helplessness and worthlessness in the countertransference that is difficult for the analyst to bear. Her mind feels under the same destructive attack as the adolescent's. Luckily Bill was interested in drawing, and in the course of the therapy he produced a wealth of drawings in which he illustrated archetypal motifs of the fight of the hero against the monster parents. Pre-oedipal as well as oedipal motifs were presented in the work and commented on, but Bill never allowed the analyst to make transference interpretations; he defended against them in a paranoid way. The therapeutic work developed in neurotic areas of the personality by strengthening the ego and making it less permeable and endangered by primitive destructive elements. Because of the adolescent upheaval, if such elements were not processed, they might have caused more severe acting out at a later date. Bill, as did Anderssen's patient, Stephan, had serious difficulties in school. He suffered from a strong inferiority complex in relation to both his older brother and his successful father. He experienced his father as diminishing him. He both loathed and loved his position of baby in the family because of the intense special relationship he could have with his mother. The motif of the wrathful oedipal father was represented by Bill as Punch the puppet who kills the baby. Mara Sidoli writes: "The oedipal battle with the archetypal pre-oedipal and oedipal representations has been the focus of the work. In spite of Bill's great resistance, the therapy helped his ego to sustain the pull of the instinctual forces, avoiding a breakdown or acting out. Within the therapy, unconscious material found symbolic representation and containment; hence Bill managed to separate in an age-appropriate way from his too close relationship with the external as well as from the internal mother which threatened his thinking capacities."

13

The Fight against Big Nose

Mara Sidoli

Introduction

Anna Freud warned that analysis of adolescents presents particular problems when she wrote:

> Since the child's immature ego is insecurely balanced between the pressure from within and without, he feels more threatened by analysis than the adult and his defences are kept up more rigidly. This refers to the whole of childhood but is felt with special intensity at the beginning of adolescence. To ward off the oncoming adolescent increase in drive activity, the adolescent normally strengthens his defences and with it, his resistance to analysis.[1]

This age group seems to require a specific approach centered on the patient's ego defenses. Interpretations directed at pre-oedipal instinctual fantasies and unconscious wishes as well as transference interpretations at the oedipal level are generally experienced as too threatening and intrusive by early adolescents, who tend to strengthen their defenses. The increased activation of instinctuality combined with the onset of hormonal and bodily changes creates extreme levels of anxiety and panic states in the ego. Augmenting the anxiety is the violence of the instinctual upsurge, which the ego experiences as attacking.

Early adolescence is a transitional stage where young people are displaced out of childhood into a state of limbo where they often feel

---

Drawings described in this chapter are available from the publisher on request.

confused, easily embarrassed, and full of shame. These feelings are well defended against and kept as far as possible from the therapist's reach. Imaginative play is seldom used by this age group to communicate unconscious fantasies. Instead, play is used to control the therapist's moves. Most of the time, verbal communications are kept to a minimum. All of these factors make the analyst's work more difficult.

However, it is possible to work analytically with adolescents if the analyst pays a great deal of attention to his or her own countertransference feelings. In this way, the therapist will have direct access to the projective identifications of the patient and thereby bypass the patient's conscious resistance. This method can be frustrating and often discouraging for the analyst because the patient may initially resist any therapeutic alliance. Therefore, the rate of progress is slow. If one manages to continue to support the young person's ego, the situation proceeds when the therapeutic alliance sets in. Supporting the achievements of the adolescent is as important as analyzing his or her anxieties and grandiosity. First and foremost, therapy for the adolescent is a way of testing out a relationship with an adult who will, above all, respect him or her and survive violent verbal attacks without retaliation. In so doing, the therapist teaches the young patients to respect themselves and others.

The Case of Bill

The following case of a preadolescent boy presents all the characteristics described above. His resistance had a silent, passive quality aimed at annihilating my attempts to communicate with him, since that communication made him anxious and insecure. Bill attended therapy once weekly for almost three years. At the start, he used some play and modeling clay, later he produced a series of drawings in which he vividly and dramatically displayed archetypal imagery related to father/son oedipal conflicts.

Bill was eleven and a half years old when he was referred to me by his father. He had expressed a wish to talk to somebody about his problems in school. The referral occurred in an unusual way because I happened to know his parents, both of whom work in the helping professions. I decided to interview the boy on his own and to have little contact with the parents. Bill came to the first interview accompanied by his mother and appeared very shy and nervous when I suggested that he follow me. Initially he was hesitant about leaving his mother behind. He was an attractive, somewhat chubby boy, with an open face that made him look younger than his actual age. His school uniform and a mass of blonde curly hair contributed toward a typical "good boy" appearance. And yet I immediately sensed his vulnerability.

We entered the playroom and I talked to him about the therapy and showed him some plasticine and drawing materials that I had assembled for him. He sat down and stiffened up, looking very frightened. A long silence followed. I made a comment on his fear and discomfort and then mentioned that his father had said he was having some difficulties in school with which I might be able to help. Bill seemed to feel reassured and told me some of his worries about not being good at math. He was afraid that he would fail his eleven-plus exams and thus not be able to enter the highly reputable private school attended by his brother, Tom, who was two years his senior. Tom was a success in every sense, and Bill felt at a disadvantage compared to him. The theme of rivalry emerged here, both with the brother and the father. His father was a very well known professional man, and Bill felt intellectually inferior to him and to Tom. He knew I met his parents occasionally for professional reasons. I felt that he did not trust me not to talk about his session to them. After he made these short comments, a thick silence dropped. Here, as in other cases, the difficulty of working with the children of therapists is increased by their feelings of being exposed and by their powerful fantasies and feelings about their parents' patients. This seemed to be the case with Bill, who sat on the edge of his chair, visibly uncomfortable, as if ready to run out. He did not utter another word until the end of the session.

In this session and those that followed, the greatest difficulty I experienced with Bill was his mistrust and suspicion of me. I commented that he might be feeling very vulnerable and exposed because he imagined I was like his father and was going to read his mind and then reveal to everybody what I had discovered inside him. He appeared untouched by my comments and the silence became increasingly difficult to break. Since he did not want to talk, I suggested that he use some plasticine. He hesitated at first, but then decided to take the whole chunk of clay. He became absorbed in modeling it, keeping his face down and obscured from my gaze. A tank began to emerge from the clay. It looked compact and on the front there was a long, menacing gun pointed directly at me. I remarked on the appearance of the tank and asked some questions about it. This seemed to please him because he decided to answer them. He seemed willing to cooperate only if he liked the sort of things I was telling him. At the same time, he was being very careful not to let himself be seduced by my apparently harmless behavior so as to avoid being controlled by me. He wanted to be in control of the session. Behind his impassive demeanor, it was clear to me that he was very fearful.

In the context of mother transference, I represented the danger and attraction of regression, and this was why the tank's gun was directed against me. When I sensed he was feeling less defensive, I suggested that the tank seemed dangerous because it was pointing its gun at me. I asked if he was warning me that he could attack me and destroy me if provoked. He remained impassive. At that point, I concluded the session and said we would meet again in a week. He quickly ran out, and I saw him reappear at the bottom of the stairs with his mother, talking very excitedly.

It took Bill a few months and much subtle probing on his part to determine that I was not a spy for his parents. In countertransference, I felt that I should avoid talking with them at all, although this was impossible due to our working connection. I am sure that my extreme attention to boundaries and my fear of leaks reflected his extreme anxieties about being exposed, thereby becoming the "messy baby" in the family.

The first part of therapy lasted for three months, during which he kept modeling clay to create scenes of battles. Gunfights were enacted by him in complete silence except for the sounds of explosions. Most of the time the guns were pointing at little soldiers who were positioned between us and were destroyed in the battle. During this period, I felt that I should watch but keep silent. Bill hardly talked at all. He kept his head down and only made sound effect noises, but he wanted my full attention and sensed any distracted behavior on my part.

During his play he modeled a variety of weapons with considerable manual skill. Two aspects seemed to be important at the time. I needed to control my wish to make interpretations about his oedipal conflicts, which seemed all too obvious, and which apparently caused him shame. I imagined he felt this shame in relation to his parents and his big brother who "knew everything." I also felt that I needed to point out what he was good at, like modeling clay, which would create the basis for a positive working alliance. However, I felt very controlled and often bored. Although Bill was communicating with me by showing me his play activity in a way that a much younger child would do, I was not allowed to interpret or comment on a personal level. I was forced to follow his pace, which seemed excruciatingly slow. This weapon manufacturing and battle phase eventually gave way to the creating of a family of worms: the mother a big fat worm, the father a thinner one, and two children of different sizes. In our conversation, we agreed these figures could represent a family like his own.

Second Stage: Oedipal Conflict and the Worm Family

The conflict had now moved to the worm family, and it centered on the father worm's wanting to lie down by his mother's side or on top of her and bite or eat the worm children if they came close to her. The oedipal conflict and rivalry over the possession of the mother was now being fully displayed in the worm family, and Bill allowed me to comment and interpret the powerful emotions and fights as he enacted them, but only in relation to the worms. Transference interpretations were unacceptable to him as were any references to his jealousy of his mother's relationship with his father and brother. His response was to stiffen and cease all nonverbal communication. If I referred to these actions in terms of his feeling annoyed and impinged upon by me, I was totally ignored.

His possessiveness towards his mother manifested itself in the maternal transference to me. He denied any private life for me outside of the realm of therapy sessions with him. He never asked about my family or my holidays and chose to ignore the existence of other patients, though he often complained about the inconveniences his own parents' patients caused him.

Third Stage: The Drawings

During this stage of therapy, Bill produced a series of over 200 drawings, drawings that represent and dramatize the psychic conflict of a young boy at the stage of transition from childhood to adolescence. It is interesting to observe how pre-oedipal and oedipal motifs are interwoven in the pictures. His fears, anxieties, violence, and hallucinatory states are all clearly illustrated in the drawings. They tell the story of his initiation to manhood by meeting and battling against his own sadism and violent instincts represented as monsters against which the hero has to battle. His castration anxieties are depicted by his terror of the bad father's retaliations. The bad father is depicted as Punch, the hunchback who in English folklore represents the sadistic father who batters and kills his own baby. Although it would be interesting to view the whole series, those pictures described show archetypal elements interwoven with developmental issues.

Picture One: This is the first picture drawn by Bill after he stopped playing with clay. The figure that he called the Jabberwocky seems to be suffering from auditory hallucination. The way the words are drawn implies that they are coming from far away, as if vibrating in the air. The figure is fierce. The eyes have a paranoid look, the ears are exaggerated aerials popping out of the head, the mouth looks cruel, and two protruding teeth are frightening. Such a mouth is reminiscent of vampires and sadistic biting. The body is absent; only two short legs support the figure and these are equipped with sharp pointed claws. On the top of the head a strange electronic command system seems to indicate the danger of a short circuit and the need for control.

As illustrated by this picture, Bill's internal picture contains many scattered, dangerous elements. Clearly this picture contains many primitive elements: it shows how the pre-oedipal part-object monster is experienced by Bill's unconscious. The picture can be seen as a representation of his early infantile fantasies about the body and its orifices at the onset of the regressive process activated by the therapy at the beginning of adolescence.

Picture Two: This picture immediately followed the first one. The interesting element here is the bleeding nose that he had initially drawn in red but quickly covered in blue ink as if the sight of blood scared him. It looks as if the focus is on the sadistic biting, and the bleeding nose is paradoxically what the mouth had been attacking. If we observe the separate elements in the picture, we can distinguish the representation of what Melanie Klein defined as a combined part object: the eyes are breast-like with clearly marked nipples in the middle and the nose looks like a floppy penis hanging in the center. Thus, the danger seems to emanate from oral-sadistic drives.

Picture Three: Here appears a typical oedipal motif: the break-in and the robbery. The robber is someone who takes other people's possessions by means of force. If we think about Bill's conflict of rivalry and jealousy with his father and brother represented in the early stage by the motif of the fight in the worm's family where the father possesses the mother by pushing the child worms away, we can see in this picture the children returning to attack and repossess the mother/house. In addition, vampire-like penises fly in the sky above the robbery scene.

From a developmental perspective, the multitude of robbers attacking from below and taking over the building represent instinctual forces that are unleashed at the outbreak of adolescence. The ego appears impotent to stop the takeover by the forces of the underworld. Nobody else is there to help. In the session, Bill took a great deal of time explaining to me how the attack on the building was taking place and how the robbers were getting away with murder.

The breaking into the house/mother is a common unconscious oedipal fantasy of boys. In this fantasy, the adolescent becomes the gangster and the father has to play the role of policeman, or else the child's own internalized censorship (superego) will need to take over to prevent the fantasized incest. Thus the gangster-police battles represent two tendencies inside the child: his regressive incestuous wish to get back inside the mother and his age-appropriate need to control the incestuous genital pull and move away from the mother. In Bill's case, his severe separation anxieties prevented him from getting away from his mother. Similarly, his wish to join Boy Scout outings was sabotaged by his bed wetting, which made it impossible for him to sleep away from home.

As a consequence of the robbery, in the picture which follows, a boy is "carried away" on the back of a rocket while a man's vision is covered by the smoke from his pipe. Like the genital energy beginning to explode in his body, this activation of sexual energy and the guilt and anxiety caused by it gives rise to the disturbing images in the next picture.

Picture Four: A boy's figure drops from a tree branch, loses its balance, and is thrown into a horrid, prehuman place full of jeering, staring, dismembered, and free-floating heads. Fierce breasts appear here and there to add horror to this frightening picture. Two elements are of special interest, the explosion at the right corner of the picture, which appears to have anal characteristics, and a devilish red Viking warrior, who seems to be enjoying the carnage from the center of the opposite side. This picture shows a great deal of chaos and disturbance in Bill's mind: his devilish baby self is triumphing over the adolescent ego. At this time, he was very aggressive at school, picking fights and failing academically, while at home he is unable to control his bed wetting. Although his anger and shame were very strong, they did not surface openly in the session.

This unbalanced state of affairs lasted for a few weeks and culminated in this picture in which two lots of space creatures confront each other in a verbal battle of jeers and insults into the midst of which a huge, scrambled piece of excrement is dropped.

In these sessions I did not make interpretations in the transference or in relation to his infantile parts; rather, I helped him tell the story of the pictures in the third person. This was the only way to get his cooperation, and he was willing to talk about them only if he felt that my comments were strictly impersonal. Outside of these sessions, he was desperately fighting to acquire independence from his mother, which meant being able to go on outings with the Boy Scouts or spending the night at a friend's house. However, his bed wetting continued to chain him to his mother in a regressive manner.

Pictures Five, Six, and Seven: A new phase in the drawings followed his victory over the bed wetting, which was marked by his first successful outing. These drawings consisted of two distinct types of figures, some very elongated male figures, mainly soldiers, and huge male faces with monstrous noses who fought against one another. The theme of the battle against Big Nose, a big face, soon acquired the traits of Punch and became the central motif of the therapeutic work.

Punch, as the representation of the archaic bad father, appears often in the fantasies of children. The puppet Punch originates in the tradition of Italian puppets and borrows his name from Pulcinella, a Neapolitan character of grotesque appearance. The most prominent features of this puppet are his hooked chin and deformed big nose. The story of Punch is extremely popular with young children and is often presented in public. The key elements of the story are as follows:

Punch is left to mind the baby while his wife, Judy, goes shopping. The baby begins to cry, ignores Punch's attempts to soothe it, and only screams louder when he chastises it. In anger and desperation, Punch throws the baby out the window. Judy returns and is furious with Punch and beats him with a rolling pin, whereupon Punch seizes the stick, beats Judy senseless and kills her. A number of fight scenes ensue with the authorities and Punch kills them all. Eventually Punch is captured and taken off to be hanged. At the last moment, he tricks the policeman, persuading him to put his own head in the noose, and then quickly pulls the rope. After this triumph over human adversaries, he is frightened by the ghost of Judy. The devil arrives to carry him off, but after a tremendous fight, Punch emerges as the victor, hoisting the lifeless body of the devil upon his triumphant stick.

The heroic inner battles to overcome the powerful, seemingly inde-structible archetypal aspect of the bad father embodied by Punch in Bill's unconscious, are depicted in a series of dramatic pictures. In Picture Eight, for instance, we can see a large portrait of Punch with a huge mouth and a little guy barely escaping from being eaten up. Surrounding the large face are other smaller ones with fierce expres-sions. In the lower left corner of the picture, one face is running after the little figure who is trying to escape. It is interesting to observe at the top left corner a much bigger figure coming out of Punch's head and literally vanishing out of his mind.

Picture Nine shows a beaten-up Punch. His nose has been crushed, and it looks as if the little boy is using the cat to scratch Punch, while keeping safely hidden on a high ledge.

In Picture Ten, Punch appears even more beaten up, his nose is flattened, his teeth are missing. The figure of the boy has grown in size and looks like the winner, although somewhat bruised by the fight.

In Picture Eleven the boy is waving the American flag and grinning with satisfaction. If one compares this last picture with the first one of the Jabberwocky, one notices how all the terrifying elements have disappeared from the portrait and it has now acquired the look of caricature. It is as if Bill is now making fun of the scary archetypal images of the past. One could say that through the therapeutic work, the primitive elements have become humanized.

Without openly mentioning it, Bill seems to have used Punch as the representation of the archetypal bad father of his early childhood fan-tasies. The possible analogy with his own father was the fact that his father had a prominent nose. In addition, he had a strong will and a considerable temper, according to Bill's reports, while Bill had a small nose that did not appear to be very masculine. In Bill's fantasy there seems to have been an equation between the nose and the penis. The sexual symbolism of the nose might have been easily interpreted but, given Bill's resistance, I chose to respect his resistance and not to interpret the drawing in sexual terms. I chose to explore with him the meaning of the image and waited to see how far he would go with the analogy.

On the whole, Bill would reveal many of his inner fantasies and conflicts so long as I did not insist on analyzing them. In this way he totally controlled my "nosiness" and "intrusive" analytic talk. At this stage in the transference, he experienced me as the diabolical father-Punch, because he felt I was forcing him to come to therapy. He was always alert, expecting some sharp comment on my part that would diminish him, as was often the case with his brother and father. As his drawings and my countertransference indicated, he was ready for a fight with me, but it never took place between us. He managed to contain and symbolize his aggressive impulses, representing them in his drawings.

In the course of our work, his negative feelings against the paternal element diminished, and this can be observed in a drawing of his Latin teacher with whom he had an authority conflict. The man looks fierce, but the face, although stern, has acquired human traits. The nose too has acquired normal proportions.

Conclusion

The oedipal battle with the archetypal pre-oedipal and oedipal paternal representation has been the focus here. The drawing phase lasted one year and was followed by a breeding phase, during which Bill developed a great interest in breeding insects, mice, rabbits, and all sorts of small pets. This interest became a hobby, one that he did quite successfully.

In spite of Bill's great resistance, the therapy helped his ego to sustain the pull of the instinctual forces without breaking down. Within the therapy, unconscious material found symbolic representation and containment. Bill managed to separate emotionally in an age-appropriate way from his mother. Following this separation, he was able to excel in the classroom and on the playing fields. As soon as he felt satisfied with himself, Bill decided to stop therapy, and we worked through the ending at his request. I agreed with his wish, although analytic work is seldom completed with adolescents. I felt that Bill had reached enough ego strength for him to be able to manage his daily life successfully, given his age. It is important that the adolescent feels enough confidence to leave therapy with the therapist's agreement, keeping the option open to return in the future. I felt that the work we did together helped Bill go through adolescence without any further upheavals. This case illustrates how the therapist's intervention aids in working through some major hurdle so that the adolescent's developmental process can be freed to proceed on its normal course.

Note

1. Anna Freud, *The Ego and Mechanisms of Defence* (London: Hogarth, 1937).

14

First Steps toward Independence: Transference Manifestations in a Fifteen-Year-Old Boy

Helga Anderssen-Plaut

Introduction

In our western culture we do not have helpful rituals for the transition into adulthood as they exist among primitive peoples in the form of rites of puberty. The tribe takes care of the individual's development and helps in an impersonal way to fulfill the necessary steps from one phase of life to the next. Among other things, these rituals involve the adolescent's "receiving the instruction which should put him in the position of living without his mother's protection."[1] Adolescents in western cultures are often left alone to deal with these phase-specific problems, especially when there is no stable family background and the inner separation from the archaic parents has been disturbed from the start.

Psychotherapeutic work represents a chance to further the inner process of changing the introjected archetypal images of parents so that they become more like human beings and are no longer feared to the extent that the confrontation with these archaic imagos become impossible because they are too fear-inspiring. The case material presented describes this process via transference and countertransference that became evident during the course of therapy, with fifteen-year-old Stephan.

When Stephan came for treatment he was stuck in the situation, typical of adolescence, between being a child and becoming an adult. As is common with people his age, he was very ambivalent towards a commitment to psychotherapeutic work. On the one hand he wanted to manage his own life, while on the other hand it was obvious, even to him, that he needed help to live through this difficult period in his life.

Symptomatology

Stephan was brought to an educational guidance center in Berlin at the suggestion of his school; he had been disrupting the class persistently and making a fool of himself over trivial matters. He forgot to bring the right books to class, his spoken answers were often inappropriate and unrelated to the topic, and at no time could he tolerate criticism. When he was spoken to about his behavior, his reaction was always aggressive and insolent, and he found himself rejected by his teachers and his fellow students alike. Although everybody had tried to deal with him, he ended up with no friends. According to his mother, the cause of Stephan's difficulties was to be found only at school, for at home she had no difficulties with him. The mother asked that we mediate with the school. Stephan stressed that he would like to come to therapy because he suffered greatly from loneliness and wanted to understand why he had no friends.

Background

Stephan was an only child. Since his birth his mother had largely left his care to others. She had spent little time with him, preferring to remain in full-time work and to take many courses in continuing education. She was working as a health practitioner. The father, a landscape designer, showed almost no interest in his son. He was often on tour for several days at a time, sometimes months, and only seemed interested in building up his career.

Stephan developed into a calm and friendly baby and toddler. There was no negative "terrible two" phase. At school he did sufficiently well. He always had some friends among his class mates. He had even been elected monitor. The relationship with his mother was very close. He clung to her, and she shared most of her limited free time with him. The parents' marriage was rather distant. Shortly after Stephan's birth the mother had considered a divorce. She could not see why she should live with a man who obviously did not care for her and their child. Nevertheless she decided to stay, since she was concerned that her son should not grow up in a broken home. When Stephan was fourteen years old she decided that it was now time for her to leave her husband and to live her own life. This included also a separation from her parents, since the family was living in the maternal grandparents' house. Stephan was to choose with which parent he wanted to stay. He chose to go on living with his father. His mother left the family and moved to an apartment of her own. Shortly after this separation, Stephan began having difficulties at school.

Psychodynamics

The symptomatology Stephan had developed since the separation of his parents showed that he lacked an age-appropriate independence from home. During the first two years of life he had not had a chance to establish a good inner object that would enable him to contain himself. His mother had spent too little time with him. Her marriage to his father was most deceptive. One might conclude that her son had to compensate for the lack of a loving husband. There was nothing conspicuous about Stephan's development as a lovely baby and toddler. But the absence of a negativistic phase could be interpreted as Stephan finding it necessary to conform to his mother's wishes in order not to lose her love. After all, she represented the only important relationship in his life, especially since the father was not reliably present because of his business commitments.

Stephan probably never solved the oedipal conflict in an appropriate way. The father never became a rival to him, as neither parent made sufficiently clear to him that the mother was the father's wife and not the lover of the son. Stephan introjected the archetypal archaic image of a wrathful father. During the latency period, Stephan and his mother could simply live their oedipal relationship without being disturbed by the father. But at the onset of puberty this was no longer possible. Stephan's forthcoming sexual development stirred up old unconscious incestuous fantasies, thus causing terrible anxiety in both mother and son. It was reported that Stephan had said he had decided to stay with his father because he felt it would do his mother good to break away from her parents at last and to realize herself. I understood this as a projection of his own needs onto his mother. On the one hand he had fled from a relationship with his mother that was too intense; on the other hand he probably also wanted a positive approach to his father to resolve the oedipal entanglement with his mother.

Unlike many other boys of his age, Stephan had asked to work with a woman therapist. I understood this as his need to come to terms with his extremely strong bond with his mother. Due to the unavailability of his mother during infancy and to his upbringing in day-care centers, he had idealized her from his second month of life onward. Consciously his mother was the most wonderful woman on earth, whereas unconsciously he feared the terrible aspect of the Great Mother who would desert him if he did not live up to her expectations. Now that his mother had actually left him, his pre-oedipal separation anxiety had been aroused. Before he came to therapy, Stephan had tried to make friends with a girl at school by sending her love letters. Instead of responding, she had told her classmates about them and they all had made fun of him. He had hoped to find the protective maternal aspect of the anima image in this girl. Instead, the manner in which she reacted disillusioned him. He had confused an adult's being in love with a baby's longing for his mother.

Therapy: The Opening Phase

Stephan's mother brought him to the first session. When I opened the door I saw an attractive slender young woman in the hall with a lanky boy in tow who looked distraught, pale, and unobtrusive. She wanted to stay during the session, although it had been clearly agreed that Stephan would come alone, and at a later date, with his consent, I would arrange a meeting with her or with both of them. He stepped in hesitantly while she withdrew, saying that she would wait outside for him. While he nodded helplessly, a picture of "mother with eight-year-old son" came to my mind. On the way to my room, Stephan's posture became more erect and by the time he sat down opposite me he looked like a young man and not a small boy. I noted that his fly was open, although it was not conspicuous because of his baggy pants. I considered telling him, but did not do so.

He began to explain why he had come to the center, using an abstract mode of speech (i.e. instead of using verbs he used nouns, a lot of foreign words, and very complex sentences that never seemed to come to an end). He underlined what he was saying with a lot of gestures. One might have taken him for an eighteen-year-old by the way he explained that he did everything wrong, both with people his age and adults. I was to tell him how to behave so he could receive the social recognition he longed for. He said he had been doing much worse since his mother had moved out, because he had always been able to confide in her. As for his father, he was seldom home, only complained about the mess in the house, and Stephan could never really talk to him. He could not relate well to his grandparents either, even though they lived in the same house. However, he wanted to deal with the difficulties at school on his own. I was not to get involved there, but he did want to come to see me weekly to talk about his feelings. At the end of the session he told me that he had bought Sigmund Freud's *The Interpretation of Dreams,* although he had not gotten around to reading it. But he found that in the photograph in the book, Freud looked strict, yet trustworthy and fatherly.

We agreed that he would come for a session once a week. Throughout the first six months of therapy there were many last minute cancellations. He was often late. Sometimes he showed up when I was not there and would have chats with my colleagues.

Comment

With his decision to have psychotherapy, Stephan took the first step towards separation from his parents. He was in search of a person he could trust, whom he could accept as a sort of "master or mistress of initiation."[2] I understood the way he continually put off the start of therapy as an expression of his ambivalence about stepping over the "threshold of initiation" and developing a relationship with me.

When finally he came to his first session he arrived as I mentioned above, with an open fly. I saw this as a nonverbal message regarding the problem area of sexuality, something he could not address at that time, but which certainly occupied and disquieted him. I did not tell him about the fly because I wanted to spare him and myself the embarrassment. It would have been treating him as a small boy and I would have been perceived as a reproachful embarrassing mother, which I did not want to enact under any circumstance. In her article "The Technique of Analysis in Puberty," Melanie Klein speaks about the enormous anxiety that is revived at the beginning of adolescence.[3]

This certainly was the case with Stephan too. By leaving his fly open he was telling me about his anxiety.

The first session was full of examples of his ambivalence about whether to be a man or a child, whether to assert that he had a penis or to deny it. If he exhibited his penis, the archetypal father might cut it off. If he hid it, he was not accepted in his social world. When he asked me to tell him how to behave at school, he was like a well-behaved son who submitted to his father. When he wanted to take school matters into his own hands, he was declaring that he was capable of asserting himself in the world, that he too had a penis of his own.

The message conveyed by the purchase of Freud's *The Interpretation of Dreams* I understood as an offer to interest himself in my profession so that, equipped with psychoanalytic understanding, we could approach his problems together. The stern Freud in the background would be the father figure whom Stephan had never had. Freud would give us the orientation in therapy that had been missing in Stephan's family life. Perhaps reading the book would even enable him to understand what was going on in therapy so that he could control the situation that might develop between the two of us during the course of treatment.

Unconsciously, he feared falling into a tremendous dependence on me in the transference. This fear expressed itself in the way he seemed to completely disregard our organizational therapy arrangements. During the first six months I felt I was a narcissistic object for him. By handling our appointments in an arbitrary way he revealed the unconscious, infantile desire that I be constantly available as a mother is to her baby. He told me that he was not annoyed to have come in vain to a session I had canceled. He had even found it interesting to meet my colleagues when I was not there. It reminded me of how small children snoop around the house when the parents are not home. In this way he got used to surroundings in which he would otherwise feel insecure. I understood this as a possibility for him to get closer to me, to gain better control of the situation and thereby more power over me, lessening his fear of dependency and engulfment. However I felt controlled by him and it annoyed me terribly. I wanted to be a dependable therapist for him, and here he was demonstrating to my colleagues that I did not care for him. Maybe he also came to make sure that I really was not there that day, that there was no betrayal, that I did not see another patient during his hour. He seemed relieved when he saw that I had told him the truth. I think that it was his jealousy that had caused my anger. I felt him acting like a possessive lover who wanted to control all my movements. This was certainly how he acted towards his mother, who encouraged this by wanting to be present at his first therapy session and by anxiously waiting for him to come home.

The Incestuous Entanglement

After a summer break of six weeks, Stephan came back. He told me that both parents had taken him abroad for three weeks—according to him—just to please him. It had been "risqué": father, mother, and son had shared a hotel room with a large bed and an extra bed. Stephan was supposed to sleep with his mother. In fact he had slept on the roof every night because of the hot climate, he said. His parents had reproached him for behaving egoistically. This made him feel very insecure. "Who was being egoistic, them or me?" he exclaimed. When they had separated they had only thought of their own happiness. Now that he thought he was doing what was good for him, they were reproachful. Had he no right to sleep where he wanted just because they had arranged this trip for him? Besides, they had not even asked him if he wanted to go. He would not have minded staying in Berlin over the holidays. But now he sounded quite angry.

The mother often met Stephan at my office after the sessions. I noticed that this annoyed me. Once, when I found her standing outside my door at the end of a session, I really felt as if she had caught me doing something forbidden. During this session Stephan had spoken about his sexual needs: he eagerly wanted to have a girl friend. Why was there no big nightclub where you could go and simply ask someone to sleep with you—just like that? If I were there maybe he could even ask me and no one would think anything of it. The only rule would be that only people who really wanted to do so could sleep with each other. As we discussed this idea, he came to the conclusion that he would really rather look for a nice young girl—I probably had a husband anyway.

During a long absence of his father, Stephan's mother moved into her parent's house again. At the beginning of a session during this period, Stephan acted confused. He could hardly speak coherently and had an agitated look. After some time he told me what had taken place: he had come home in the evening and found his mother and her recently acquired lover in an embrace. He said he had "caught them being very intimate," and they were startled by Stephan's sudden appearance. They had quickly pulled away from each other, and Stephan had been seized by a terrible fury. He had run to his room and thrown himself screaming onto his bed in a temper tantrum. Yet when he came into the living-room later, everything was "normal" again and the three of them had dinner together. While telling the story he regained his composure and could speak coherently. It was incomprehensible to him that the whole thing had made him so angry. I said that he had felt anger at a specific moment and that it was then that it had its justification for him. He answered that he knew his mother had a boyfriend, and that was all right with him, but he had just never seen it so clearly as he did now.

In the following sessions he expressed his annoyance with his mother's overprotectiveness. She was no longer living with them and he did not want to be called twice a day any more; he wanted to take care of himself when his father was away. When he told his mother this, she felt insulted. However, from then on she called him less often.

After this argument with his mother he began to get a foothold in school. He joined the staff of the school magazine and also found a friend. They got together to try to meet girls under the pretext of writing an article for the school magazine. They did not achieve the desired results, but it was fun nonetheless. The relationship with his father improved. They often had a chat in the evenings. On one of these occasions his father told him about his own youthful dreams of being a famous writer. When his father was out of town Stephan cooked for himself and enjoyed it. He could relax alone in his room, sitting at his desk with some strong tea, classical music, and a candle—writing stories.

Transference and Countertransference

Stephan's report of the trip abroad with his parents demonstrated the incestuous atmosphere in the family, especially the incestuous bond between Stephan and his mother. She did not have the capacity to set limits and establish boundaries. Unconsciously she seduced him, and his father even seemed to encourage the situation.

My distinct countertransference reaction when I met the mother at the end of the session in which Stephan had spoken about his sex-club fantasy could be understood as an indication of the unconscious incestuous motivation that made her overprotect her son in this way. She handled him like a small boy in need of being sheltered from the world. As long as he stayed the small boy he had always been it was natural that they sleep in the same bed in a hotel room. There was no danger of losing control of the situation. I felt as if I had been caught in the spider web of very strong archaic emotions and I wondered if the three of us would ever have a chance to escape from it.

In this sex-club session, as well as in previous sessions, Stephan had transferred libido from his mother to me in the framework of a positive transference and had projected his image of the anima onto me. (One can often observe this when a very young man chooses a somewhat older woman, who could represent his mother, as his first sexual object.) Because in reality there existed no incest barriers between us, the incest fantasies could be projected onto me and expressed in the transference. This comprised a small step in the direction of consciousness of his anima image. During this session we had discussed what sort of partner he would find at the sex-club and neither his mother nor myself were his choice; he concluded that he would much rather look for an attractive young girl.

Jung points out that the anima will be projected so long as it is unconscious: "The first bearer of the psychic image is always mother."[4] Stephan gained some inner freedom by projecting this image onto me. Thus the first step towards separation from his mother had been taken. The atmosphere of the sex-club would guarantee that it involve only a sexual relationship between us. Perhaps he hoped to be initiated in this way and become a man through the sexual act with a woman. Love did not enter the picture.

In a way this sex-club fantasy was like a "land of milk and honey" on a sexual level. As a baby he had never experienced being fed whenever he wanted. In the day-care center he had received his bottle on a regular schedule in a way that did not correspond to his inner needs. Now he dreamed up a demand-based feeding situation around the fulfillment of his sexual desires. Because of the introjected wrathful father imago and the terrible aspects of the "Great Mother," there was no room in his inner world to create wish-fulfilling fantasies that were also emotionally related. By telling me his fantasy he started to create a space in between his instinctual needs and the longed for fulfillment. This space he could now fill with illusions, made possible by the transference of his anima onto me—the anima being the archetype of relationship.

It had become clear to him during this session that he could not have a sexual relationship with me. Nor did he have to wait long for evidence that his mother also was not available. My countertransference to this consternation at the beginning of the session after that startling encounter with the mother and her lover had enabled me to listen to him in an amicable and supportive way. I was not afraid to examine reality with him, and this enabled him to put into words what had happened. I allowed him to be angry with his mother's "betrayal," and he was thus able to gain greater distance from the experience and deal with it more appropriately. It was at this point that he found a friend. For me this was connected to the fact that his anima image was no longer identical to that of his mother. By means of the intermediate stage projection onto me, his anima became free to be further projected onto an "attractive young girl." He could make friends with a young man, because having projected his anima image he was no longer in danger of becoming identified with his feminine side and therefore in danger of becoming homosexual.

He did not need his friend as a homosexual partner but rather as an ally. With him he no longer felt lonely and consequently was not as dependent on his mother's care. When he started to cook for himself and arrange his room so that he could feel comfortable, he realized an approach to his own feminine/motherly side, to his own capacity to take care of himself.

Dealing with the Father

Stephan managed to get closer to his father due to the fact that his anima was no longer projected onto his mother. When he no longer fantasized stealing his father's wife there was no more need to fear the wrath of his rival. Thus he could see his father more as a human being, which probably brought about a change of the introjected father image as well. This made it possible for Stephan to identify with his father by writing stories.

Having worked on the inner separation from the mother, he now seemed ready to deal with the inner separation from his father and accept his own masculinity. He took to this issue in the last session before the summer vacation, one year after the start of therapy. The content showed his ambivalence about the obviously necessary confrontation with the father. He had written a detective story in which he vividly showed how violently the conflict with the introjected father raged in him. There was a lot of fighting going on between an old man and young man. It was a question of life and death between them, and Stephan was frightened.

The other side of the ambivalence was expressed in a retreat fantasy. He wanted to live in the Alps alone for a year. With this fantasy he avoided the confrontation with the father and hoped to become a hero without a struggle.

The Last Phase and the Resolution of the Transference

When he came back after the summer vacation, he told me that his friend had gone to Australia for a year. He said that he wanted to stop seeing me and try to cope with his life on his own, but he wanted to come two more times so as to put our work into perspective. However, we agreed to continue until Christmas and then stop. This meant that we would have approximately ten more sessions. In fact he only came five more times, due to cancellations on his part.

He seemed more mature than before the summer. Even colleagues told me "Stephan has become a real man." This comment was only partially true. It was still difficult for him to assert himself and to manage his own life without the protection of his mother. He considered leaving his father and going to live with his mother, if only she had had a larger apartment. "At least there is love there," he said. But then he would feel like he was under a bell-jar; it would be suffocating. However, staying with his father meant more clashes with him; he feared these without the support of his friend.

In another session he dealt with our mutual relationship. He wanted to know whether I had only a "financial interest" in him. To my question of how he would like the situation to be, he replied it would be nice if I were there simply because I was interested in him. On the other hand this would not be so good, either; his obligation would be too great and he would have to be grateful to me. Of course he would be grateful to me anyway, but 'not all that much." The best situation would be somewhere in between. I should be paid for my work but I should also enjoy doing it. Then he expressed his anxiety about need-ing to tell me things so that I would not be bored during the sessions. At other times he feared that I might be a sort of mind reader, able to know all the things he did not want to share with me. He wanted to have his secrets and did not want to tell me everything. Yet he would also want me to sometimes understand him without words.

Discussion

In this last phase of therapy, regressive and progressive tendencies struggled with each other. He still wanted to be contained by his mother (and in transference by me). Yet he wanted to be independent. His friend's departure did not make things easier for him. His friend had been his ally in the struggle for independence and his absence reinforced the regressive tendencies as well as his fear of assertion.

I understood his wish to stop working with me as an attempt to move towards separation: he would gain distance and rid himself of the illusions he had experienced through the transference. If he were able to say "thank you" instead of having to be grateful, this would mean more autonomy. And if I had not been bored by the things he had told me throughout therapy, then there had not only been receiv-ing but also giving on his part.

In view of the reported sex-club fantasy we may assume that Stephan had sexual fantasies in which, instead of playing an active role, he was passively seduced. In asking me if I could mind read, he really wanted to know if he could be punished for such fantasies. This could mean that his secret was an identification with the feminine sexual role. He still had difficulties with this side of himself. By understanding him without words I made it easier for him to accept and partly integrate the sexual aspect of the anima, which could also help him in writing.

He summarized his inner conflict quite accurately: He wanted to be independent, to have his own identity. But he was worried about the sacrifices he would have to make in exchange. I was relieved when during the last session he asked me if I knew of a youth therapy group where he could sort out his problems. This was a positive idea and it demonstrated that he understood that he needed the support of people his own age so that his development towards manhood could proceed.

Conclusion

In the introduction to this chapter I referred to initiation rights that are used in primitive cultures to help young people negotiate the intermediate state between childhood and adulthood. The case of Stephan came to mind because in this phase of life, very strong primitive archaic emotions are involved that if unaided are very difficult to deal with. The almost archetypal affects and emotions that accompany the physical development take hold of and dominate the psyche as a whole, so that there is not much room left for reflection. Sometimes the archaic emotions are so powerful that they infect the people dealing with these adolescents like a virus. I think that is what happened to Stephan's mother and to myself in the course of the therapy, especially at the time when I felt caught in the spider web of incestuous transference.

Notes

1. J. Jacobi, *The Psychology of C. G. Jung* (New Haven, CT: Yale University Press, 1942) p. 180.
2. J. Henderson, *Threshold of Initiation* (Middletown, CT: Wesleyan University Press, 1967).
3. M. Klein, *The Psycho-Analysis of Children* (London: Hogarth, 1932).
4. C. G. Jung, "Anima and Animus," *Two Essays on Analytical Psychology, Collected Works* (London: Routledge and Kegan Paul, 1953, rev. ed. 1966) v.7.

PART II

Inpatient and Outpatient Adolescent Psychotherapy in Institutions

Introduction to Part II

The five chapters of this second part discuss severely disturbed adolescents who temporarily need an institutional setting for treatment, and the application of analytical psychology in institutional settings. The chapters also show how nonanalytic methods can be integrated in an analytic frame.

Carl Jung was critical, if not disapproving, of group mentality, and he was not interested clinically in group dynamics; however, his concept of the collective unconscious and of consciousness as a kind of general sociopsychological concept is a helpful basis from which one can derive some ideas about the mutual process of individual and collective development. As are other archetypal pairs of opposites, the individual vs. the collective is such a pair, even if until now we have had no name for this archetype. Another perspective for understanding the dynamic of institutions is the opposition of internal vs. external reality, or internal vs. external psychic space. In analytical psychology it is a basic assumption that the transcendence of these opposites is achieved by the forces of the self. Thus the self is not only a concept of individual psychology, but also of the collective psyche. The family, the group, institutions, or even the whole society can represent collective aspects of the self.

The main focus of this book is on the development of individual adolescents and the intimacy of dyadic psychotherapeutic relationships and the inner world of the adolescents. However, one should not forget that in adolescence an important developmental step is the transition from the family into the greater society, and the important function of the peer group as a transitional space is a significant element of this development. Adolescents often "solve" their confused emotional or mental states by "a flight into group life," where the various parts of themselves can be externalized and projected onto members of their peer group. This dynamic can be used therapeutically in institutional treatment when the group and/or the institution functions as a container.

In Gustav Rovensiepen's chapter, "The Clinic as Container," the idea of the institution as a container is illustrated and applied to a hospital that treats adolescents suffering from severe disturbances such as psychoses, borderline personalities, and psychosomatic diseases. Most of the patients have severe problems functioning in groups and have no age-appropriate relationships to peers. They live, both internally and externally, in a regressed state of dependency and they are tied to their primary objects with a very strong ambivalence. Because institutional treatment intensifies the problem of dependency, emerging conflicts and primitive affects such as greed, envy, rage, jealousy, helplessness, and the fantasies related to them surface faster and in a more vehement way than they do within family structures. The adolescents try to overcome them by externalizing and projecting them onto the clinic, their peers and the adults. If the clinic functions as a container, represented by the staff and by the physical structure of the building, it promotes in the adolescent patient the feeling of being held. In our view this is an absolute precondition for individual or group psychotherapy to be effective. Like the container the mother provides for the unbearably intense affects of her baby, we understand the day unit and the inpatient unit to be an extended container into which such affects can be projected. Our primary goal is not the development of a trusting therapeutic relationship between *two people* but the creation of a "good enough" container function. The different kinds of container/contained relationships within the structure of the clinic are described. If one assumes that there is a strong relationship between inner and outer reality, this model helps the adolescents to differentiate their psychic structure according to their perception and emotional experience of the outer reality of the clinic. The main task of the psychotherapist is the work with the caretakers and teachers. Permanent and frequent external supervision (by external analysts) for the staff is necessary and available. Some remarks are made on some typical countertransference problems of the careworker staff.

After describing the theoretical and clinical model as well as the organizational structure of the hospital. Bovensiepen uses a case vignette to show, from the perspective of individual psychotherapy, how Tom, a seventeen-year-old adolescent, experiences the container function of the clinic.

The reader will meet Tom again in the chapter by Heide Heidtke and Michael Neumann-Schirmbeck on "Group Therapy in a Day Care Setting." These authors are coworkers of Gustav Bovensiepen in the same clinic described in his paper. For purposes of the day clinic setting, they have developed a special form of group psychotherapy for adolescents that is a combination of analytic group psychotherapy with elements of psychodrama techniques. The authors' basic assumption is that the group serves as an external representation of the group members' "self." Parts of the adolescents' inner world and their interpersonal relationships with each other are projected into the group, which has a containing function. Heidtke and Neumann-Schirmbeck distinguish between what they call the "open group milieu" and "group therapy" in the strict sense. The adolescent's daily life in the day unit and in the school is managed by the open group work as opposed to weekly group therapy in a closed group. The open group work helps the adolescent to have new social experiences, whereas the group therapy is the setting for corrective emotional experiences aimed primarily at producing intrapsychic change. Both situations influence each other, but it is impressive how the adolescents often show completely different behavior and emotions in the open group than they show during group therapy. In contrast to the open group in the unit, group therapy, and especially the presence of the therapists as parental figures, creates an extended family.

The authors focus also on the difference between transference within the group process and in individual psychotherapy. They write: "In comparison with groups of adults transference is much stronger and develops instantly. In individual psychotherapy, the therapist is used much more as a figure of the adolescent's inner life, as an object of his fantasies, projections and identifications. In group therapy, the therapist is more of a 'real person' for the adolescent's orientation." The presence of two therapists facilitates splitting mechanisms, especially of parental transferences. This is seen by the authors as desirable because this defense has a protecting, ego-supporting effect against the adolescents' psychotic anxieties. Because group therapy functions as a closed group, the splitting can be worked on in the course of the therapy. In contrast to group therapy with adults, the authors stress the necessity to work with adolescents by more active intervention and ego-support. The main tools to achieve this support are psychodrama techniques.

Psychodrama techniques make it possible to guide the adolescents from imagination to action, thus helping them to build up a link between their experiences (including actions) and their inner situation during the group therapy sessions. The two main forms are role play and improvisation. During this phase of therapy, the adolescents act out their stories, rather than tell them. The role play can be either a protagonist-centered acting, in which one adolescent expresses clearly what he is concerned with, or a group-centered acting, where the therapist perceives a group fantasy or emotion and guides the adolescents to enact it. The more developed the containing function of the group, the more it becomes possible to apply improvisational plays. At the beginning of the group session and during the enactments, the two therapists comment and interpret verbally in order to link the acting with analytic understanding.

In their chapter the authors give detailed descriptions of three sessions to illustrate their techniques. They understand the group as an intermediate area or an intermediate playground in which the adolescents develop their own space and imaginative capacity.

The third paper in this section is Geoffrey Brown's paper. "Borderline States: Incest and Adolescents." This paper addresses several interesting theoretical questions, but Brown's main concern is to determine what specific role traumatic external experiences play in precipitating the severe developmental distortion and delay that are observed in some severe psychopathological states during adolescence. He illustrates his theoretical reflections with a case history of a sixteen-year-old girl he had seen first as an inpatient and, after discharge, in outpatient treatment. The traumatic experience of this girl was caused by repeated incidents of sexual abuse from her fifth year on.

In the clinical part of the chapter Brown tells us about his patient, Amy, who was referred to him when she was sixteen years old, following a suicide attempt. Amy had a long history of disruptive and disturbed behaviour since her entry into primary school. The therapist found her surrounded by a crowd of professional helpers largely unaware of each other. This is a typical situation one meets when dealing with severe psychopathology and acting out in adolescence. It may reflect the dissociated state of mind and the splitting tendency of the girl who has projected her inner state onto the outer world in order to liberate herself from confusing and destructive emotions and anxieties. Brown shows how Amy gradually became aware of her feeling states, which before were completely disassociated and acted out in the inpatient therapeutic milieu. Thanks to the safe container the unit represented, it was possible to limit Amy's self-destructive behavior. In the individual therapy she gradually developed a trusting maternal transference and could "disclose" the abuse by her father. In this phase of treatment her perceived father image changed from a figure to be feared to a figure with warm nourishing qualities, "like golden sunshine." Brown describes the split of this father image and how he experienced it in a positive transference with a psychotic quality. Much of Amy's inner chaos, in terms of inconstant and split objects, she enacted within the therapeutic milieu of the unit. But slowly the chaos began to subside, to be replaced by a strong attachment to the therapist and to the unit as whole. Since discharge, she is now in her sixth year of psychotherapy. She is able to have a stable relationship with a young man and has sufficiently distanced herself from father.

In the theoretical part of the chapter Brown agrees with other authors who link the emotional experience of chronically abused children like Amy to their disturbances in thinking and symbolizing and to their preferred mechanisms of splitting and dissociation. Brown's reflections about "disclosure" when dealing with sexual abuse victims are very important and helpful concerning treatment techniques. He understands disclosure as a "process taking place within the framework of a relationship between patient and therapist: it is not just a statement made once." He illustrates this in the work with Amy. She first told him she had been abused by a stranger; then followed a series of statements spread over some months, leading up to disclosure of abuse by her father. To reach the most emotionally loaded complex (the father-daughter incest) is often a long process and requires a safe and containing environment such as are provided by the unit and by the emotional containment within the therapeutic relationship.

Brown discusses the similarity between psychopathology and the phenomenology of post sexual abuse syndrome (Briere), borderline personal disorder, and adolescent turmoil. He assumes that "some degree of borderline functioning is inherent in the adolescent psyche. This is not to say that adolescence is the cradle of borderline functioning." Like most of the authors in this book, Brown sees severe psychopathology in adolescence (e.g., borderline functioning) as a result of experiences of severe deprivations in the early mother-infant relationship.

The fourth chapter in this section, "Sandplay Therapy and Verbal Interpretation with an Anorexic Girl" is by Gianni Nagliero. This chapter, like Neumann and Heidtke's chapter on group psychotherapy, discusses how nonanalytic techniques can be applied and integrated within an analytic understanding. Sandplay therapy as a psychotherapeutic method of analytical psychology was developed by Dora Kalff in Switzerland. Sandtray as a diagnostic and therapeutic tool was "invented" during the 1920s in London by Margaret Lowenfeld with whom Kalff studied in the 1950s. When Nagliero writes Kalff "places great trust in the self-healing potential of the individual psyche when favorable conditions are created," he is referring to the basic Jungian assumption of the autonomy of the unconscious and the archetypal dynamic of the self. Thus one can understand sandplay as an imaginative technique that links the ego with the forces of the unconscious. When the patient creates a scene in the sandtray, the scene can be understood as a representation of an aspect of his or her inner world, of which the patient may only be partially conscious. Nagliero emphasizes that by talking about the scene, "the patient can address internal problems without becoming conscious of them. Thus the words of the therapist seem less dangerous than direct interpretation. This aspect of the therapy is particularly important for patients who have strong paranoid defenses." Nagliero stresses the patient's sensitivity to what may be experienced as intrusive. Because of their longing for autonomy, adolescents immediately react defensively when they feel threatened by external interventions, which they experience as intrusive. This is well-illustrated in the case of thirteen-year-old Carla. Carla suffered from anorexia nervosa, and the therapy was partially conducted during her stay in a children's psychiatric ward. In the first part of the chapter, Nagliero presents several of the sand pictures Carla had made during her therapy. The first pictures of the series indicated that Carla regressed quickly and came into contact with her world of infancy where she often felt alone and lacked a containing relationship with her mother. This inner situation and a canceled session by the therapist led to a deep depression accompanied by an increase in her anorexic and bulimic behavior and her paranoid anxieties. As a consequence of her split between "spirit and body," a part of her seemed to identify with Jesus, and another part with a "negative, frightening devil" in the form of a "sweet doll." Nagliero shows that the more this process deepened the more transference/countertransference feelings intensified; using words became more and more essential in the therapeutic relationship. Becoming aware of the discrepancies between her external life (and worsening symptomatology) and the images she made in the sand, Carla could put into words her inner state as well as speak about her suffering from isolation and her anxieties about becoming a woman. The last six months of the therapy developed into a verbal psychotherapy indicating that Carla could "sacrifice" her infantile dependency and could work on her problems of separation.

Nagliero comments that sandplay therapy, "which makes possible the expression or precocious aspects of the relationship seems to be able to respond to the need to contain the patient, while verbal interpretations seem to respond to the need to use the mind in its discriminating function and consciousness-raising abilities."

In the last chapter in this section, Janet Glynn-Treble shows how difficult it is to practice analytic psychotherapy in an institution that is not primarily conceptualized and organized according to psychoanalytic and group dynamic principles. Similarly to the first two papers in this section, this paper applies Bion's concept of the container/contained and Jung's concept of the *vas hermeticum* on an institutional dynamic. It is very interesting how Glenn-Treble understands the dynamic processes within an institution in terms of alpha and beta functions. First she draws a broad picture of the history of residential treatment institutions for severely disturbed adolescents in Great Britain. She distinguishes and gives examples of two types of institutions: the educational institution and the psychodynamically-oriented institution. Like the other authors in this section, she focuses on the difficulties that arise when children and staff alike are acting out, but the staff has not been helped to reflect on the significance (have a reverie, in Bion's sense) of the children's destructive projections and abusive behaviour. Usually in the more educationally oriented institutions, the superego of a staff member will try to control the children's behaviour by punitive and repressive methods that eventually become sadistic. Thus the institution operates in the same sick fashion as the original families, and the maturational processes of the adolescents cannot be helped.

Glynn-Treble then proceeds to describe her experience as a child therapist attempting to set up a program of individual psychotherapy within one educational residential school for disturbed adolescent girls. The emotions that this stirred up—envy, jealousy, rivalry, aggression, competition and opposition among both the staff and the girls—are clearly described and illustrated with examples. This resistance to offering psychoanalytic attention to an individual child made her feel impotent, helpless, and often persecuted. The situation was extremely difficult to endure both for the therapist and for her patients. Disruption and attacks on the frame of the therapy by the staff and the girls were an everyday occurrence as academic studies and sports were given priority over psychotherapy. In these attacks Glynn-Treble could sense retaliation on the part of the staff exasperated by their own helplessness and frustration in their attempts to control chaos both externally and internally. These difficulties can be understood as attacks on the institution's capacity to "think"; that is, the capacity to create an internal and external space for the staff to reflect on their work and their feelings and try to relate these to the behavior of the children.

Glynn-Treble feels that the work of a therapist within such an institution can offer an opportunity for the infantile projections and needs of both patients and staff to be responded to appropriately, rather than defended against.

15

The Clinic as Container

Gustav Bovensiepen

Introduction

It is striking how ineffectually child and adolescent psychiatry has dealt with the treatment of young people in their middle and late adolescence in Germany. As a result, many of these young people turn up in departments of adult psychiatry, which have neither the psychotherapeutic nor educational means to deal with the special dynamics of adolescents. Because many adolescents attack the psychoanalytic setting, some psychotherapists are not particularly enthusiastic about treating them. The difficulties presented in these cases may lead frustrated therapists to Freud's conclusion:

> It almost looks as if analysis were the third of those "impossible" professions in which one can be sure beforehand of achieving unsatisfying results. The other two, which have been known much longer, are education and government.[1]

The analytic treatment of adolescents in institutions requires an intimate and complicated cooperation of two of these impossible professions: education *and* analysis.

In my experience working as the psychotherapeutic and medical director of a psychotherapeutic clinic for children and adolescents from the ages of eleven to twenty-one. I have been impressed by the value of applying Bion's container/contained concept to the institutional treatment of adolescents.[2] In order to understand the concept of the treatment program, the external structure and the setting of the clinic has to be described.

The clinic offers exclusively long-term treatment, from one to three years, for severely disturbed children and adolescents with structural ego-disturbances, such as psychoses, borderline personality structure, and severe psychosomatic diseases. These youngsters need a social-educational treatment as well as an analytic-oriented psychotherapeutic milieu. Adolescents with drug addictions or severe delinquency are excluded from treatment since the structure of the clinic offers too many possibilities for regression and acting out of antisocial tendencies.

The clinic has four small units: two inpatient units each for eight adolescents from the ages of fourteen to twenty-one; one day unit for ten adolescents and one day unit for eight children from the ages of ten to thirteen. The clinic can treat the whole spectrum of adolescent development from ages ten to twenty-one. Most of the patients come from the lower or the lower middle class and grow up in socially and/ or emotionally disintegrated families.

The schedule and structure of the four units are very similar. The structure can best be understood by a discussion of the schedule of the adolescents in the day unit. These adolescents stay in the unit from 8:00 a.m. to 5:00 p.m. Monday through Friday. When they arrive, they have breakfast and then go to the school groups with the inpatients where they have three to four hours of classes. Great importance is attached to school as a social and reality sphere. During the intervals between classes and lunch and between lunch and afternoon activities, there are individual sessions and free time. The afternoons are structured in the following way: Monday: sports, swimming, or aikido; Tuesday: occupational and creative therapy; Wednesday: group psychotherapy; Thursday: occupational therapy involving hand crafts; Friday: special leisure activities or field trips selected and planned during an all-clinic meeting on the preceding Monday. Every afternoon except Friday, meetings with families after clinic time occur. As a rule, a family meeting with two therapists takes place for each adolescent every week. The frequency of individual therapy varies from one to three sessions a week: all are group activities except the individual therapy.

The staff members meet regularly, usually in the morning, and confer every two weeks with a consulting psychoanalytic colleague. The staff of each unit consists of nurses, social workers, teachers, and a female and male psychotherapist who are psychologists and/or medical doctors either fully trained or analysts in training. To facilitate the adolescent's identity development, great importance is attached to a balanced ratio of female and male staff members. Because of the autonomy of the small staff of each unit, a great deal of group cohesion and exchange of information exists. This is an indispensable prerequisite to creating an adequate containing function of the unit.

The program of the inpatient units differs slightly. Here the adolescents together with the care-workers cook for themselves and perform domestic chores. The caretakers work according to the primary caretaker system; this means that each adolescent has a primary caretaker with whom he or she may develop a more personal relationship within the functioning of the group.

Admission to the units takes place after several interviews, which include family sessions and a trial visit of several days. After several months of treatment, some of the adolescents attend a regular school outside the clinic, while others attend a vocational school for professional training. The clinic has a network of connections to a variety of businesses where the adolescents do several three- to four-week practicals.

Object Relations, Projective Identification, and the Container

The psychopathological dynamic of the adolescents treated in the clinic has a specific characteristic that the treatment concept must take into account. The "flight into the peer group" is typical of adolescence.[3] The adolescent subculture, the peer group, serves as an organization into which desires, fantasies, and relationship needs can be projected. The peer group can take in all those externalizations that help adolescents extricate themselves from unconscious incestuous entanglement. This flight can only happen if the adolescent has developed a sufficient hunger for relationships. For many of the adolescents in the clinic, the struggle for independence is not the central issue. Most are in a state of regressive dependency; thus, the theoretical understanding of this state forms the basis for analytic work. Quite a number of adolescents have infantile needs and desires as well as great difficulties in distinguishing between inner and outer reality. For example, they tend to treat all people indiscriminately according to the dominant internal object relation, so that they hardly differentiate between the functions of doctor, psychotherapist, primary care-worker, or nurse, let alone the individuality of these people. The transference is archetypal rather than personal, and so it has a particular force that is difficult to handle.

Jung's essay, "Marriage as a Psychological Relationship," has relevance here. In it, Jung makes an interesting observation about the problems of relationship in marriage in which the more developed personality functions as a container and the less developed personality as the contained. One person, he argues, can contain a part of someone else.[4] Jung refers to this idea again in his 1946 essay, "The Psychology of Transference," in which he locates the effectiveness of the unconscious emotional contact in the analytic relationship in the "participation mystique" of unconscious identity between analyst and patient.[5] In the same year, Melanie Klein described for the first time an analogous process taking place in the mother-baby relationship which she called "projective identification," and which refers to a number of distinct yet related processes connected with splitting and projection.[6] Projective identification can be used as a defense: it is used to rid the self of unwanted parts. It operates in the area of unconscious fantasy and can include the fantasy of omnipotently intruding into another in order to be fused or confused with the object, the concrete fantasy of passively living inside the object, and the belief of oneness of feeling with the object. It can also be used for the expulsion of tension by someone who has been traumatized as a child by violent intrusion.[7] In projective identification, there is an element that is projected, the contained or object, and the container. Projective identification is also used for communication. Widely acknowledged by the majority of psychoanalytic schools is the idea that the dynamic of emotional and fantasy exchange taking place between a mother and a baby at a preverbal level also develops in the analytic relationship. The concept of the container and its relationship to the idea of projective identification as a preverbal form of communication has been developed by the English post-Kleinian analyst W. R. Bion. He has written about the various forms of container-contained relationships and from this theory he derived a developmental theory of thinking.

One of Bion's three models of thinking is built on Klein's ideas that innate knowledge is based on the inherent expectation that the union of two objects, the oedipal union, creates a third that is more than the sum of the two parts. In the generation of thought arising out of emotional experience, an innate preconception, the neural and anatomical expectancy of the mouth for a nipple, meets a realization when the real nipple enters the mouth. The result is the formation of a conception.[8] Conceptions form satisfying conjunctions in which a preconception meets an adequate realization.[9] Conceptions are then available for thought processes. Bion's theory has the great advantage of relating psychotic disturbances of the thinking process to the early mother-baby interaction and thereby facilitates the analytic understanding of such disturbances.

The Regressed Adolescent Patient

Since the adolescents treated in the clinic have severe disturbances and live, both internally and externally, in a regressed stated of dependency, they have no age-appropriate relationship with their peers. The archetypal dimension of the severity of this kind of regressive dependency can be illustrated by the beginning of a Russian fairy tale called, "The Tale of the King of the Woods, Named Oh."

> A long time ago there was an old man and his wife who had only one son. But their son did not turn out well, and he was terribly lazy. All day long he did nothing at all, not even wash himself with cold water but spent all his time lying by the fireside running his fingers through the millet seeds. He was already twenty years old, but still he sat by the fireside without his trousers on and never moved away from it. The sad parents wanted him to work and earn money, but he wasn't interested in working at all and just kept sitting by the fireside, running his fingers through the millet seeds. The father apprenticed him to a tailor, but after three days the boy ran away, crept back to the fireplace, and ran his fingers through the millet seeds. His father beat him and sent him first to a shoemaker and then to a blacksmith but the boy ran away time and time again. Finally his father decided to take the lazybones into another kingdom and give him away to the first person he met.
> After a long hike, the father and son came to a big, dark wood. To rest a little, the father sat down on a charred tree stump and groaned, "Oh, I am so tired." As soon as he had spoken these words, a little old man with a long, green beard crawled out of the tree stump and asked the father what he wanted from him. The father was astonished and wanted to send him

away, but the old man said, "So you didn't call me. . . . but of course you did call me. I am Oh, the King of the Woods. Why did you call me?"

After some discussion, the father agreed to apprentice his son to the King of the Woods. They agreed that the father was only allowed to take his son back after a year if he could recognize him. If not, the son would have to stay with the King of the Woods for another year. Then they parted and the King of the Woods led the son into another kingdom underneath the world and into a green cabin. . . .[10]

The story has a happy ending: the son marries the daughter of the czar. In psychoanalytic terms, the King of the Woods represents an archetypal father figure, a magician who initiates the transformative processes. In the clinic, adolescents are rarely transformed to the point that they can no longer be recognized, but they live, like the Russian son in the fairy tale, in a state of internal and external infantile dependency on their parents. The patients' demand for care and their defensive passivity often take the character of a total defense against any chances for development at all. This is what distinguishes them from most adolescents in their peer group at an age when changes in development occurs rapidly and risk-taking behavior occurs frequently.

An example of this total dependency can be seen in the case of a mother who not only prepares lunch for her son to bring to the day unit but also bathes and washes him. This almost incestuous, or at least para-incestuous, relationship corresponds to a very infantile relationship with his mother in the boy's internal world. In their thinking, feeling, and actions, these adolescents experience themselves as indistinguishable and unseparated from their parents. Erich Neumann, an Israeli Jungian analyst, has described such regressed states of minds in terms of the relationship of the ego to the collective unconscious. Such states correspond to a mythological one in which consciousness is totally under the "domination of the Uroborous"[11] because separation from the "world-parent" has not yet taken place:

> Owing to the distortion of the infantile ego, the pleasure-pain components are experienced inseparately from one another, or at any rate the object of experience is colored by a mixture of both. The nonseparation of opposites and the resultant ambivalence of the ego towards all objects evoke a feeling of fear and impotence. The world is uroboric and supreme, whether this uroboric supremacy be experienced as the world or the unconscious, one's environment, or one's own body."[12]

This attitude is often revealed in individual therapy, a prime example being when adolescents cannot imagine their parents as a couple. In fact, the concept of a couple simply does not appear in the fantasies they bring to individual therapy. They resist and are repelled by the emergence of such fantasies, often in a schizoid way. One boy was completely convinced that only a computer could have given birth to him. Another adolescent, who had strong doubts about whether he was the natural child of his parents, expressed it in the following way: "If it wasn't done artificially, it must at least have been real torture for my parents to produce me, and now they are stuck with having to take care of me." The lack of an inner image of the parents as a sexually active couple is an adolescent defense against the infantile aggression that wishes to attack the union of mother and father and gain sole possession of one parent.[13]

The difficulty arising from this lack of differentiation from the parents lies in the fact that the state of nonseparation is not necessarily experienced as paradise. The dependent relationships of early childhood are characterized by longing for this very state of "heavenly passivity," yet at the same time it is felt to be threatening. Situations of dependency cause early affects such as greed, envy, rage, jealousy, and helplessness to develop much more rapidly and intensely than in situations that are less characterized by total dependency (which to some extent an institutional treatment facilitates). The adolescents do their utmost to prevent these feelings of dependency from becoming conscious. As a consequence, their passivity often has a pronounced aggressive character. Aggressive passivity as a defense against changes that are necessary for development is very effective, because it also nurses the illusion of autonomy, omnipotence, and strength.

Many of the teenagers we work with still live, psychically, in a state of incest, and are tied to their primary objects with very strong ambivalence. This state of mind has a disastrous effect on the development of their identity, in that they have not developed sufficient self-representation; their self is still widely fused with the self of their mother. This situation may result in an internal concept where the parents have the character of archaic part objects. In an inpatient setting that promotes regression, these concepts are quickly mobilized and projected into the structure and the staff in a splitting manner. At first, the reintegration of these split-off elements is more difficult than in an outpatient setting. On the other hand, the fabric of the clinic, and the many facilities for creative work, offer a relatively impersonal relation to the threatening objects, which is experienced as much less frightening than in a traditional therapeutic relationship. The individual psychotherapy, as well as relations between teachers and adolescents, are deliberately managed in a rather distant way for long periods of time. As psychoanalysts and staff members, we understand ourselves to be objects that restrain and direct the anxiety. Attacks on the physical or psychic qualities of the clinic and staff are understood as attacks on internal objects, and when they take place, the primary care worker tries to arrange a therapeutic conversation in the actual context of the adolescent's life. The American analyst, Redl, called this situation a "life space interview."[14] It is a noninterpretative way of talking with adolescents that presupposes a certain knowledge of their inner world and the history of their object relations. Unfortunately, this technique is very difficult to learn.

The Clinic as Container

It is helpful to apply the model of "container-contained" to the therapeutic milieu when treating severely disturbed children and adolescents in institutions because institutional treatment itself intensifies the problems of dependency. When conflicts emerge within the institution, primitive affects and the fantasies related to them surface faster and in a more vehement way than they do within the family structure. The clinic as a container, represented by the staff and by the physical structure of the building, promotes in the adolescent patient the feeling of being held. Just as the mother contains aspects of the baby's experience that he cannot yet tolerate, holds them, thinks about them, gives them a name, and returns them to him in "digestible" form, so too the clinic and its staff contain the fantasies, feigns, and projections of the adolescent patient, transforming, purifying, and decontaminating them before they are given back to the patient in the form of educational or therapeutic interventions. Through this intensive psychic process of exchange, the container too changes in the way that Jung once described: "When two chemical substances are combined, both are altered. This is precisely what happens in the transference." The changes in the clinic as container can be observed in the fantasies and intense feelings aroused in the psychotherapists during individual therapy and in the staff during the daily running of the clinic.

An example from a staff meeting illustrates these changes: one discussion centered around a boy who had managed successfully to manipulate the staff members. He did this by splitting off violent, aggressive, and persecuted parts of his personality that he could not tolerate in himself and projecting them into the institution by distributing them, in a set of multiple transference relationships, among the members of staff. This led the staff to articulate a feeling of paralyzing resignation and a general wish, more or less openly expressed, to get rid of the boy as soon as possible. During the discussion among the members of the staff involved in working with this boy, the group managed to put together again the parts of him that he had split off and projected into them. As a result of this group process, the image of the boy's "monstrosity" diminished to manageable proportions and the intensity of the anxieties related to him decreased so that they could be contained and did not need to be acted out. The working through of this dynamic during the staff meeting transformed the emotional atmosphere completely. Such a change produced a different attitude in the staff towards the patient resulting in a subsequent positive effect on our therapeutic and educational approach when dealing with him.

As far as the patient is concerned, the group functions as a container for the totality of his self, and the patient will be able to experience in the course of treatment a state which Jung describes as "his own indivisible unity." As a result, we attribute the same importance to the influence of the adolescents on the therapeutic setting as we do to the influence of the setting on the adolescents. Even though we try to make the everyday life of the clinic comprehensible to them by a relatively firm structure in which the interpersonal boundaries are clearly drawn, the adolescents' regressive attitude and way of functioning, as well as their marked tendency to split off and disown large parts of their personalities, do strongly influence the emotional climate of the clinic. The only way to prevent a fragmentation of the therapeutic team, something which continually threatens to happen as an outward expression of the adolescent's tendency to fragmentation, is to practice a very detailed exchange of information during the supervision of staff, along with intensive psychodynamic thinking and reflection. Like the container the mother provides for the unbearably intense affects of her baby, we understand the day unit and the inpatient unit to be an extended *container* into which a great deal can be projected. Our primary goal is not the development of a trusting therapeutic relationship between two people. In the best cases, that relationship gradually develops during the adolescent's stay.

Individual Therapy in the Context of the Extended Container

In order to give the reader an idea of how an adolescent experiences his situation in the day unit, I shall outline a case from the point of view of individual psychotherapy. The same case will be described from the point of view of group psychotherapy in the paper "Group Therapy in a Day Care Setting" by H. Heidtke and M. Neumann-Schirmbeck.

The Case of Tom

Tom was seventeen when he was admitted to the day unit. He lived with his mother and his older sister; his father had moved out two years earlier. He suffered from severe anxiety attacks, hypochondriacal fears of becoming ill, and several compulsive symptoms. He had no contact at all with peers or other people outside his family. In spite of his intelligence and because of his symptoms, he had hardly attended school for several years. He never left the apartment alone, and inside it there was no privacy: the door of his room had to remain open all the time. Whenever he felt frightened, he slept next to his mother in the parental bedroom.

He was admitted to the clinic under pressure from legal authorities. Otherwise his parents would have lost custody of him through a court decision, because they had already broken off or boycotted several in- and outpatient treatments for him. Because of this very difficult initial situation, we were quite skeptical about the chances of his remaining with us at all.

At the beginning of treatment he reported the following dream:

He, his father, and the teenagers in the day unit had all gone swimming near his apartment. The lake turned into a muddy mush consisting of mud and liquid manure. While all the others went on swimming, he and his father were unable to move; they were stuck in the mud up to their chests. After a while he was able to escape to a higher place.

At the beginning of the session. Tom had talked about his fear of dying or being injured. When questioned about the dream, he only made the dry remark, "I think this dream is crazy." But since I expressed interest in this "crazy stuff," and he was an obedient boy, he began to show some interest in the dream too. He said that he and his father had never in their lives been able to keep up with the others, and that somehow they were always stuck in the mud. At this point I did not interpret the dream communication about the transference to me but explicitly referred to the group situation in it. This was done to allow time for a positive experience of the extended container to develop, within which the transference to the psychotherapist can bloom spontaneously. I pointed out that his decision to come to the day unit had really got him involved in quite a dangerous adventure. After that, and during the following weeks, he repeatedly described a traumatic experience: at the age of fourteen he had been taken against his will to his first appointment in a child psychiatric inpatient unit and some violence had been used to overcome his resistance. For months he used the individual therapy session to talk about this violent separation from his mother and to discuss his father's shortcomings. During this period of therapy, no progress was made.

He said that his father was "a zero, or even a minus zero, if there is such a thing. My father is a seller of souls." He expressed his thinking and feelings in terms of binary computer logic: for him there was only one answer to everything, either yes or no, 1 or 0, for the mother or against the father. He tried everything to make me feel like a 1, which meant good, and he turned his father into an absolute 0. Whatever I said or did, it was always right and good, and he turned everything I said or felt about him into something positive. This massive resistance in the form of a mother-transference was as effective as if he had turned all my comments into something negative. I never had the impression that any of my remarks, feelings, or fantasies really got to him, even though he accepted everything that was presented to him quite willingly and obediently. In this way, at first, he succeeded in completely preventing us from working on his identification with his mother and his dependency on her. These avoidance techniques were perfectly understandable: the anger, depression, and retaliation anxieties caused by his disappointment in his mother and his initial separation from her would have been impossible for him to bear at that time.

After eight months he told me a dream in which he was again swimming with the whole group of teenagers from the unit:

When he was in the water he could see how eggs hatched and baby ducklings hopped into the lake. He felt an intense impulse to take care that the ducklings did not drown, because he was not sure if they were able to swim such a short time after leaving their eggs.

When commenting on the dream, he said, that he had felt utterly relaxed, "so removed from everything," as he put it. In a previous sessions he had for the first time made a critical remark about the attitude his mother had shown during a family session. Meanwhile he had developed a more differentiated attitude towards the other adolescents in the day unit, although he was still quite isolated. He tried to make himself useful by doing all sorts of errands for the others. I now suggested that he might have felt good in the dream because, contrary to his own expectations, he had found that he really was able to swim after leaving his home-egg and coming to the day unit. He said that at home it had actually been much worse than at the day unit, and he felt as if he were in the bilge of a sinking ship when he was at home. When I said, "In the bilge of a ship in which you were locked?", he replied, "I would have sunk, together with my mother, without even getting wet!"

His metaphor of the sinking ship symbolized the "claustrum," that Meltzer, a post-Kleinian analyst, discusses in his work.[15] Tom was locked in projective identification inside his mother's body, specifically the bottom part of her body. The image also illustrates his situation in the external world. In the day unit he was completely isolated: there were no windows or doors through which the other adolescents could come into contact with him. Because he transferred his inner state of mind onto his relationship with me in the therapy, he became more aware that the group of adolescents and adults in the day unit was not a dead, locked up "claustrum." Instead it was a place full of life, rivalry, feelings, and relationships. He had split his internal mother into two archetypal images: the death mother, (figured as the bilge of the sinking ship), and the mother full of babies, (the ducklings and his siblings in the day unit) whom he wished to protect. He projected the death mother into our relationship, and this caused extreme transference resistance in individual therapy. The first step for Tom was to develop a positive archetypal image of the container, the clinic. Then, as a second step, he was later able to develop this image in individual psychotherapy by fulfilling his negative archetypal expectations in the modifying container of his ordinary, human, and personal experience with me.

The defense of splitting also enables the adolescent to make a helpful separation between the archetypal and personal aspects of his objects. Since the clinic, as an extended container, triggers not only negative but also positive archetypal patterns, the adolescent has much more freedom to project his split-off parts in a kind of rotating system into a variety of people. This may be the reason he feels less frightened and persecuted in the group situation. Young people often try to escape from home into the peer group, which serves as an important container for their projections. For this reason, within the overall therapy provided by the clinic, individual therapy is often dominated for a long time by extraordinarily intense resistance.

Countertransference of the Care-Workers

As much as the container function of the clinic is held by the individual and group psychotherapeutic setting, the structure and behavior of care-workers is an important part of the extended container. Unlike teachers and therapists, the primary care-workers are involved with the day-to-day care of the adolescents and have to react promptly to their behavior and handle it in a practical way. The regressed adolescents will always try, by means of projective identification, to turn their primary care-workers into "baddies," slave drivers, or dictators, according to their own unconscious expectations. The type of projective identification employed here is usually the violent evacuation of painful states of mind: in fantasy the adolescent forcibly enters the object for immediate relief, often with the aim of gaining intimidating control of the object. The same is also true of their unconscious positive expectations which the staff feel impelled to fulfill. As psychotherapists one is accustomed to being experienced as the horrible parents by the patients, and it is often very difficult to endure. The nonanalytic members of staff who have not had our experience and must deal with the day-to-day care of the patients are constantly in danger of being pushed, unconsciously, into action, because their mode of care is active, and not reflective. As recipients of the adolescent's projective identifications, primary care-workers may find themselves acting out or embodying certain archetypal roles. Because the patients often cannot distinguish between the concrete and the symbolic or the personal and the archetypal, little problems of daily life can assume an archetypal dimension. For example, some frustration about the "wrong" bread at breakfast can cause an eruption of aggression towards the worker who is seen as a monster parent, an ugly witch who lets the children starve or wants to poison them. To counteract this, the nonanalytic staff members tend to bend over backwards; this seems to he a tendency found more in a psychotherapeutic clinic than in other settings. At the same time, the process works with positive projective identifications, and it can be tempting for the care-worker to identify with the all-nurturing good mother, or the one with perfect understanding who is infinitely superior to the other clumsy and imperceptive staff members. The adolescents' demands for infantile dependency are great. Shift changes and the time of the routine daily staff meetings provide a means of measuring and evaluating the degree of autonomy achieved by the adolescent group. During these times, the adolescents may use direct or indirect maneuvers to disturb or hinder the meeting by uttering complaints like, "You never have time for us!" The situation may also change quickly. Once, when the inpatients had several love affairs with each other, with a consequent shifting in couple alliances, they did not have the slightest interest in finding out what the adults were doing behind closed doors. In fact, they were perfectly happy that the adults were out of the way, while the adults themselves began to worry about a striking silence in the unit and wondered what the young people were up to. The adolescent group had for a short time, so to speak, progressed beyond the oedipal stage.

In adolescence both pre-oedipal and genital wishes manifest themselves at the same time, and this can create further complications for the primary care-worker. Early, childlike regressive wishes to be dependent and cared for could be mistaken by the care-worker for erotic genital wishes, and he or she might distance themselves out of insecurity or anxiety. On the other hand, the adolescents' sexually seductive behaviour could be mistakenly treated as exhibitionism and dealt with by mothering them as if they were little children. In both cases the danger remains that the seductiveness of the adolescent may be responded to by the staff with sexualized signals. As in individual therapy, a regularly and systematically applied team supervision by an external supervisor helps the situation.

Conclusion

To apply the concept of the container/contained to groups enriches the psychodynamic work with adolescents within an institution. The adolescents live in a transitional space between their family and an established position in the society. Normally their relationship to peers and groups of all different kinds helps them to cope with this transitional stage. In the institutional treatment of severely disturbed adolescents who often cannot appropriately relate to peer groups, it is very helpful to create a group situation where the group can serve as a container to hold together all their defensively split-off parts.

There are different kinds of container/contained relationships in the structure of the clinic: first, the clinic as a whole in its physical, personal, and psychic appearance; second, the special unit (inpatient or day-care unit) where the adolescents live together with their care-workers; third, the container/contained relationship within the individual psychotherapeutic relationship; fourth, the intrapsychic container/contained relationship as it grows through development and differentiation of the internal object relations in the patients. If one assumes that there is a strong mutual relationship between inner and outer reality, this model helps the adolescents to differentiate their psychic structure according to their perception of the outer reality of the clinic. It is our experience that without systematic work on the container function of the clinic, even the most sophisticated individual psychotherapy will not be successful. On the other hand the psychotherapists' knowledge about the internal world of their patient helps them to understand the transference the staff has on the patient and thus helps them to counsel and support the care-workers in their daily work with the adolescents.

Notes

1. S. Freud, *Standard Edition,* v.10.
2. W. Bion, *Attention and Interpretation* (London: Tavistock, 1970), p. 72.
3. D. Meltzer, "Identification and Socialization in Adolescence," in *Sexual States of Mind.* (London: Clunie, 1973), p. 42.
4. C. G. Jung, "Marriage as a Psychological Relationship," in *The Development of Personality, Collected Works* (London: Routledge and Kegan Paul, 1954, rev. ed. 1964) v.17, para. 331–2.
5. C. G. Jung, "The Psychology of Transference," in *The Practice of Psychotherapy, Collected Works* (London: Routledge and Kegan Paul, 1954) v. 16, para. 376.

6. M. Klein, "Some Notes on Schizoid Mechanisms," in *Envy and Gratitude and Other Works, 1946–1963.* (London: Hogarth, 1975).

7. R. Hinshelwood, "Projective Identification," *A Dictionary of Kleinian Thought* (London: Free Association Books, 1989) p. 187.

8. W. Bion, "Attacks on Linking," *Second Thoughts* (London: Maresfield Library, 1967).

9. Hinshelwood, p. 190.

10. H. von Beit, *Gegensatz und Erneuerung in Märchen,* (Bern and Munich: Franke, 1972).

11. The "Uroborous" is a primal state of wholeness and undifferentiatedness symbolized by the snake or dragon that bites its own tail.

12. E. Neumann, "The Great Mother," *The Origins and History of Consciousness.* (London: Routledge and Kegan Paul, 1954), p. 41.

13. See M. Klein, *The Psycho-Analysis of Children* (London: Hogarth, 1932).

14. F. Redl, "The Life Space Interview," *Working With Difficult Children* (London: Free Press, 1966).

15. See D. Meltzer, *The Claustrum,* (London: Clunie, 1992); *Sexual States of Mind,* (London: Clunie, 1973); *Studies in Extended Metapsychology,* (London: Clunie, 1982).

16

Group Therapy in a Day Care Setting

Heide Heidtke and Michael Neumann-Schirmbeck

Analytical Psychology and Group Psychotherapy

Analytical psychology has paid almost no attention to group psychology and forms of psychotherapy that are based on group processes. One reason for this is that Jung was critical of group mentality and negative about group therapy. Instead, the psychotherapy of analytical psychology focuses on the development of the individual:

> I therefore consider it the prime task of psychotherapy today to pursue with singleness of purpose the goal of individual development. So doing, our efforts will follow nature's own striving to bring life to the fullest possible fruition in each individual, for only in the individual can life fulfill its meaning.[1]

From Jung's perspective the value of a group lies more in its educational aspects than in any therapeutic experience:

> From my point of view group therapy is only capable of educating the *social* human being.[2]

Only in the last twenty years have Jungian analysts written about group psychotherapy with adults. One major objective in working with groups is that the group has to learn to be aware of the parallels between inner processes and external social interactions. A basic Jungian approach to group psychotherapy is to focus on the opposites individual/collective.[3]

A further Jungian approach to group therapy deals with the self of the group and takes the group as the external representation of the self in the child's and adolescent's inner world.[4] This approach is derived from Jung's idea about the self and the family; Jung points out that the individual in childhood is

> still a long way from wholeness. Wholeness is represented by the family, and its components are still projected upon the members of the family and personified by them.[5]

The Open Group Milieu versus Group Therapy

The day unit is part of a psychotherapeutic hospital for children and adolescents. The psychotherapeutic concept and organization of the hospital is described in "The Clinic as a Container" by Gustav Bovensiepen. Participation in group therapy starts immediately after an adolescent is admitted to the day unit. Individual therapy can be delayed for a while. Initially it is important that the patient becomes accustomed to the adolescent group and finds a place within the milieu of the unit. Thus we consider all our work in the hospital to be open group work (Gruppenarbeit) as opposed to group therapy in the sense of a closed group. The general group dynamic in the unit is experienced as the mediator of a corrective social experience. We see this experience as the irreducible foundation for the success of what we offer therapeutically, because the dynamic forces within a group of rather disturbed adolescents are massive and need to be constantly structured and managed by the staff. By contrast, group therapy becomes a space for corrective emotional experiences aimed primarily at producing intrapsychic change.

Against this background, the group dynamic of the unit (the open group) takes place in an arena where the adolescent can act out. What he does, therefore, is up to him. In acting out, the adolescent gains new social experiences. These experiences are very important for our adolescents because most of them live in an extremely withdrawn situation at home. The adolescents in the unit act in a way that is comparable to the acting within a peer group.

To further understand the group psychodynamic, it is helpful to apply the container/contained model. Even though this model is derived from the dyadic mother-child relation, we can apply it to the group situation in the unit: the open group of the unit is the container where the group psychotherapy, the containment, occurs. As the fantasies or feelings are projected into the mother/therapist, they will be transformed and then given back in the form of educational or therapeutic interventions. Our experience is that the group therapy (the contained) has a strong effect on the open group of the unit (the container). Conversely the dynamic of the unit (as a container) influences permanently the dynamic of group therapy (the contained). By contrast to the open group in the unit, the group therapy, and especially the presence of the therapists as parental figures, creates an extended family.

The difference between the open group and the therapeutic group can be illustrated by describing the "pecking order" that emerges. A patient who plays the boss of the group in the unit appears as a little boy in the group therapy. Here he may be very insecure and anxious, while outside the therapy he tries to compensate by acting out. Another adolescent frequently tries to come close to the girls in the unit with a strong "macho" approach; he wears fighting dress, walks broad-legged and seems to be bubbling over with energy. However in the group therapy he appears as a little boy, vulnerable, full of anxieties, and with feminine traits. When the girls address his "macho" behaviour in the group therapy, he can only react by crying.

The group therapy session lasts ninety minutes, once a week, and takes place in the room where patients also have their family therapy sessions. All the adolescents in the program must attend group therapy as well as other group activities. This means that they must be present in the room, but are not compelled to engage in the process. For example, it can happen that an adolescent sits in the corner of the room with his back turned to the group or remains silent during the session. One of the group psychotherapy techniques we apply is psychodrama. This technique makes it possible to guide the adolescent from imagination to action, thus helping him to build up a link between his experiences (including actions) and his inner situation during the group therapy session. The adolescent's capacity to enact demands a relatively stable ego to contain and give form to crowding unconscious impulses.

In groups with adolescents a minimal structuring of the process facilitates the therapeutically effective regression: the interventions are ego-supportive compared with the technique used in analytic groups with adults. One cannot always wait "until something happens"; rather the therapist acts as a real "other" to the adolescent and must act as authentically as possible. Authenticity and spontaneity, while keeping the necessary distance, satisfies the adolescent's need of genuineness in contact and his need to orient himself in relation to adults.

An important question is how to deal with the silence of the adolescents in the group meeting. It is difficult to handle this kind of defense analytically. However, for the group dynamic, it is not helpful to abstain from intervention completely because the adolescents' anxieties increase to a dangerous level. This is why we try to interpret the initial silence very early. On the other hand, transference plays an essential role because of the need for regression in the group process.

Transference within the Group Process

In comparison with groups of adults, transference is much stronger and develops instantly in adolescent analysis. In individual psychotherapy, the therapist is used much more as a figure of the adolescent's inner life, as an object of his fantasies, projections and identifications. In group therapy, the therapist is more of a "real person" for the adolescent's orientation. The adolescent seeks an authority in the therapist with whom she or he can both progressively identify and with whom he can fight. In our group therapy setting, two therapists always work together. This gives the adolescent more space to react. We think this is more effective because the adolescent has to protect himself less than if only one therapist were present. It is clear that this "protection" is a result of splitting mechanisms, which unfold better in the presence of two therapists. Also, the constellation of a female and a male therapist promotes the parental transference. This approach also relieves the burden on the therapists because they can share roles spontaneously or tactically. However we have to pay attention to the danger of always presenting ourselves as a united front; otherwise a striving for harmony will predominate and hinder lively, conflict-oriented work. Only when the group members can recognize conflicts and rivalry between the group leaders will their fears of the "strong parental figures" lessen. In the group, sibling rivalry and primitive oedipal fantasies come up directly, and the therapist couple triggers the unconscious fantasy of the combined parents being locked up in permanent intercourse.[6] The English analyst, Melanie Klein, sees the combined parent figures as the most threatening persecutors in the inner life of the child.[7] There is also the other side of the coin: severely disturbed adolescents have the possibility of experiencing not only their anxieties and their envy, but also an ongoing process of unlocking and locking up within the couple. This is according to the archetypal need for a functioning couple, the image of the *hierosgamos* in alchemical terms.[8] In our view this need is not simply persecuting: it facilitates the adolescent's ability to distinguish between father and mother and to establish a good relationship with each parental figure, even if, at the beginning and during a long period of therapy, the transference is dominated by a splitting of the "good" and the "bad" object.

On Psychodrama

Our group's psychotherapeutic approach to the specific characteristics of adolescence is the combination of analytically-oriented group therapy with psychodrama techniques. The specific characteristics are: striving for autonomy, identity problems, separation anxiety, model seeking, and low threshold of fear due to a relative ego weakness. It is necessary to sort out a sense of the group process through analytic observation, while psychodrama techniques help to reach the desired goal by psychodramatically working through the offered material.

Psychodrama provides helpful and clear boundaries between phases of the process; these are warming up, acting, and closing, and they help the adolescent to act out unconscious conflicts within a given framework. These supportive boundaries facilitate regression and help contain anxieties. At the same time, the presence of the others provides ego-support, because the adolescent can split his transference and distribute it among his fellow actors. If one, exclusive transference relationship predominated, it would be much too threatening and would inhibit group interaction.

There are two main forms of psychodrama: roleplay and improvisation. We often use future-oriented themes; this enables the adolescent to experiment with his fantasies and imaginings without too high a risk that he will get stuck either in the consequences of his actions or in one set of feelings about himself and others. Compared to analytic psychotherapy, in psychodrama the adolescent enacts his story, he does not tell it. The Austrian psychotherapist, Moreno, who developed the psychodrama technique, stated: "Enacting is more healing than talking"[9]; here enacting is understood as a preliminary stage of knowledge. The enactment happens strictly in the here and now, and this meets the adolescent's defensive tendency to cling to the present. The play as a form of imagination makes it possible that the remembered, the hoped, the dreamt, and the feared, both past and future, can be brought into the present, beyond real life. Through the dramatic living out, a "cathartic action," deeper levels of the psyche become available that are often closed off to verbal remembering and to the dawning of consciousness. The representation in psychodrama is a form of enactment that needs to be clearly distinguished from "acting out" as psychoanalysis uses this concept.

Classical psychodrama proceeds in three phases. Warming up creates the mood in the group for the events to come. We usually begin with what we call the "flashlight": the adolescents say a few words about what they are mentally working over and whether they have brought a theme for today. The play acting phase creates the frame for group or protagonist-centered acting. At times, one scene may be enough to get to the heart of the problem, at others, many scenes need to be enacted for the therapeutic process to get started and a catharsis to be reached.

A protagonist-centered play happens when, during the warm-up phase, an adolescent has been able to express clearly what he is concerned with and what is on his mind. On the other hand the readiness to enact may be manifested nonverbally, for instance through motor restlessness, facial expression of agitation, and other physical signs such as sweating, shivering, or crying. Sometimes the readiness is reinforced by the group on a more social level. For example, when one patient absolutely refuses to submit to a special regulation in the daily life of the unit and the group suffers from the consequences of this behavior. When a group member is ready to play a single protagonist, there are a variety of modes of working through: a dream, a fantasy, a symbol or a scene from the past or the present may be represented. In our group it has often been an actual experience in the present that kicks off the play; for example, a problem with the mother on returning home, a misunderstanding with the teacher in class, or a fight among the adolescent group members.

Psychodrama requires the adolescent to identify in succession and in a variety of ways with the various people of his drama. The repeated role changes promote his capacity to identify empathetically with different roles and this is a way to come closer to an emotional experience of facets of inner objects which are projected in the play onto members of the group. Even if this is not interpreted within the group process by the therapist, it facilitates the adolescent's capacity to work on it in individual analytic therapy.

Role changes apply to the technique of being a "double": here a peer or a therapist works for a short time behind the protagonist and tries to "feel into" the protagonist and to verbalize thoughts, fantasies, or feelings that the protagonist does not yet know or does not dare express. The capacity to "double" requires an ego structure which is not too deficient. Thus it is understandable that in a group with severely disturbed adolescents it is often the therapist's task to double or to facilitate role changes. The closing talk phase of the group therapy immediately follows the psychodramatic action and serves as a working through and an integration of what has just been experienced.

In "sharing," the group members tell the protagonist experiences from their own lives that are the same or similar, so that the protagonist feels understood in a special way and can recognize that one is not alone with the particular difficulties. In "feedback," the actors speak about their different experiences in playing their roles. Whether as audience or as actors, they will have identified with one or more of the characters being portrayed, and they are encouraged to speak about these identifications. The actors will have asked themselves, or we will ask them, what it meant for them to be chosen by that particular peer for that particular role. They are asked if they have recognized anything familiar about themselves. Sharing, telling of the same or similar experiences, comes rather easily, but feedback is more difficult and is often mixed with sharing. Thus in this final phase, working through of the psychodramatic events takes place and is intended to be an integration of new experiences and an awareness of present experience and behavior. However, this ideal final phase does not often occur with the adolescent patients in our day unit, but all group members are more or less involved. If it is sometimes not possible for the adolescents to describe things verbally, they can do it by painting the most scary, the most exciting, or the most beautiful scene of this session. In Moreno's approach the therapeutic effect was reached when the group members and the group leaders are able to give feedback about what they have experienced during the play, their feelings, thoughts or fantasies as actors as well as audience. In addition to this "classical" psychodrama technique we do make analytic interpretations, but we clothe them in comments about "sharing" or "feedback."

Paul: A Protagonist-centered Play

The psychodrama represents within the therapeutic group a form of alpha function: affects, body sensations, actions (Bion's beta elements) are transformed by the members of the group (and probably by the group-ego) into dreams, imaginings, and thoughts, which then can be verbalized and enacted.[10] We have the impression that the unfolding of the group's alpha function is a special advantage of the group therapy and can serve as an indicator of the group's capacity for containment and of the maturity of the group's cohesion. In Jungian terms it throws a light on what Jung called the transcendent function, whose main function is to create links between different psychic states and attitudes.[11] According to Jung the transcendent function represents the individual's capacity to symbolize.

The following case illustrates how the group can provide the transcendent function for a group member in case this group member is not capable of symbolizing its overwhelming affects and psychosomatic sensations (beta elements). This case also shows the technique of a protagonist-centered play.

Paul was adopted at the age of twenty months by his parents. This adoption was finalized against considerable opposition on the part of the local authorities, among other reasons because of the couple's age, the father being fifty-four and the mother fifty-two. Paul joined our program shortly before leaving his secondary school; he was seventeen. His adoptive parents described him as having always been a difficult child. His development had always lagged behind the average; for example, he had not started talking before the age of four. Throughout his childhood and teenage years he was very withdrawn, a "loner." All free time activities were undertaken with his mother. At home Paul and his mother shared the bedroom and the living room while the father had his own room in their home, which he himself had planned and built.

When Paul started school, his parents reported problems with motor coordination and speech. He had not been given professional help. Since his father, who had a degree in engineering, considered him less talented than his mother did, these difficulties justified the mother's dedicating all her time to help Paul with his schoolwork. This family arrangement carried on until the father reached retirement. After this point Paul's symptoms increased and his performance in school worsened to such an extent that the school authorities had to intervene. The father's retirement had apparently threatened and partially destroyed the "harmonious relationship" with his mother. Paul found himself in competition with his father, who confronted him with considerable demands. Paul reacted by asking questions that seemed to be crazy. This drove the very compulsive father to despair and reinforced his conviction that this kid was "insane." The father's performance standards resulted in Paul's being consistently expected to perform beyond his capacities. Paul tried to compensate by a regressive clinging to his mother. The mother, just as clinging and anxious, colluded with his behaviour and prevented him from achieving age-appropriate development. The change was so striking that, in spite of the fact that he had only another half year of school to complete, he was no longer able to manage school. The "real couple" in this family was formed by Paul and his mother. In family sessions, it soon became clear that the father was experienced by both of them as the trouble-maker.

At this stage of therapy, we noticed in Paul increasingly delusional fantasies, leading to grandiose ones. He described the home milieu with his father and mother as a "balance of terror" and the confrontation between his family and the day unit as a "fight of giants." This language indicates that Paul lived in an inner world of alternating grandiose fantasies and terrifying visions. In his individual therapy sessions, the themes shifted from prehistoric men to Watson's double helix to environmental issues. These fantasies went along with a state of agitation; his hands were in constant motion, and when excited he tended to grimace.

During his stay in the day unit his infantile ties to his mother could be increasingly loosened and his latent aggressive feelings against his parents came more to the fore. These changes led to an open opposition of the parents to the clinic. The father declared that Paul's low performance and his "strange behavior" was inherited, since he was not his natural son. In the daily life of the group in the unit Paul appeared to be very submissive. He was seldom oppositional, although what he did was usually explosive and not appropriate to the situation. In stress situations, he tended to grimace, which could be easily misinterpreted as laughter or shiftiness, as he tried to interpret his way out of difficulty. In such a situation Paul produced a pungent body odor which we understood as his way of expressing aggression.

During the group therapy sessions we could clearly see the style of his aggressive confrontations with his father. He expressed annihilation fantasies and stated, "the old man is crazy." Despite his aggressive tension he could follow the themes of the group therapy. In the beginning when he felt threatened, he would abruptly leave the room for a short time. In the end he could tolerate such situations and was also able to contribute some themes of his own for the group process. He became able for the first time to recognize and accept the solidarity his peers expressed to him. He continued to avoid engaging in competitive situations, although it became obvious that his own aggressive impulses and fantasies were coming much closer to consciousness. Once Paul reported at lunch that his parents were so worried about him that they wanted to take him out of the program. In the "flashlight" phase of the next group session it was intriguing how this theme moved everyone with varying degrees of intensity. Paul reported that his parents were very upset because after one year in the unit, from their point of view, his symptoms had not improved. They also complained that the clinic was messy because two bicycles had been left outside in the cold winter snow and had not been sheltered in the cellar.

The group session continued as follows: The group makes a proposal for tackling the theme; Mark and Ann suggest that Paul's family therapy meeting, planned for the next day, should be enacted in the group now. The others agree; they keep asking whether Paul really wants to go home? If not, then they must "toughen him up" with the play action. But one boy, Tom, refused the group's proposal; he had just joined the program. It became clear that he was very frightened of Paul's theme. The time of his stay in the unit had been too short to enable him to use the group situation as a protective and experimental space. On this occasion he withdrew to one corner behind the audience.

The session went on: Everybody then moves into one corner of the room, while Paul and one therapist remain in the space on the "psychodrama stage." First of all, they set up the room for the family session. Paul puts five chairs in a circle. Then he chooses the players, his ego-helpers. After some hesitation he chooses Susanne to play his mother, Jan his father, and makes them sit in the chairs. He wants the therapists to play themselves. Basically we handle it so that one therapist can have a role in the play while the other leads the drama. However, this time we felt that our model would not work well as we could see from the role casting that both the protagonist and the other players were going to need supportive doubling. We explain this to Paul and the group and Paul decides then to choose Mark and Martina to play the therapist's roles. The players need information in order to play their roles. Paul is therefore asked to stand behind Susanne who will play his mother, and double her, talking about her in the first person: "I am Paul's mother, I'm sixty-nine years old. Since Paul came to our family I have not gone to work; I have always been there for Paul." In order to expand the information, one of the therapists interviews Mrs. R., the mother, doubled by Paul: "How are things with you now that Paul isn't there? What do you do the whole day? How do you get along with your husband, since he is retired and is also at home during the day?" For a while Paul is thinking about these questions and seems to be surprised about his answer: "I miss Paul, I feel lonely without him. My husband stays in his summer house during the whole day and is occupied with his hobby, or he sits alone watching TV."

After this scene Paul doubles his father, a seventy-one year old, rigid, compulsive man, who frightens him. Obviously he has more difficulty talking about his father and is inhibited by his anxieties. Jan, in the father's role, says in a firm voice: "All right Paul, your mother and I have decided to take you back home." Paul, upset and unsure says: "Mummy how are you feeling at home? Are you lonely without me?" The mother confirms this and wants to say more but is interrupted by the father supportively doubled by a therapist, who, turning to the male therapist, says, "Mr. Neumann, you must admit that Paul is getting worse, he is even more confused and talks only of space travel and spacemen. We are going to take him home now. After all, he has a proper home. And when we die, he will have to go in a residential home anyway, because from the way it looks now he will not be able to take care of himself." Paul acts as if he had not heard his father's words, and returns to ask his mother who, supported by a therapist, describes her situation: she sits alone in her living room, which she used to share with Paul, the father has his own living room for himself which he does not want to share with anybody. She reminds Paul of the past good times they had together, how she always helped him with his homework, played with him, brought him his food. Questioned by the therapists, she describes how empty her life is now, how she is unable to get anything going with her husband, she just cannot reach him. The father keeps repeating harshly that Paul must come now, that the stay in the clinic has done him no good. It becomes clearer from the mother's reiteration of the "good old times" why it is that Paul is to be taken home: mainly to maintain the balance in the parental relationship. The five adolescents, who had no role to play in Paul's drama, are emotionally involved in the action. Two girls are crying and one keeps her fingers crossed for Paul. Irritated but fearful of his father and guilty about his mother, finally Paul says, "I want to stay on here, as least until Easter, while it is so cold" (it is November).

The drama is over and the four players are released from their roles and we ask them to say, "I am again Susanne, Martina, Jan, Mark." Then the group members reform their original circle. Everyone is still very affected. They tell Paul stories of similar experiences such as, "My mother is just like yours" or "Sometimes I think too that without me my parents would not know what to do with each other." Several urge Paul to tell his parents tomorrow just like he did today, and Mark adds at the end of the meeting with emotion, "We want to keep you with us!"

The psychodrama feedback techniques are intended to protect the protagonist from "interpretations" and advice but in the working through of Paul's psychodrama we allowed such expressions because they were making clear to Paul that the others liked him and wanted him to stay. Paul experienced for the first time in his life that in a group of his own peers he was appreciated and taken seriously. When specifically asked this, Paul verified that it was true.

Tom's Imagination of the Future: An Improvisation Play

Group play or an improvisation occur more frequently than a protagonist-centered play in our therapy. Usually the therapists try to formulate a motif that has developed out of the unconscious group fantasy during the warming-up phase. The topic and the place for the action are set. The adolescents must develop the play spontaneously and without any preparation.

The following segments of a session followed the discharge of a boy whose future seemed secure in the eyes of the other adolescents. In the opening round of the session, which involves making a resumé of the events of the preceding meeting, anxiety about the future and group fantasies about "visions of the future" become apparent. The therapists suggest a fantasy on the theme. "A glance into the future— five years from now," which will be presented as a vignette. Two adolescents, who are higher in the group hierarchy than Tom, come forward and present their dreams of the future. This obviously decreases Tom's anxiety about exposing himself. When it is his turn to make a presentation, with the help of a therapist he begins to imagine his future. In his imagination he builds his desk in an office of Daimler-Benz (Mercedes), his dream company. There are only a few items of room equipment, chairs and some squares of foam rubber—all the rest has to be imagined. He furnishes his office while informing the others of what he is doing, namely creating a first class manager's office, which has the most expensive computer—his true passion—deep, soft leather chairs, and a bar. Sitting confidently behind his enormous desk he reveals to the group members that he has familiarized himself with the Daimler management. Then one of the therapists enters the office and wishes to interview him on the life of a manager.

Tom reports that he is married, has a small daughter, and lives in a house which he owns. He drives a Mercedes and intends to work his way up to the very top. What is not clear is whether he aspires to a top position in business management or in politics as a member of a right wing conservative party in the European Parliament. Once a week he takes care of his mother. Before he came to the clinic, he spent his entire free time with her and for two years never left home without her. His mother is allowed to baby-sit his daughter when he and his wife wish to go out.

After this play-acting all the adolescents come back into the circle. Tom, smiling, comes out of his role and says, "Now I am myself again." In the course of the "sharing," some of his peers make comments like, "I don't know what I want as precisely as you know it" or, "I've never seen such a big desk at all." Close to the end, the male therapist remarks that today only three boys but no girl had responded to the theme. Tom looks at him and, turning in the direction of the female therapist, comments, "Well, women only decorate the living room sofa like lapdogs with bows in their hair!" The therapist responds, "Of course you must start letting out your aggression against women in this circle; I can understand that here it is certainly easier than at home with your mother."

Tom's behavior in his psychodrama illustrates this aspect. The initial withdrawal is followed by an involvement with his peers, facilitated by his grandiose and omnipotent ideas about becoming a top manager of Daimler-Benz. The involvement leads to an enlargement and strengthening of his ego. From this position he now becomes able to engage in the process of separation from his mother and can develop perspectives about his future with less anxiety.

A New Room is Arranged—a Group Dynamic Play

In the course of the stay in the day unit, a form of competition inevitably develops between the day-unit setting and the adolescent's family setting at home. In the case of Tom, he cannot bear this conflict and his solution is to withdraw completely from the group therapy meetings as well as from the day-to-day life of the group in the unit. This withdrawal serves to keep an inner balance, and in our view this corresponds to a strong defense of his self. This mechanism is especially apparent in Paul's family play. This withdrawal does not fit with the adolescent's archetypal need for development (the deintegration of the self) and has led to admission to the day unit of many of our adolescents.

In the beginning it is often easier for our adolescents to engage in a peer group dynamic play rather than to enact a family situation. Because of their separation problems and their regressed dependency on their parents, their capacity to symbolize is very restricted and an inner psychic space that could be used as a "stage" for their imagination is not available. Furthermore, conflicts in the here and now of the day unit are much more accessible to their consciousness and can easily be brought into the group therapy sessions. Sometimes acute group conflicts in the daily life of the unit "spill" into the therapy sessions. This overlap gives us a good chance to bring together the psychoanalytically-oriented milieu therapy with psychoanalytic individual and group therapy.

Whereas the protagonist-centered play and the improvisation play focus on the dynamic relation between the individual and the group, the group dynamic is the main focus of the following situation and resulting play. The background of the situation is as follows: a part of the big terrace has been converted into a living room, because we needed more space in the day unit. After three months of construction work, this new room is finished and there is much discussion among the adolescents about how this room should be used and equipped. During the "flashlight" round, none of the adolescents want to introduce an individual topic, so the therapists suggest that we might use this session to try to arrange the new room. Our suggestion meets with unusual unanimous enthusiasm. As a first step we ask the adolescents to imagine that we can do with the room whatever we like, we need not be concerned with any costs, feasibility, or size restrictions. Nineteen suggestions are made stretching from a billiard table to a waterfall. The next step is to reach agreement about which of the equipment items can be dropped. We are left with nine suggestions, one for each adolescent in the group.

Now the adolescents are asked to imagine which object of the chosen nine they would like to represent or pretend to be. If there are several volunteers, the selection is made in the well-known way: think whom you want to vote for, then close your eyes and point with stretched arm to the one you want to vote for. In the discussion about which objects will be used to equip the room as well as in the voting process, the position of each member in the group becomes clear: who gets his or her way, who is insistent, who gives up. This also shows the ranking within the group. Through the meaning and the symbolism of the individual objects, contents are carried that are not available in the day-to-day situation and that are hard to express. For example, Mark's identification with a billiard table reflects the extent to which he serves as the "motor" of the group; he is always responsible for entertaining activities. Chris's choice to be a pillow shows his limpness and passivity in the group. The other adolescents usually spare him with the excuse, "He doesn't feel well." However, behind this gentle treatment one can sense some anger about his passivity; his defensively split-off aggressiveness is projected into his peers and they transform into words what they feel.

The next task is to position the imagined objects in the room; this mirrors the inner space of the group. Mark as billiard table and Jan as music box spontaneously create an "entertainment corner," the good object with which it is possible to play. Peter as bed with stereo equipment would like to be right besides them, but for lack of space he has to move further away. Susanne as radio stands looking unhappy and unrelated in the middle of the room, while the others group themselves in a cosy corner. Tom as a shower wants to hang on the door, being an automatic shower. After everyone has positioned himself or herself, the next step is to find out how they feel and how they experience their distance from each other and whether that situation suits them. Here it becomes apparent that the self-chosen or attributed position reflects the real relationship of each individual within the group. Several members of the group express their wish for a change of place and there is the possibility now to act these and to move about.

After this change, they relinquish their acting roles and resume their seats in the circle. To their amazement the young people realize that they have resumed the same position in reality. They can now express directly their wish for changes. Anna tells Martin that she finds him very "encapsulated" and would like more closeness and contact with him. Martin can show himself pleased about this. Chris can say in his very shy manner that he would have liked to be closer to Tanja. She expresses emphatically that she does not want him close to her. Finally Peter expresses his disappointment that in the day-to-day life of the unit he never succeeds in getting closer to Jan and Mark.

Conclusion

There exist, as far as we know, almost no publications about group psychotherapy with adolescents from a Jungian point of view. Also, we have the impression that "classical" analytical group psychotherapy is not suitable for application with severely disturbed adolescents. On the other hand, if we take seriously the importance and power of the group experience, be it peer group or delinquent gang, and its influence on and fascination for the adolescent, we should use it as a helpful therapeutic tool. Our group therapeutic approach is based on two major assumptions: first, the therapeutic group can serve as an external self-representation for the adolescent, and the relationship between the individual and the group can be treated as an external analogy to the ego-self relationship. Second, in terms of space and separation, we assume that the individual's capacity to relate to a group (we distinguish between "relation" and "fusion") corresponds to the individual's capacity to maintain inner, psychic space, which presupposes a "good enough" separation from the primary objects, the parents.

In both these areas, the adolescents we treat in the day unit are basically disturbed: the deintegration/reintegration processes of the self are restricted and defenses of the self predominate.[12] The adolescents' imaginative and symbolizing capacity is restricted, and they still live in a very regressed, psychologically incestuous state with their parents. The Jungian analyst, Plaut, points out that "the capacity to imagine constructively is closely related to, if not identical with the capacity to trust."[13] But this is an experience that most of our adolescents have never had. Between this internal situation and the outer collective world with which the adolescent is confronted, no bridge exists for these adolescents to walk on. The English psychoanalyst, Winnicott, speaks of a potential space, an intermediate area, that is lacking or is not sufficiently developed.[14] Psychodrama, as a play technique in combination with the containing function of the group and the unit, can provide an intermediate area or an intermediate playground to help the adolescents develop their own space and imaginative capacity. By combining group therapy with interpretation, as a form of translation of the individual's language into the language of the group and vice versa, we hope to help these adolescents to take their first steps out of their isolation, so that they can experience action, life, and relationships in a new, and not simply subjective, reality.

Notes

1. C. G. Jung, *Psychology Today. Collected Works* (London: Routledge and Kegan Paul, 1954) v. 16, para 229.
2. C. G. Jung, *Briefe II: 1946–1955*, ed. A. Jaffé (Freiburg v. Olten: Walter Verlag, 1972) p. 452.
3. R. Seifert, "Die Gruppentherapie im Rahmen der Analytischen Psychologie," *Analytische Psychologie* 5 (1974):30–44.
4. R. Strubel, "Selbstwerdung und Gruppenselbst," *Analytische Psychologie* 12 (1981):138–150.
5. C. G. Jung, *Psychology and Alchemy, Collected Works* (London: Routledge and Kegan Paul, 1953) v.12, para.152.
6. M. Klein, "The Role of the School in the Libidinal Development of the Child." *Love, Guilt and Reparation* (London: Virago, 1988) pp. 59–76.
7. M. Klein, *The Psycho-Analysis of Children*, (London: Hogarth, 1959).

8. C. G. Jung,"The Psychology of Transference," *Collected Works* (London: Routledge and Kegan Paul, 1954) v. 16.

9. G. A. Leutz, *Psychodrama* (Munich: Pfeiffer, 1974) p. 145.

10. W. Bion, "A Theory of Thinking," *Second Thoughts* (London: Heinemann, 1967) pp. 110–119.

11. In this respect, the transcendent function is a function of the self and does, in our view, also work for groups. (See note 4).

12. For details of the clinic see Bovensiepen's paper in this volume, "The Clinic as Container."

13. F. Plaut, "Reflections on Not Being Able to Imagine," in *Analytical Psychology: A Modern Science,* ed. M. Fordham, et al. (London: Heinemann, 1973) p. 127.

14. D. W. Winnicott, *Playing and Reality* (London: Tavistock, 1973).

17

Borderline States, Incest, and Adolescence: Inpatient Psychotherapy

Geoffrey Brown

Introduction

The occurrence of borderline functioning within the adolescent phase of development, both as a manifestation of psychopathology and as a characteristic of normal adolescent psychology, has been a subject of fascination for me, especially as seen in a National Health Service setting where severely disturbed adolescents are treated on psychodynamic principles. In settings where the children and adolescents are the focus of therapeutic attention, sexual abuse has become an emerging important factor. From a relatively peripheral issue, child sexual abuse has come to occupy a central place in our daily work. In 1990, 33 percent of our new cases were known to be victims of past sexual abuse. Currently over half of the adolescents in the treatment program have a history of child sexual abuse. This statistic has become typical. Most agencies working with adolescents have similar figures, whereas estimates in children's homes are even higher.

The widespread contemporary attempt to respond to this phenomenon is producing repercussions on many levels, from child-rearing practices mandated through social legislation, to reexamination of theoretical formulations. Many of the response measures have produced pain, controversy, and confusion in a collective attempt to assimilate an aspect of collective shadow. Explorations of the impact of sexual abuse on development and its effect on the adolescent life stage are urgently needed.

One such inquiry is a paper entitled "The Effects of Childhood Sexual Abuse on Later Psychological Functioning" presented at the Third National Conference on Sexual Victimization of Children by J. Briere.[1] In it, he presents the results of a survey on a random sample of adult female "walk-in" psychiatric patients. He found that 67 women out of 153 reported a history of childhood sexual abuse. Statistically when compared to a nonabused group, these women were more likely to be taking psychoactive drugs, to have a history of alcohol or drug abuse, to have been the victim of battering in an adult relationship, and to have made at least one suicide attempt. In addition, the sexual abuse victims were more likely to report dissociative experiences, sleep disturbances and nightmares, along with feelings of isolation, anxiety, fear of men or women, sexual dysfunction, and the impulse to self-injure. Briere referred to this pattern of chronic symptomatology as a "Post-sexual Abuse Syndrome" and pointed out the similarity to the phenomenology of borderline personality disorder as described in the third edition of the *Diagnostic and Statistical Manual of Mental Disorder*.

History

The term "child sexual abuse" has been adopted in the contemporary attempt to assimilate the significance of the finding that many people have been involved in sexual acts with adults during their childhood. Implicit in the term is the notion of a damaging misuse of the child within the context of a relationship normally characterised by dependence and trust.

There is growing evidence of highly significant links between childhood sexual abuse and subsequent emotional, behavioral, and psychiatric disorders.[2] However, no consensus is to be found among the differing causal models. Explanations based on learning theory and those based on the similarity with post-traumatic stress disorder provide valuable but incomplete accounts.[3] Briere's "post-sexual abuse syndrome" is descriptive rather than explanatory, but raises a parallel with the phenomenology of borderline personality disorder. Summit, writing in 1983, describes the child sexual abuse accommodation syndrome.[4] In his lucid and valuable paper he describes the circumstances as well as some of the coping strategies employed by a child victim. However, the distorting aspects of the abused child's environment and the impact of this on psychological development are implied rather than discussed. Beyond the effects of the sexual act itself, such as pain, fear, overstimulation, and physical helplessness, he stresses the consequences of an atmosphere of secrecy and denial. An aspect of the child's bodily and emotional experience is denied access to parental mediation and empathic assimilation. The abusing father or mother cannot be turned to through fear of disbelief, retaliation, or threats. In this way, the abused child becomes emotionally orphaned.

Within the psychoanalytic literature there is an overwhelming body of writing on the subject of incest and abuse. In 1896, Freud presented his paper, "The Aetiology of Hysteria," in which he proposed that the origins of neurosis lay in the experience of sexual abuse in childhood.[5] This theory was met with shock and disapproval, and he abandoned the point of view, going on to develop his theories of the inner world. The unconscious wish for an incestous relationship with a parent became a central theme in his thinking in which the significance of external events subsequently played a smaller part. In 1932, however, Ferenczi read a paper in which he gave an account of his treatment of patients who had been sexually abused. "Insufficiently deep exploration of the exogenous factor carries with it the danger that one resorts to premature explanations in terms of disposition and constitution," he warned.[6] This was an early counterblast in a debate that has a contemporary ferocity, especially as seen in the writings of Masson.[7]

In his paper "Child Abuse and Deprivation: Soul Murder," L. L. Shengold provides a vivid analysis on the developing child. He draws a sharp distinction between external and internal experiences in his opening paragraph:

> Soul murder is my dramatic designation for a certain category of traumatic experiences—those instances of repetitive and chronic overstimulation, alternating with emotional deprivation that are deliberately brought about by another individual. Children can be broken much more easily than adults, and the effect on them of torture, hatred, seduction, and rape—or even of indifference, of deprivation of love and care—is the devastating one of developmental arrest.[8]

Shengold goes on to describe two psychological mechanisms that the abused psyche can employ in its defense. The first is that of blanking out somatic and emotional feelings, a dissociation from consciousness. In describing the second mechanism, he points out the helplessness and confusion of the abused child who can often only turn to the abuser for relief of distress. In his view, when a child is chronically exposed to an abusive environment, these mechanisms of dissociation and splitting can become permanent fixtures.

Jung wrote extensively and creatively on the part played by the idea of incestuous union in the development of personality. Although he does not take up the consequences of actual incest, he explores its unconscious significance in *Symbols of Transformation.*

> The basis of the "incestuous" desire is not cohabitation, but, as every sun myth shows, the strange idea of becoming a child again, of returning to the parental shelter, and of entering into the mother in order to be reborn through her. But the way to this goal lies through incest, i.e. the necessity of finding some way into the mother's body. One of the simplest ways would be to impregnate the mother and beget oneself in identical form all over again.[9]

What is important in relation to child development is the idea that "the incest prohibition makes the creative fantasy inventive," which leads to development of greater consciousness. "It was only the power of the 'incest prohibition' that created the self-conscious individual, who before had been mindlessly one with the tribe." The conflict between the wish to regress and be fused with the mother and the need to separate and be conscious has always struggled for expression and is not solely "motivated by what is narrowly and crudely conceived as 'incest.' We ought rather to conceive the law that expresses itself first and last in the 'incest prohibition' as the impulse to domestication, and regard the religious systems as institutions which take up the instinctual forces of man's animal nature, organize them, and gradually make them available for higher cultural purposes."[10]

Jung's recognition that "the incest prohibition makes the creative fantasy inventive" is related to Hanna Segal's idea on symbol formation. She notes that when a desire has to be given up and suppressed because of a conflict, a capacity for symbol formation can develop.[11] It is essential for the child's development that the parents do not give in to the child's unconscious desires when they are expressed during the oedipal phase. This idea can be further linked to those of D. Meltzer who states that the child's oedipal wishes are linked with procreation and that the parent's refusal to yield to seduction and the child's biological incapacity are primary in forcing a resolution of the oedipal conflict in psychic reality. As a result of this loss, the parents and their generative capacity can be symbolically internalized. The incestuous enactment of these unconscious wishes make them concretely real and causes disturbances in thinking, arresting the capacity to symbolize. The result is concrete thinking and particular difficulty in establishing a reparative process.

"Incest in Psychic Reality" is the focus and title of a paper by C. Gluckman who examines the age at which sexual abuse begins in relation to "the disturbances of generations" and the amount of psychic damage sustained.

> In general the evidence suggests that the earlier it starts and the more prolonged its duration, the more damaging are the consequences. Its early onset may lead to massive body/mind confusion and the lack of ability to differentiate self and objects. The geography of the body and its mental imagery is likely to be obscured with particular confusion surrounding anal, urethral and vaginal functions. A desperate response of the small child may be a distortion of the thinking process and a shift towards psychosis as a way of coping with unpalatable reality.[12]

Gluckman's description of the consequences of early and prolonged sexual abuse is born out by my account of the history and therapy of a female patient, here referred to as Amy, which reveals a pattern of dysfunction.

Case Material

Amy was the older of two daughters in a racially mixed marriage. When she was referred to me at age sixteen, following a serious overdose of paracetamol, I found that she was already surrounded by professionals, each with a special relationship to her yet largely unaware of each other. They included an education welfare officer, an individual psychotherapist, a child psychiatrist, and a general practitioner. Amy had a long history of disruptive and disturbed behavior dating back to her first entry into primary school. Concerned adults were paralleled by persecutory figures, a pattern established early in her life. Some adults, like one of her elementary teachers, felt that she was an impossible, malignant child; whereas others felt that she was misunderstood and in need of protection.

Her problems, primarily school-based to begin with, escalated over the years from fighting and vandalism, to stealing and alcohol abuse. Special placement in off-site units, intervention by the Education Welfare Service, and two years of individual psychotherapy from age fourteen to sixteen did not abate her disruptive and violent behavior. Her referral followed a period of strife in her relationship with her mother, and continuous intoxication culminating in a serious overdose. In the first assessment meeting, she appeared with her mother who seemed depressed. Amy looked boyish and chubby. Here, as in her first individual session, she presented herself with a mixture of serenity, warmth, and good sense. Initially, she stated that she needed help to stop drinking; however, she added that she drank to get rid of her other self. She described herself as split: "It's as if there are two of me. The other one takes me over, a monster who no one can help."

Amy had been born when her mother was nineteen years old, and her sister was born eighteen months later. Her parents had never married, separating finally when Amy was ten years old. Her mother felt bewildered and claimed never to have understood why Amy had such difficulties at school. At home, her mother said, Amy had been a good and supportive child up to the age of fourteen. Since then their relationship had become a source of anguish to her. Her other child, she asserted, was perfectly normal.

After some weeks in our weekly individual psychotherapy sessions, Amy tentatively disclosed a long history of sexual abuse. This content emerged intermittently over subsequent months. Sexually abusive relationships with men dated from age five up to the time of admission to my office. She began her admissions with a peripheral anecdote about a park keeper. When she was ten years old and her parents had separated, Amy wandered into a local park in an attempt to avoid her mother's misery. The park keeper, a stranger, appeared kind and friendly and took her into his keeper's hut where he pressed her into a sexual act.

This incident has three levels of significance. It is a statement about an external event and a communication of a fearfully kept secret. It can also be viewed as a communication about the transference: the therapist appears to be well-meaning and invites a troubled girl into his room, but what are his intentions? In addition, the anecdote functions as a sort of screen memory; like the content of a dream, it tells of an internal structure or a pattern of object relations. These differing levels of meaning, common to all communications when viewed psychodynamically, have a special importance in work with victims of child sexual abuse. The communication of a factual event may have statutory child protection significance and therefore raises ethical dilemmas for a therapist. The possibility that the therapist's intentions are sexual and that interaction will proceed towards a sexual act is not simply a fantasy, it becomes a real possibility when viewed from the patient's model of what happens in a dependent relationship with an adult. The patient's past experience of the transgression of boundaries by the behavior of adults surpasses that of nonvictims.

While the content of sessions, including the material that constituted disclosure of abuse, was told largely without affect, Amy's behavior on the ward included episodes of destructive acting out, sleep disturbances, nightmares, and visual hallucinations, the manifestations of what she called her "other self." To begin with, Amy disclaimed any feelings associated with session material or the disturbed behavior. She denied the validity of any of my interpretations and denied her own feelings. In time, her disruptive, aggressive, and destructive behavior gave way to episodes of fearfulness, especially at night. Fear was the first feeling that she identified as belonging to herself.

At this time, Amy was able to reveal more of her past history. From age twelve up to her admission to the ward, Amy had been regularly sent to baby-sit her mother's sister's children. Part of Amy's duties included spending time with her aunt's second husband once the children were asleep. What occurred was perverse physical and sexual abuse with a marked sado-masochistic quality. Amy's level of disturbed behavior escalated at this time. With great difficulty, she moved towards facing the central trauma of her early incestuous relationship with her father. At times she appeared to have forgotten what she had recalled, and at times she denied earlier disclosures as lies or madness. Once her sister was born, the baby seemed to have become her mother's favorite, while Amy became her father's pet. At this time, her parent's relationship began to deteriorate. A pattern of sexual abuse began when Amy was five and continued for at least four years. Her position was fixed between a hostile, nonempathetic mother and an abusing father.

The role of the hospital adolescent unit as a container for her chaos, pain, anger, and helplessness cannot be overemphasized, especially during the first eighteen months of treatment. Because the unit team was in close communication with me, it was possible to avoid the myriad diffusion and splitting, which Amy had employed as coping strategies for survival prior to admission. The unit, as a safe container, also separated her from current abusing adults and provided an environment that could meet her needs in concrete ways. Control of visitors and staff to those who could limit the effects of destructive acting out against themselves and the patient, and the provision of a safe context for interaction, stimulation, and play were among the most positive features of the institution. These features symbolize a "good enough" maternal environment. For Amy, internalization of this experience was a slow and painful process and was mediated by the individual sessions.

The quality of the maternal transference was indicated by a dream Amy discussed after having been in treatment for nine months. She remembered one good memory from the past, which involved fishing outings with a safe and caring uncle. Her dream dealing with this material is as follows:

> I come to a beautiful pool in the bend of a river and realize this is a fine place for fishing. Many others have seen the value of the spot and are already happily fishing. They are mostly young, about my age, both boys and girls. They seem happy and excited as they fish. Longing to join in, I prepare my tackle, but when I make the first cast, my body feels strange. I try again and have the same frightening feeling. It's as if my arm is coming off my shoulder. I feel as though my body is splitting apart though I feel no pain. I realize I cannot fish, and feel upset.
>
> I see my mother standing near and tell her what has happened. She approaches and without a word moves to touch me. I think she wants to see what is wrong. She touches me with her finger-tips on my chest. Her hand seems to slide right into me, making a great hole. Inside I realize that I am quite hollow, and I draw back from her in panic and revulsion.

While this dream had a nightmare quality for Amy, it was different from the many terrifying dreams of nameless fears that caused her to resist sleep and yet were beyond recall by day. For the first time, she was also able to join me in thinking about the content. Her first association was with sad thoughts she recently had had about her plight. She saw other adolescents getting on with their lives whereas she felt stuck. The following statement by her illustrates this sentiment: "They are able to take advantage of the good fishing while I am not. I don't understand what has happened to me." I asked her about the mother in the dream, and she said she had never let her mother touch her for as long as she could remember. She was able to accept my interpretations that she felt there was a danger in turning to me for help with her damaged part. My attention and closeness brought fear of further intrusion and damage.

D. W. Winnicott's concept of the true and false self describes Amy's defense. In this dream both the age-appropriate developmental challenge and contact with a maternal object threatened the fragile cohesion of a false self structure, exposing a split and empty self image. The point of origin of the "false-self" is in a defense against that which is unthinkable, namely the "exploitation of the true self, which would result in its annihilation."[13]

Following this dream, Amy's endearing smile began to fade. She became outwardly sullen and depressed. Much of the content of our sessions focused on night fears and free-floating anxiety during which she was often inarticulate and frozen; it was as if she were unable to move or leave. In the countertransference, I experienced an empathic connection with feelings of pain and fear and felt compelled to create a calming, soothing, and safe experience for the child within the adolescent. When I spoke about the fear of violation or abandonment that she was experiencing, Amy expressed hatred of this part of herself, saying "she is bad and crazy and should he killed." For a long time her behavior reflected this self-destructive inner state of division. Yet she seemed to experience a sense of being held and was able to disclose the abusive relationship she had with her father.

During this period of her treatment Amy's father was serving a prison sentence, and she was out of contact with him. Once she had begun to acknowledge the fact of her incestuous experience with him, she quickly moved from perceiving him as a feared figure, who had enforced compliance and silence, to expressing her feelings of emptiness and longing caused by his absence. She described him in glowing terms, attributing to him a warm, vital quality, "like golden sunshine." The numinous quality of the father-imago was strongly present and, for a time colored her vision of him and her past. Amy appeared to be split into a pure child longing for her spiritual emptiness to be filled by a God-like father, and a demonic child who insanely claimed or imagined that she had had a sexual relationship with him. She saw me in much the same light. On the one hand, there developed a positive transference with a psychotic quality between us, and on the other, I was associated with the guilty, demonic child who spoke of carnal incest. Turmoil and confusion reigned, and different oppositions were constellated in which I was felt to be either a potent source of good, or an intrusive source of danger. A dream in this period illustrates some of this painful confusion that overwhelmed the patient's fragile ego-function, producing visual hallucinations. In this nightmare, she dreamt of being attacked and raped. In the struggle, she could not identify the assailant at first but knew the gender. At the height of her helpless submission to the rape, she caught a glimpse of his face. It was that of her trusted female nurse keyworker, towards whom she had begun to show a dependent attachment.

In terms of inconstant and split objects, much of Amy's inner chaos was enacted with a variety of people within the therapeutic milieu of the unit. A person whom she had appeared to trust became feared; someone to whom she had turned as a good maternal figure became a target for her aggression. In our sessions, I tried to operate as an auxiliary ego; commenting and confronting when possible and making reference to the confusion experienced by the child-like part of her. A sudden pang of anxiety over a sick pet guinea pig left at home in the care of her mother offered an opportunity to interpret the plight of the enraged and neglected baby within her. Very slowly the chaos began to subside and was replaced by a strong attachment to both me and the unit as a whole. Acting out happened more often during holiday breaks and when I was absent. This behavior became more of an issue when she was about to be discharged from inpatient status. Her attempts at controlling me and the staff through manipulation of her self-destruction took on a more goal-directed quality.

For many months following her discharge, panic and fury at her sense of abandonment dominated the continuing psychotherapy sessions. At times, respite admissions to an adult psychiatric hospital were needed. During this phase she came to outpatient sessions with stories of further self-destructive behavior involving alcohol abuse and theft, incidents which resulted in court proceedings. Frequently she returned to the unit in a drunken aggressive state demanding readmission. Before this behavior subsided, I spent many months interpreting this angry attack on me and the unit as her anger at abandoning parents.

After discharge, Amy moved in with her mother, living out an enactment of concrete dependence. Eventually she was able to express her anger directly to her mother, and during the ensuing months of depression she moved away and began to live in a flat of her own. A dream she retold during the fifth year of treatment illustrates the shift in content.

> I return to my flat to find a stranger in my living room, an unpleasant-looking man. I protest that he should not be there, but he takes no notice and in an enticing way he offers me some food from a bowl. I look in the bowl and see some foul, rotten material and shrink back in horror and nausea. I rush out to find my neighbor, a nice middle-aged woman. When I pour out my story with disgust, fear, and outrage she appears unconcerned. She returns with me to the flat. The man has died and has become a rotten corpse. The smell is foul, but the woman seems to be saying, "So what, why all the fuss?" I am desperate to get it out of my home."

I did not address the content with the patient in terms of the transference because it would have risked damage to my role as a dependable good figure and auxiliary ego. In the context of pursuing goals towards the promotion of separation and individuation, it was better to invite her to think about the dream as a statement about her internal world as it related to the past. At first she was overawed by the dream and felt it to be an expression of feeling haunted by an outside evil that would never leave her. Eventually she was able to see the symbolic content: the intruding father offering food that proves to be damaging; an unsympathetic mother figure unable to help and unable to see. Most interesting about the dream is the ending in which the father has died but left lingering feelings of anger and disgust. He no longer has the power that he once had when he was either the golden sunshine or the overpowering abuser.

In contrast to the much earlier dream of the "rapist mother," this one involves a much greater sense of differentiation and structure. There are three distinct figures: a rotten father image, a nonempathic but basically harmless mother image, and an ego-dreamer. The action takes place in a space that has boundaries and subdivisions, but the dreamer has the power to move between these spaces and to voice protest, and in so doing experiences a range of affects: fear, disgust, rage. After our discussion of this dream, Amy recalled how she did not know what her feelings were when she first came to see me, but now she was all too familiar with a whole range of them, nearly all unpleasant.

At the time of writing, Amy was still in treatment undergoing her sixth year of psychotherapy. She faced the need for ending with misgiving and recognized that her abandonment fear remained a dominant inner construct. However, she had made a stable relationship with a young man of her own age and had managed to distance herself from her father. Her mother appeared to offer some reparation in the form of her continued but nonintrusive support.

Discussion

In the case material I have presented, the primitive defense delineated by Shengold and Gluckman are apparent. They are, I believe, exemplified by Amy's image of herself in the first dream in which she is both split and empty. Much of her behavior up to this time appeared to be formless chaos. This hyperactive round of disruptions and destruction was fueled by her need to evacuate her inner turmoil of feelings into the world around her. In Bion's model, beta elements derived from the child's physical and emotional arousal, are placed through projective identification into the mother who can, through her receptivity and ego function, return them in a modified form.[14] This process, referred to by Bion as alpha functioning, was largely missing in Amy's earliest relationship with her mother and father. Hence there is a double parenting failure in child sexual abuse; for while the father is irresponsible, abrogating his parental role and his place in the adult sexual couple, the mother's failure to acknowledge the reality of the situation and inability to protect her child puts her in the category of an absent parent. This makes the abuse worse, for there is no real parent present for the child. The failure of Amy's mother to provide containment for the overwhelming affects produced by the abuse led to the formation of persecutory bizarre objects, which the nurse-mother rapist image in the second dream symbolizes.

In Amy's world, good objects were placed for safe keeping outside, through projective identification, into idealized, distant people. This coping mechanism often elicited the assiduous care and concern for Amy's wellbeing that she could not exercise herself. On the contrary, she had been possessed by the other, split-off, persecutory part object and was compelled towards punitive self-destruction (cf. Bovensiepen,

"Attacks on the Body as a Containing Object"). The sado-masochistic relationship with her abusing uncle can be seen as an expression of this impulse. Such profound division of the internal world, correspondingly split part-object relating projected into the environment, is a characteristic consequence of severe early trauma and deprivation. It provides the basis for the commonly observed pattern of victim behavior in such patients.

Amy's means of disclosure, those statements made by the patient that broke through her habit of secrecy and accommodation and communicated information about sexual abuse, further illustrate the need for containment. Her first disclosure was of abuse by a stranger. This was followed by a series of statements leading up to the disclosure of abuse by her father. This sequence, from the most peripheral and least emotionally-loaded recollection towards the intensely charged and repressed memories of father-daughter incest, forms a recurring pattern in work with sexual abuse victims. Disclosure, therefore, is best understood as a process taking place within the framework of the relationship between patient and therapist: it is not simply a statement made at one point in time. The precondition for the therapeutic unfolding of this process appeared to be the concrete safety and containment provided by the adolescent unit following her admission to the hospital. The subsequent phases of the process depended on the development of an experience by the patient of an emotional container. As a signpost, the stranger-abuse anecdote pointed towards the central theme of sexual abuse. In the transference, this disclosure also raised questions about the nature of the therapeutic relationship. Only when Amy's issues around the inherent danger of intimacy could be addressed could the therapy proceed.

Conclusion

I find it difficult when working with a survivor of sexual abuse to extend reconstruction back to early stages. The power of the central trauma of incest blocks the view. There is little doubt, however, that Amy experienced inadequate mothering predating her sexual abuse. At the very least, consistent and empathic parenting was lacking and this nonfacilitating childhood environment led to a fixed maladaptive personality structure corresponding to a borderline personality organization.

Amy's father, through his own immature needs, had responded to the child's emotional availability with seductive enactment of her barely conscious impulses evoked by her encounter with the power of the father archetype in the context of the oedipal stage of development. In this intrusion into her psyche-soma, her father violated and sabotaged what should have been a healthy struggle to integrate archetypal material. By making the motif of incest concrete, Amy's father precipitated her into states of overwhelming affect where her frail ego was unable to act on experiences and was thus abandoned through parental disregard of her true self. Amy, therefore, dealt with the experience by employing primitive defenses; splitting, dissociation, evacuation of psychic content through reenactments, idealization, and projective identification. Progress on the path of development was arrested because true relating in vital libidinal areas had become impossible. The persistence of the abusive relationship through critical years of childhood maintained the conditions for the consolidation of a borderline personality structure.

As a survival strategy, Amy employed a false-self relationship with her mother up to the age of fourteen years. She used the environment outside the distorted relationships of the family as a receptacle in which to evacuate and enact split-off parts of herself. However, with the resurgence of the need for separation and individuation, under the influence of her own sexual maturation, this unhappy equilibrium was disturbed. Further encounters with archetypal themes intensified and embellished the power of the already nonassimilated, split-off fragments. In this way, persecutory, invasive, and self-denigratory feelings could not be defended against without an escalation of self-destructive behavior. Her false-self relationship with her mother collapsed, revealing something of the truly damaged mother-child dyad. Hostility towards her mother and suicidal self-destructiveness, presented as her symptoms at referral, can be seen as the emergence of an impulse towards maturation and repair.

Summary

In this chapter an account of the history and psychotherapy of a severely disturbed adolescent girl is presented and used to examine the impact of child sexual abuse on child development. My own attempt to reevaluate theory and technique is presented against a historical background of confusion over the validity and significance ascribed to disclosures of child sexual abuse. Briere's post-sexual abuse syndrome fits in with the phenomenology of borderline personality disorder and thus provides a link through which the destructive effects of child sexual abuse on emotional development can be examined.

Some implications for technique arise from this premise. Disclosure is shown to be a process that occurs over time and forms an integral part of therapy. It is facilitated by the provision of a concretely safe and emotionally containing setting. In this case, different levels of meaning of disclosure material were considered.

The trauma of sexual abuse in childhood is shown to produce adverse developmental consequences emerging in adolescence in the form of borderline functioning. An incapacity to transcend the fusion-abandonment opposition limits the capacity for relating. Split-off destructive part objects perpetuate either self-destructive behavior or victim behavior when evacuated in the environment.

Notes

1. J. Briere. "The Effects of Childhood Sexual Abuse on Later Psychological Functioning," Paper presented at the Third National Conference on Sexual Victimization of Children. Washington, D.C., 1984.
2. See J. A. Stein, et al, "Long-Term Psychological Sequelae of Child Sexual Abuse: The Los Angeles Epidemiologic Catchment Area Studies," in *Lasting Effects of Child Sexual Abuse,* eds. G. E. Wyatt and G. J. Powell (Beverly Hills, CA: Sage Publications, 1988); R. Oppenheimer, et al, "Adverse Sexual Experience in Childhood and Clinical Eating Disorder." *Journal of Psychiatric Research* 19:357–361.
3. D. Finkelhor, "The Trauma of Child Sexual Abuse: Two Models," in *Lasting Effects*; E. Deplinger et al, "Post-Traumatic Stress in Sexually Abused and Non-Abused Children," *Child Abuse and Neglect* 13 (1989):403–408; J. R. Wheeler and L. Berliner. "Treating the Effects of Child Abuse on Children," in *Lasting Effects.*
4. R. Summit, "The Child Sexual Abuse Accommodation Syndrome," *Child Abuse and Neglect* 7:177-93.
5. S. Freud, *The Aetiology of Hysteria* (London: Hogarth, 1962) orig. pub. 1896.
6. S. Ferenczi, "Confusion of Tongues Between Adults and the Child: The Language of Tenderness and Passion," in J. M. Masson, *The Assault on Truth: Freud's Suppression of the Seduction Theory.* (New York: Farrar, Straus and Giroux, 1984).
7. J. M. Masson, *The Assault on Truth.*
8. L. L. Shengold, "Child Abuse and Deprivation: Soul Murder," *Journal of American Psychoanalytic Assn.* 27 (1979):533–599.

9. C. G. Jung, *Symbols of Transformation, Collected Works* (London: Routledge and Kegan Paul, 1956) v. 5, para. 332.

10. C. G. Jung, *Symbols,* para. 415.

11. H. Segal, "Notes on Symbol Formation," *International Journal of Psycho-Analysis* 38(1957):391–397.

12. C. Gluckman, "Incest in Psychic Reality," *Journal of Child Psychotherapy* 13 (1987), no. l.

13. D. W. Winnicott, "The Theory of the Parent Infant Relationship," *International Journal of Psycho-Analysis* 41 (1960) 585–95.

14. L. Grinberg, et al, *Introduction to the Work of Bion* (London: Clunie, 1975).

18

Sandplay Therapy and Verbal Interpretation with an Anorexic Girl

Gianni Nagliero

Introduction

My work with children involves a combination of sandplay therapy and an analytical approach. The patient has a choice: to create a sand picture, to communicate with me verbally, or to combine these methods. This combination seems to be particularly suitable in the psychotherapy of adolescent patients. The analytical approach allows for a coming to consciousness on the part of the patient, mediated by the analyst's interpretations of the relationship.

Sandplay therapy, a psychotherapeutic method developed by D. M. Kalff, allows the patient, "by means of figures and the arrangements of the sand within the area bounded by the sandtray, to set up a world corresponding to his or her inner state."[1] The therapist attempts to make sense of the symbolic content of the patient's play, but typically does not verbalize it to the patient. Instead, the therapist dwells on what each scene represents in reality, and encourages the patient to amplify and speak about what he has created.

In Kalff's model, verbalization between patient and therapist is always regarded as secondary to the real healing work of the therapy, which she regards as deriving directly from the patient's expression and reworking of internal images. Instead of stressing the potential

Pictures described in this chapter are available from the publisher on request.

significance of the transference and countertransference, Kalff urges the unconditional acceptance of the patient by the therapist and places great trust in the self-healing potential of the individual psyche when favorable conditions are created. For Kalff, the work performed during sandplay can itself bring about the revitalizing encounter of the ego with the forces of the self. This can be a "numinous experience," which frequently finds its expression in religious symbols used in sandplay.

The therapy room is generally furnished with two sandtrays of pre-established dimensions that correspond to the field of vision of the person who is doing the sandplay (52 cm. x 72 cm. x 7 cm). One contains wet sand while the other holds dry sand: the patient can work with either. There is also a collection of miniature objects such as houses, characters, machines, animals, and trees.

Since adolescence involves the transition from predominantly play-oriented physical activity, to predominantly verbal, intellectual activity, the sandplay and analytic techniques seem to be particularly suited to aid in the transformative process. Kalff suggests that by building scenes in the sandtray in a special atmosphere created by the therapist, the patient is able to rework a process of development blocked in the early phases of life. The first stage of this development, which often involves regression and presupposes a maternal, accepting role on the part of the therapist, consists of establishing contact with the self. This contact eventually leads to the self-healing and guiding that will lead the patient towards individuation. In addition, the representation of one's inner world by means of the sandtray can make it easier to depict terrifying contents since this form allows a patient to objectify these contents. Because the patient fashions the scene, they have a modicum of control over the events they depict. The scenes depict the patient's own inner world, one which the patient may only be partially aware of. By speaking about the scene, the patient can address internal problems without becoming conscious of them. Thus the words of the therapist seem less dangerous than direct interpretation. This aspect of the therapy is particularly important for patients who have strong paranoid defense mechanisms.

Clinical History

Carla was thirteen and a half when we first met. She was the second child in a family of three: the older sister, age fifteen, was of low intelligence and suffered from depression; the younger brother, age six, suffered from secondary enuresis. Until she was five, Carla's family lived in the country in a beautiful farming area. They moved to the city where her father worked as a concierge. The family, including the paternal grandparents, lived in cramped accommodations consisting of one bedroom and a kitchen.

Apparently, Carla's mother's pregnancy was uneventful: Carla was breast fed for six months and weaning was begun at five months. She had no language problems and socialization and schooling went well until the onset of anorexia, four months before she began therapy with me. Her periods started at twelve but were abnormally irregular. At the time of hospitalization, she was not menstruating, weighed forty-four kilos (97 lb.; 6 stone 13 lb.) and was one meter, 75 cm tall. (5 ft. 8 inches).

Her anorexia is connected with a visit Carla made to see her cousins in the country village where she had grown up. While eating a cookie, as she later told me, she suddenly saw herself as fat and decided to lose weight. This critical moment occurred in a place Carla considered to be a lost paradise. This idealized paradise represented a regressive wish to go back to early childhood because of her inability to tolerate strong feelings of guilt related to the changes in her body and her mind. These changes evoked feelings of guilt at the possibility that boys might be sexually interested in her and feelings of anxiety at her own sexual desires. When she returned home, her family noticed that she became easily angered and started eating less. First she stopped eating bread and then she refused to eat or drink anything at all. Her parents noticed that she had become "closed, sad, and uncommunicative."

Carla was referred to the child and adolescent department of a university hospital and was diagnosed as anorexic. She was offered psychotherapy but rejected it and was eventually moved to another hospital. She remained in the hospital for a month because of her serious physical condition. Carla exhibited delusions of persecution, a phobia related to a distorted body image, and catatonic states of being. Her mental state was marked by confusion compounded by the new emotional experiences brought on by the physical and mental transformations of adolescence. At the time of admittance to the hospital, her paranoid projections and isolation then represented an extreme form of defense against the outside world and her inner anxieties.

My first impression of Carla was of an extremely deteriorated girl. Pale, immobile, and apparently unreachable, she lay on her hospital bed. I introduced myself and invited her to explore the option of therapy. Following this meeting, there was a series of appointments requested by her during her last few days in the hospital. However, she canceled them all and refused contact. I continued to offer my services. Even though anorexia is a dramatic situation demanding urgent help, it is important to allow for a mental space, free of pressure and anxiety from the therapist so that the patient's desire for therapy can grow. If this state of mind is achieved, there is a greater possibility for a relationship that allows for separation. Complicating Carla's case was the use of medication, which was helpful in the early part of therapy because it helped to lower the level of the patient's delusions of persecution and paranoia. However, the medication is supervised by the psychiatrist. Especially when working with adolescents, the analyst needs to recognize the effects so that medication does not become a chronic factor, inhibiting the autonomous growth of the patient's faculties of attention.

The Sandplay Method

At her first regular session, I noticed Carla's empty and distant look accompanying her sad expression. Her face was thin and drawn, and her big eyes seemed to bulge out of her head. Her height accentuated her thinness. She wore a heavy, ugly anorak, which she did not remove, even though the room was overheated. She seemed out of proportion and unworried about her appearance. During the initial sessions, I felt unable to help, and Carla's expression and lack of communication with me seemed to mirror this sentiment. Although I did not have much hope, I was prepared to accept what would happen. Meanwhile, silently, Carla began to make her first picture. In the first year of therapy, Carla made fifteen sand pictures, eleven of which are discussed here.

Like her words, Carla's first sand picture expressed her conflict and depicted the place where her development suffered a blockage. The country house, her idealized world, seemed to be a lively place because everyone looked busy, but actually nobody seemed to be making contact with anyone else. One little girl, representing the patient herself, stood alone. She was not firmly on the ground and seemed to represent the thin, fragile figure of the ballerina, an image that is frequently constellated by anorexics. The theme of feeding, often found in the first sand picture of anorexics, was represented here by dead chickens killed for eating, which, I thought, symbolized Carla's unexpressed aggression. Other animals representing instincts were notably absent. Carla's instinctual life appeared to have been sacrificed. The men, here the knife-sharpener and the woodsman, were either cutting or sharpening their blades, while the women were holding the chickens in their hands. Thus the sacrificed instinctual aspect was connected with female fertility as represented by the hens.

When Carla finished the picture, she said. "This is a little village ... I like silence," as if to invite me to be quiet. I said that she could use her session time to be silent, if she liked, but I needed to know more about her life if we were to work together. She then told me about her life in the village where she had been happy. Carla showed some precocious paranoid aspects when she described "a frightening teacher [who] frowned at me." With this picture, Carla came back into contact with five year-old feelings. In contrast with her feelings about the present, she used to be safe and isolated.

The second sand picture, done a month later, represented a positive regression. Horses, which Carla loves, were moving towards the water, which represents life. While the instincts seem to be capable of revitalization, the tigress in the upper left side could represent unintegrated aggressive instinctual drives.

In the next sand picture competed a week later, water appeared again. When discussing this picture, Carla said, "I like the sea, but this is like where everyone goes to get water for their homes ... a man who lends water to everyone ... he gives it, just gives it away." I made special note of the protection provided by the double fence. A state of great psychic fragility, even latent psychosis, can be indicated by a border made all around the sandtray. In this case, the double fence was only found in the upper half of the sandtray picture, and it seemed to represent an element of containment: the patient was simultaneously protecting herself from anxiety about the important experience and risking the possibility of reliving elements of her early life when she was a lonely child without adequate maternal protection.

A week later Carla made the fourth sand picture. When she finished. I remarked that it was a big house where each person had his or her own space. Carla replied that this was a dream. Once again, people were separated by wide spaces, seeming to indicate a lack of relationship between people. However, she had begun to hypothesize relationships as signified by the existence of communication between the various rooms.

The following week she came in with a dark face. After a period of silence, she asked me to ask her something. I reminded her of our pact to keep silence if need be. While we were talking, she made concentric circles in the sand with her left forefinger, then she added some water and made two hills where she put some houses and a bridge. She then told me a friend of hers had scolded her because she dropped the ball while playing. "Doesn't she know I am weak?" Calla added, "My parents too scolded me." Another part of Carla seemed to be coming to her awareness, one that functioned as the strict and demanding superego. Perhaps she felt that my reminder of the rule was a strict, parent-like demand.

During this time she had anorexic and bulimic phases mixed with depression. Unfortunately, I had to cancel our next appointment. I suggested that she might feel abandoned. She nodded. The sand picture also showed a feeling of depression, but something deeper was revealed. The bridge represented a link. Perhaps this depression was caused by the recognition of the good and bad aspects of her mother (or the therapist when he performs this function). The bridge showed the possibility of integrating both aspects, but the perception of this provoked depression.

This depression can be seen in the following sand picture done immediately after the missed session. Before making the sand picture, she picked up the devil and then left it and created the picture. When she finished she picked up a small black doll and exclaimed, "how sweet this is!" The sand was preceded and followed by contact with the shadow in its double archetype, the black of the negative, frightening devil, and the black of the "sweet" doll. The depression dramatized in the sand picture seemed to lead to the possibility of integrating the shadow, her dark side, which entailed a long journey in the desert to reach the water of the oasis. But this was for the future: in her everyday life, her depression was intense.

The following week in April, Carla started moving the sand around with an air of concentration. She then picked up the tree house but put it down again, then took three huts and fashioned the house of her dreams. The fences were now open. She said that the house and black horse were two things that she wanted, but "Jesus is standing in the way."

Although the sand picture conveyed a certain degree of well-being, Carla's exterior life had worsened. Her anorexia and paranoia had increased and she refused to attend school. In this period, she increasingly showed her ambivalence about her adolescence. She wanted to be on her own and become a woman while simultaneously recovering a period of total dependency on her parents. The figure of Jesus and her comments on his role indicated the conflict between the spirit and the body. We talked about religion in a way that addressed her feelings of guilt about the body and desire.

Easter break interrupted our sessions, and Carla returned thinner than ever. For the next two months she was either absent or refused to come into the room. She returned at the end of June and drew a train coming out of a tunnel, left her finger prints in the lower right-hand corner of the sand, and left. She then left for summer camp and returned a month later, disoriented and confused. I was worried since the beginning of June and the summer holidays were approaching. Unconsciously she seemed to sense my worry and answered it with the next sand picture.

Carla put Snow White and the dwarves near a house, then moved two dwarves to the right and put a witch near the house. While the protective dwarves were away at work, Snow White had to face the witch on her own. Carla seemed to have to face alone the image of her internal witch/mother.

My notes here read; "She is depressed but getting better." In this session, for the first time, I became conscious of a "strange erotic interest" in her. Carla's bodily transformation was related to her internal body image as well as her physical appearance. The combination of a change in body form with a change in body image could only occur in a mental space that is unencumbered by the analyst's desire for gratification and the patient's search for approval and affection. In this context, a major obstacle to therapeutic progress was the patient's desire to change as a means of satisfying the desires of the analyst's unresolved "complexes." Since problems occur in the transference, the maintenance of a therapeutic environment requires the therapist to become conscious of his own countertransference and continually analyze it. This analysis will allow all the true origins of the desire to surface along with any discouragement, anger, jealousy, or eros, any of which may intrude, often very subtlety, upon the therapy.

I had registered my own "strangely erotic interest" in Carla, thus defining my vision of Carla as a woman as something strange. The apparent foreignness and strangeness of this feeling reveals that a new image was making room for itself, both within my own mind and the patient's. This picture was to take the place of the clumsy, unattractive image of her that corresponded more accurately at the time to the physical reality. The accepting space of sandplay therapy allowed for the birth of a new image, which was independent of any judgment on the "pathology" manifested in the patient's everyday life. The new image representing Carla's sexuality was experienced within the relationship, where the patient experiences the possibility of being loved and the analyst perceives her as an attractive woman.

After a holiday break of a month and a half, Carla immediately told me a dream about Jesus who saved her from the devil, and then depicted it in the sand tray. A plowed field, ready to be seeded, is shown in the sand tray. The sand shows the possibility of uniting two opposite parts: on the left, there is a completely closed house, while on the right we see her "own house," as she called it. In this space, there is an encounter with the devil, with occult forces, with the shadow. In the center is baby Jesus who represents the possibility of uniting these two parts. The therapy could be the medium for Carla, through which she could bring about this confrontation with the shadow and reintegrate it. In this way, she could once again contemplate the possibility that instead of experiencing her own body and sexuality as a danger, she might discover how the suffering of adolescence can turn into the joy of being a woman. The earth, representing her body, was here depicted as ready for fertilization.

She could now begin to distance herself from the distorted perceptions of her body, which had previously become obsessions, by acknowledging that she was not fat in other people's eyes although she still felt fat. She also recognized this discrepancy as a problem and wanted to overcome it. Her primary association with being fat was her mother. In connection with previous associations, I suggested that she might have seen her mother as being fat when she was pregnant with her brother. "Full of wrinkles . . . old," Carla added.

The following week she did not construct a sand picture, but left a hole in the lower left hand corner of the tray. During the session we talked about the resistance that a part of her exhibited towards therapy and becoming an adult, a part that was having a hard time growing.

Somewhat desperately yet decidedly, Carla answered, "But I want to grow up."

A few sessions later, she appeared with short, badly cut hair which she had cut herself. However, for the first time she arrived on her own. She spent the entire time hurling accusations at me, saying that I had broken confidence and talked to my colleagues who, in turn, had told her mother. Carla's ambivalence was illustrated by her contradictory impulses: when she decided to come on her own and behave like an adult, the part of her that was afraid of being attacked and betrayed reemerged and perceived me as being an ally of old parental images.

A number of sessions were dominated by the interplay of these two parts. She both accused me of telling her mother everything and let on that she had told her mother everything. Each time she came closer to me in our relationship, she counteracted that step forward with words and gestures. She said that she did not want to come any more but asked me to continue to help her with a stuttering problem. This apparently chaotic emergence of pairs of contrasting feelings was something that she had to experience and integrate. Surprisingly enough, she seemed to feel more attractive and was more communicative. We talked about the difficulty of liking herself, and I told her that she often filled her mind with thoughts of unattractiveness in order not to appreciate herself or have others appreciate her. She responded with the next sand picture.

Here she showed the possibility of integrating her two split parts, body and soul. There was an upper and lower half connected by a bridge that spanned the river, itself a visible sign of both penetration and fertility. As she left, for the first time she thanked me.

Carla could now depict a house where a new birth has taken place. A new religious context emerged from the unconscious and was represented here by the shepherds coming out of the sea in a festive spirit. This was Carla's last sand picture, and it concluded the first half of her therapy. It was possible to observe the great discrepancies between Carla's external life and the images that appeared in the sandtray. Her symptoms were worsening, adding to her lack of self-esteem and sense of guilt. She fell into a depression that kept her isolated at home, while in her sessions she complained about how terrible she felt. What stood out more and more in the sand pictures was the integration of opposites and operation of the transcendent function. It is interesting to note that Carla did sand pictures for a little over a year, as if she wanted to clear a space in this early phase for an unconscious, bodily process while recovering a whole series of physical sensations. During the second part of her therapy, Carla worked much more analytically, focusing on relationships and developing her consciousness of her problems.

She also became aware of confused aspects of herself through drawing. For example, the women she drew had always been thin, ethereal, models. Now, she had begun drawing women who were rather out of proportion. She traced and retraced the outline of the figures, especially the breasts, hips, and thighs. Through the drawings she managed to touch upon sexual problems. Once she drew a woman and then she drew a swim suit, but then, in an unusually emphatic way, she erased the whole thing. When I asked her why, Carla said "She is dirty."

I asked her about her about her own sexuality, interpreting her drawings as portraying sexuality as something dirty. I added that I thought she considered her own sexuality to be dirty and added that this problem was related to her anorexia and her own refusal to become a woman so as to avoid being sexually active, become pregnant, and become a mother like her own. She was ensuring that she stay an adolescent eternally.

The Analytic Element

In the last six months, our work became more and more analytical, a process during which, as requested by the patient, I tried to utilize interpretative language and the analysis of unconscious contents while paying attention to my own countertransference feelings and interpreting them in terms of our relationship. A session which took place before the conclusion of our therapy illustrates the direction of our work. My reflections are recorded and italicized under Carla's communication: this format reveals the conscious and unconscious dialogue between the therapeutic pair.[2]

Carla came in and stated that she had missed the last two sessions because she wanted to go out with a friend of hers, someone with whom she talked and shared some intimate things. I reminded her that she had a commitment here, one she had decided to undertake. She answered, "Yes, it's true that I have this commitment, but now I feel well, and I don't need to come so badly any more." I pointed out that, as we had seen once before, she often stopped attending when she thought everything was better. After a few moments of silence, she started speaking about the problems she had with her mother (and other older people in general). "My mother is always reminding me what I should or shouldn't do, over and over again, but I have a head on my shoulders."

Indirectly I felt she was telling me that I was behaving just like her mother who did not believe she was telling the truth when she said she felt fine. I became her old, clutching mother who did not want to let her go, who did not want her to grow. In this same indirect way she was asking me to let her go because she felt ready.

She went on, "My father's musical tastes are different from mine . . . even if everyone says he's such a genius . . . that's O.K. But my tastes are just different. My father likes melodious Neapolitan songs, but I like modern music."

She was telling me that she was separate from the father/therapist; that she had her own identity now, even though she did not dismiss her father's tastes. She recognized the difference because she now appreciated her own particular nature.

Carla said that she wanted to throw a party at the end of the therapy. "Thanks to you because you helped me, but thanks to me, too, because I gave it all I had." I nodded and smiled in agreement with what she said. She told me a story about scolding a thirty-year-old woman with a baby in her arms who had unjustly attacked a girl. Carla thought that on the one hand, the woman had been right to insist on having a seat, but she should never have taken the liberty of pulling the girl's hair. She added. "Now I speak up when I feel like it. I don't say things behind people's backs."

She was saying that now she was capable of standing up for herself, even when she had to face a mother with a small child, whereas in the past she was blocked by strong guilt feelings connected with the jealousy aroused by her brother's birth. Now she seemed capable of seeing two sides of a problem.

Continuing, Carla said, "I'm doing well at school, and I like it even though there are some subjects that I have trouble with." She said that now she jokes and kids around with the boys. Then she spoke about a friend of her father's whom she had liked and with whose son, she joked and talked to.

In the past, this affection for the friend of her father clearly repre-

sented a feeling of affection for the therapist which had been displaced onto this man. Now, however, it was directed towards his son, some-one more age-appropriate.

The patient said that they joked about her big feet, size ten. She herself joked about it.

I noticed that she was speaking just like an adolescent.

During the next session, she showed me a photo of a boy with whom she had "sort of a commitment," to which I responded that things were going well for her, and it was no wonder that she wanted to stop coming to therapy. After a few moments of silence, she spoke as if she had just remembered something. "My mother's always telling me the same thing. She's afraid, like all mothers who don't want their children to grow up and be independent." I was surprised at how clearly her language revealed the unconscious. So I let her take her own path. In that last session, she also told me in an indirect way what her relationship with her therapist was like. She did this by speaking about a boy she had met in the hospital who had left without saying goodbye. In contrast, she had left her address to the others upon leaving.

She was telling me that she was not fleeing, but that she could bear the separation and give me her address. Here she could admit that she was leaving.

Carla then commented that I looked pensive. At that time I was thinking about the beginning of her sexual relationships. I asked her to tell me of her fantasies and she said that I was probably thinking of the problems she would have when she became a mother.

She seemed to get further than I did. I was moved by the fact that she was now able to think about her own maternity, especially since she originally came to me because she wanted to remain eternally sixteen.

Then she commented, "I kept tossing and turning in bed . . . maybe because it was the last . . ." I told her that she might have been think-ing about saying good-bye, the kisses and the hugs of parting, and I added that we had spoken very little about her sexual fantasies in connection with me. She shook her head, but I continued, saying that such feelings are normal after making this sort of journey together. Then she nodded and recalled the example I had once used of an exploratory journey undertaken with the help of a guide, one which she would now have to take on her own.

In this process of self-determination, as the world of childhood is left behind, the adolescent often has great difficulty in facing up to adults, both the parents and the therapist. What seemed to clash most harshly with Carla's own demands to leave the dependency of therapy was, not so much my careful outlining of those aspects related to separation, but the interpretation of these aspects as being necessarily depressive and related to mourning. For Carla, it seemed that the end of therapy was not a moment of mourning at all, but one of celebration in which an infantile element was sacrificed. This naturally brought with it an element of sadness, one that was precisely necessitated by the development of her adult side. However, I could not help wondering if this understanding might conceal a denial of mourning on the part of both the patient and the therapist, so that both could avoid the problems of separation. In the session previously reported. Carla showed a state of mind in which the joy of the new world opening before her took precedence over the sadness of separation.

Conclusion

The particular suitability of this modality of working with adolescents depends on the characteristics of the adolescent, torn as they are between the desire for maternal, nonverbal experiences and the desire to understand and to gain access to the amazing and mysterious world of the mind. A special relationship between sandplay therapy and analytical work exists, and this correlation deserves to be studied in greater depth. At times, these two approaches seem to be distinct and distant from one another, but the above case history illustrates their significant points of convergence. One such point might be the attention that is given to the unconscious relationship in the therapeutic pair, particularly to the requests of the patient, to the patient's unconscious expression in the sandplay, or by the carrying on with verbal interpretative work.

The psychoanalytic research conducted in the last few years has been paying more and more attention to the study of those mechanisms by which both the patient and the therapist perceive and induce something in the other. The involvement of the more precocious aspects of the relationship is being hypothesized with growing frequency. Attention to the tone rather than the content of interpretations has led to further reflections on the more archaic levels of development that can affect the analytic pair.

Sandplay therapy, which makes possible the expression of precocious aspects of the relationship, seems to be able to respond to the need to contain the patient, while verbal interpretations seem to respond to the need to use the mind in its discriminating function and consciousness-raising abilities. It is necessary to offer the patient a chance for an emotional and cognitive understanding of what is happening in their inner world in order to proceed on the way towards individuation.

Notes

1. D. M. Kalff, Sandplay: A Psychotherapeutic Approach to the Psyche (Boston: Sigo, 1991), p.9; "Introduction to Sandplay Therapy," Journal of Sandplay Therapy 1, 1:9–15.
2. See M. Sidoli, "Separation in Adolescence," The Unfolding Self (Boston: Sigo, 1989).

19

Individual Psychotherapy in a Residential School for Girls

Janet Glynn-Treble

Introduction and History

The purpose of this chapter is to explore the difficulties in providing therapeutic transformation for disturbed adolescent girls both in a residential setting and within individual psychotherapy. As is the case with other chapters in this collection the theoretical foundation of this approach is informed by Bion's concept of maternal "reverie" and its use by the infant in transforming "beta elements" of physical sensation and primitive feelings into "alpha elements" of images and thoughts. Bion puts forward the idea of alpha function, of which "reverie" is a factor, as a major tool and task of therapeutic transformation.[1]

In addition to Bion's theories, the literature about residential therapeutic institutions for children and adolescents is rich and varied. There is a tradition of provision of residential therapeutic education in England, the psychological approach of which draws upon psychoanalysis. Although he later developed his own ideas, A. S. Neill has described the work at Summerhill, which was originally inspired by his contact with psychoanalysis.[2] Barbara Dockar-Drysdale has written about work at the Mulberry Bush School, whose therapeutic approach stems from the ideas of the psychoanalyst Donald W. Winnicott.[3] Additionally, there are a growing number of residential therapeutic communities that can provide care fifty-two weeks of the year, if necessary. These communities provide "intensively nurturing . . . settings which can be fine-tuned to meet an individual's psychological, social, educational, and physical needs" with a psychological approach that "might be broadly described as psycho-dynamic."[4] Drawing from his experiences at the Cotswold Community, Richard Balbernie has written a thorough analysis of many aspects of the difficult task of residential work with children.[5] More recently, Melvyn Rose has written about work at Peper Harow.[6] In the United States, the work of Bruno Bettelheim and the Orthogenic School at the University of Chicago is well known.[7]

In such settings the aim is overtly therapeutic. Thus a commitment and willingness exists on the part of the staff to examine feelings and projections that are usually of a persecutory or depressive nature. Examination of these issues within themselves, the institution, and their clients provides a means of gaining a greater understanding of how to proceed therapeutically with their clients, thereby enhancing the therapeutic potential of the setting.

However, there are many settings where the primary aim is not overtly therapeutic: that is, social care provision or special education. In such settings there is an expectation that clients will be helped to change and mature by professionals who endeavour to work therapeutically with children and young people. However, the structure and support of staff groups and consultation designed primarily to examine unconscious emotional processes within the institution are not usually available, and therefore a commitment to examine feelings and projections is absent. In such cases, it falls to the individual worker to attempt to process these experiences. Group consultation outside the work setting can greatly enhance an individual's capacity to work therapeutically and withstand projections and institutional defenses. If processing work is not attempted, individuals and institutions are liable to fall prey to the anxieties projected into them from their disturbed clients, and are subject to experiences of fragmentation, the erection of rigid defenses, or the acting out of projections from clients and colleagues alike.

If severely disturbed clients in residential establishments are to be helped towards maturation, then the institutions and individuals in them need to perform a containing function for them, rather than developing systems that deny the impact of primitive, projected beta elements. Needless to say, the obstacles to achieving such a state of "containment" where the projected material is temporarily accepted and actively worked with are legion. The stresses involved in working in residential settings for disturbed children and adolescents are enormous, yet methods are developed to deal with this stress. In their book, *Therapeutic Work with Children and Young People,* Copley and Forryan describe some of these methods. They write about "the sensitive approach of a school in its therapeutic endeavour to relate to the needs of disturbed children." For example, a school can overcome the impulse to eject a child. It can provide continuity and reliability in children's contact with staff, nonjudgmental listening time, structured time for children's verbal expression of their feelings and experiences, tolerance of and efforts made to understand erratic behavior. This approach is in direct contrast with one that "might attempt to enforce standards of behavior at the expense of providing space for thinking about anxieties and difficulties . . . where the defensive rules of the place . . . take precedence over the task of understanding its clients."[8]

Other difficulties of providing a therapeutic experience of "reverie" for disturbed children in day school settings have been described by Jackson, Dyke, and Woods. Woods draws attention to the ambiguity of the teacher's role in having to meet the anger, violence, and despair of the disturbed child on a daily basis while also attempting to educate and control. The importance of separating the treatment element from the educational is made clear in his article, "The Boundary between Psychotherapy and Therapeutic Teaching."[9] Developing this theme in his article, "Referral and Assessment for Psychotherapy in a School for Children with Emotional and Behavioural Difficulties," Dyke discusses the additional difficulties inherent in the referral and assessment process for psychotherapy within a school setting.[10] Using the day school setting, Jackson writes about establishing the boundaries of the therapeutic setting and the impact of projections from disturbed children on their teaching staff, particularly the need to disentangle those elements of despair teachers often feel are their own from those that are projected into them by the children.[11]

The Residential Setting

The previous references help to form the historical and intellectual underpinnings of a residential school setting for educationally and behaviorally disturbed girls. The main task of this setting is educational; however, there are some confusions in defining the aim of the school, since the girls are expected to develop emotionally during their stay. There is an additional confusion in the minds of both staff and clients that the purpose of the place is also mildly punitive, although clients have not committed offenses. This latter image is fueled by the unconscious fantasy projections of the clients. These confusions about educational, therapeutic, correctional, and punitive functions give rise to misunderstandings in the management of the girls on the part of the staff who are also unsure about their role as containers and their capacity to provide an experience of reverie.

The girls are admitted to the school for a variety of reasons. Sometimes they have experienced deprivation and abuse in their family setting. Sometimes they are almost beyond their parents' control and are at risk in their community. Often they have not been containable in previous schools. Although most have had a psychiatric assessment, the school is not considered to be a treatment center. The school takes up to thirty-five girls, aged eight to sixteen, who are divided into four classes according to age. A full school curriculum and individual lessons are provided. In addition, a wide range of extracurricular activities is offered outside school time.

The staff is organized into four teams. Child care staff look after the girls outside school hours. Teaching staff conduct classes but are also assigned residential duties during the evenings and weekends on a rotating basis. The psychiatric team, consisting of a psychiatrist, a psychologist, a psychiatric social worker, and a child psychotherapist, provide assessment and treatment. The psychiatric social worker provides a valuable link between the school and the girls' family, which may be miles away. The domestic staff is composed of cleaners, cooks, gardeners, caretakers, sewing and laundry ladies. All are known to the girls and have personal contact with them. Normal school holidays and term times are adhered to by all staff members and students; additionally, the school is closed during some weekends. The accommodation consists of purpose-built classrooms, shared bedrooms for two to four girls, and common rooms. There is considerable mix between the educational, administrative, and "home" functions of the school buildings.

It is important to consider how the parenting function for the girls is split among many individuals. A good deal of fragmentation, both external and internal, occurs. This is especially pronounced during the weeks preceding and following school holidays. For the girls, in addition to their internal distress, stresses arise from being removed from the parental home, friends, and locality and being placed in a close-quarter living situation with other disturbed girls where bullying, infantile behavior, and acting out are constant occurrences and where they are parented by many people. They often come from chaotic and uncaring home situations where drugs, prostitution, abuse or neglect are prevalent. For the staff, long hours and unremitting infantile behavior take their toll in terms of physical and emotional illnesses, accidents, domestic difficulties, and frequent staff turnover. One of my patients had four different teachers in the twelve month period of our psychotherapy. These stresses become persecutory for both staff and girls who experience claustrophobic symptoms. A prevailing shared fantasy among some staff, jokingly expressed in the staff room, is how to escape. The girls sometimes either manage to get themselves suspended for bad behavior or actually run away in an unconscious attempt to escape from their internal difficulties. Often internal images of intolerable parents are projected onto the school and staff. Otherwise, these persecutory and claustrophobic fantasies seem to be dealt with by a manic furor of activity in which no one has time to stand still.

Beyond the educational curriculum, the main targets for management within the school are the actions and behaviors of the girls. Very little time or mental space is given to feelings or thinking of the staff or the girls. One can see how the disturbances that the girls bring can attack the thinking and feeling capacities of the potential containers, i.e. the institution and the individuals within it. Difficult behavior such as violence, verbal attacks, and destructiveness, is managed by a privilege system in which the right to outings and pocket money is earned or lost according to behavior. The privilege system provides a clear structure within which staff, who are not analytically trained, can be supported in their management of girls. Those girls with a developed ego derive satisfaction from their achievement in this system. However, for those girls with more infantile needs, the privilege system is a daily reminder of a failure to achieve, and thus the system takes on a persecutory aspect. Because of the rigidity of the system, a girl can find herself on a downward spiral toward greater and greater deprivation, and a correspondingly increased feeling of persecution and desire to withdraw or retaliate. This is one major area in which the institution's self-protective mechanism takes precedence over the needs of clients.

Therefore, the institution fails to function as an adequate container since it cannot accept what has been projected into it.

Some value is given to thinking and talking as the girls are offered weekly counseling sessions with key social workers. These sessions, however, lack containment, in that they are not given a specific time and place for meeting. Additionally, the staff meets weekly to review the girls. Discussion centers mainly on behavior rather than feelings, and there is not time to allocate more than three or four minutes to each girl. The six-month review of girls by staff members entails a much more extensive description of the physical, social, and educational aspects of a girl's life. However, it focuses on the progress and achievements or failures, rather than the needs of the girls and is often presented in a condemnatory light.

The Practice of Psychotherapy in the Institutional Setting

Due to the financial reorganization with the National Health Service, psychotherapy had not been provided for some years, and thus the psychotherapy program had to be created anew. Initially, both the staff and the girls projected magical powers onto me, causing them both to fear me and to form unrealistic expectations. My countertransference feelings about the institution as a whole was akin to the feeling of the "new girl." I was bewildered by the number of people and personalities to relate to and their constantly changing composition. There were numerous rules and rooms. There was a general air of mistrust and imminent damage illustrated by the fact that all rooms were locked and members of the staff walked around with bunches of keys. There were numerous activities and a constantly changing timetable. Girls continually acted out, resulting in phone calls from the police with complaints of fire, theft, or fighting. Girls were running away, staying out all night when home, experimenting with drugs, and failing to return to school after holidays. In short, I had feelings of confusion, fragmentation, and bombardment projected into me. Using Bion's terminology, there were a lot of beta elements, and very little alpha processing was occurring. It is likely that much of the institution's functioning is an attempt to defend itself against the massive projection of helplessness, fragmentation, and attack from the girls.

In providing individual psychotherapy, one attempts to provide a setting in which beta elements can be transformed by the therapist's alpha function, or reverie. In order to fulfill my task of providing individual psychotherapy within this setting, I had to try to create a firm framework within which some therapeutic containment could be achieved. My experience of being inadequately provided with the necessary materials was indicative of the lack of mental space allocated to the girls' emotional growth. Since the boundaries were unclear, a secure physical space was required. Apparently, there had been no time to think about providing a room for psychotherapy, and physical space was in short supply. Eventually, a room was suggested. However, it was difficult to find furniture. Other staff felt the furniture was needed elsewhere, and I found myself in the position of a needy child who had rivals. Eventually, I succeeded in obtaining what I required, including a locking cupboard for the safe storage of individual therapy materials. Previous therapy materials had been lost or destroyed. Physical space and materials for therapeutic work seemed to be a luxury as did the provision of psychic space for emotional work, in spite of the fact that psychotherapy provision was highly valued by the senior staff.

Having procured a physical space, I was confronted with the task of providing a secure professional basis from which to work. This included issues about regularity and continuity of therapy, boundaries, sharing, confidentiality, choice about treatment and referral procedures, many of which were under threat as a result of the institutional setting or the disturbances and feelings of fragmentation in the girls.

Referrals came in various ways. To begin with, the head teacher or staff were quite keen for me to start working with some of their most difficult girls. The social worker and psychiatrist mentioned some names, and I heard names repeatedly cropping up in staff room conversations. Some parents requested psychotherapy for their daughters; some girls either asked to see me or accosted me in the corridors and made overtures. Senior staff members at the school were *in loco parentis* and made referrals in conjunction with parents when possible.

All lessons were attended on a timetable, and originally a girl referred for psychotherapy was expected to withdraw from class to attend an individual session. This gave rise to displays of hostility masking deeper anxieties. Some were quite eager to talk with an adult, while others found psychotherapy alarming. Eventually I found that therapy progressed more successfully if preparatory work was done with the girl by someone who knew her reasonably well. I asked the adult to introduce the idea of therapy to the child and think with her about what therapy entailed and why it had been recommended. The adult then accompanied the girl and introduced her to me, in much the same ways that a good parent would. Thus the girl could feel part of the process and avoid feeling imposed on: central anxieties about helplessness were thereby contained.

The establishment of regular and continuous supplies of psychotherapy time was unbelievably difficult to achieve. I believe it reflected, in my countertransference feeling, the frustration, deprivation, confusion, and helplessness experienced by my clients. In addition, I struggled against the rhythm of the school year, with its frequent holidays and recurrent manic activities connected with end of term festivities. Session times became fragmented at holiday times so that "holding on" to therapy sessions before and after break was difficult, and the tendency to reject what was offered, as it appeared unreliable, increased. Additionally, the girls were frequently absent from school after holidays and home weekends. Sometimes they were suspended because of their behavior. Illnessess, school outings, and timetable changes also used up therapy time. I tried to establish a forty minute session, rather than accept that twenty minutes or half an hour was enough, and this seemed to work well for me even though it did not fit neatly into the school timetable.

It was also important to establish the spatial boundaries of therapy to be clear that it was not something which we did in classrooms or corridors or whenever somebody felt like a chat. Withdrawal from class presented problems. It was difficult to extricate a girl from her involvement in a class activity, especially since the practice in the school was for girls withdrawn to be accompanied by a staff member. I was often escorting girls to and from class, and my calling at the classroom publicized psychotherapy to classmates. This publicity often heightened persecution anxieties or provided the opportunity to publicly denigrate the therapy, therapist, or therapeutic needs. Sometimes a quiet word from the teacher was more effective, but I preferred the girls to take responsibility for coming themselves, which happened once therapy was underway.

In order to contain the therapeutic relationship within the consulting room, I did not mix with girls outside sessions, a factor both the girls and staff sometimes found difficult to accept. In such a small, closed community, the transference feelings arising from sharing the same therapist could run high. Several of the girls I saw shared the same classroom all day and a bedroom at night. I knew they compared notes and quoted me to their friends, so I tried to be alert to their denied feelings of jealousy and their intrusive rivalry that sought to find out and destroy my other babies. Susan Dyke has written about the heightened transference feelings that occur from the first session in an institutional setting, which arise from patients' very active feelings of rivalry.[12] She adds that the child's "means of entry and meaning of entry into the therapy room" is a central theme in therapeutic assessment sessions in a special school setting. She found that most of her assessment sessions were concerned with the themes of breaking in or rivalry with those who were already in, and the opening and closing of doors or being shut out. She writes that "the transference is already tremendously powerful and cannot be ignored in one's own interpretations," and, therefore, assessment in an institution differs radically from assessment in a clinic setting. This description corresponds closely with my own experience.

The girls were constantly testing my capacity to remain an adequate container. Both the staff members and the girls expected me to make another appointment if a session was canceled due to illness or absence, so I continually had to reestablish this boundary and preserve the integrity and confidentiality of their sessions from fantasized or real attack by peers. Because the girls projected their own rivalrous, destructive fantasies into peers and staff members, confidentiality was also a difficult issue. They were not always willing to believe that information would be treated in a caring way. Certainly some information, such as drug abuse or pregnancy, needed to be shared, but I tried to share only my general understanding of each client with other staff members rather than specific information about what transpired in sessions.

The question of choice and the voluntary nature of psychotherapy became a complicated issue. Some girls needed to believe that we were able to cooperate in the process of our discussions. Others became very persecuted by their hostile projections or anxieties and holding them in attendance was difficult when all staff and girls knew that I was the only person in the school who offered a choice about attendance. Staff members differed in the degree to which they were willing to be firm about attendance in the face of a negative transference, and I was largely dependent upon them to do what they could to help. Understandably, they were sometimes unwilling to face hostile confrontations with girls about therapy that was neither compulsory nor their business. Transition from teacher to therapist involved temporarily giving up someone good they already have, the teacher, which some felt as an experience of infantile loss.

Sometimes the differing expectations of the privilege system and the therapeutic attitude caused confusion for the girls as well. Much of their behavior, language, and attitude, arising from a full-blown persecutory projection, would evoke condemnation and loss of privileges from other staff members. I felt compelled to interpret these incidents but found that this approach could activate sadistic attacks on the "soft" element in therapy. At times, I felt that I was a fool to have any caring feelings. The sadism in the personalities of severely deprived girls takes full advantage of the nonretaliatory nature of psychotherapy until more internal controls are established

Having a therapist in an institution to think about the meaning of a child's behavior can support the efforts of other staff to arrive at understanding rather than mere control. In his article "The Boundary between Psychotherapy and Therapeutic Teaching," John Woods has described how the therapist's attitude can support staff functioning:

> The child's attacks on the school's authority easily provoke retaliation or despair in the teacher. The therapist has the function of showing how such reactions can be modified to reveal what is hidden by the child's disordered behaviour. Retaliation or defeat is a repetition of earlier damage for the child . . . The staff group tends to look . . . to the therapist as an example of how to bear the uncomfortable experience of loss of protective authority. Through an increased ability to tolerate the arousal of fear, anxiety and despair, teaching staff are in a better position to reassert their personal authority with the child.[13]

The splits in a girl's personality can powerfully divide the institution, some team members taking a softer, more maternal attitude with a girl, while other team members, who are receiving the brunt of her hostile attacks, are provoked into a much harder and more punitive stance. It is not surprising that the staff sometimes adopts a punitive overall response or develops a fairly hard, self-protective crust. The middle way of firmness combined with continued care for the girl, rather than ejection, is difficult to achieve in the face of massive and continuous projections. Therefore, the therapeutic attitude must model this middle way.

Many of my countertransference feelings were experienced by other members of the staff who, without the advantage of psychoanalytic training, had a considerable burden carrying these projections. From the girls, I was often the recipient of their denied and projected feelings of denigration, neglect, and helplessness. In their eyes, I was often seen as useless and stupid and was coldly dropped or angrily attacked by them. From the staff, I received attitudes that corresponded to the girls' needy and infantile parts which I represented. They were too busy and therefore unavailable for me. The question of how best to support staff sensitivity to the needs of the girls in the face of these projections is difficult to answer. Two of my most difficult tasks in my own act of reverie consisted of managing my countertransference feelings of fragmentation and denigration projected into me by the girls and the institutional functioning, and retaining my therapeutic sensitivity. There was a massive disregard, both by the girls and within the institution, of infantile needs for reliability and concern, of feelings of dependence and vulnerability, and of meaningful attachments. "Toughness" seemed to be the dominant behavior advocated by the staff and the girls, and I had to be on my guard not to collude with this attitude.

Through this morass of denial of needs and projection of feelings of denigration, fragmentation, and helplessness, it was often difficult to retain the perception, both within the therapy and in the institution, that the girls were extremely defensive against rejection or abandonment anxieties and were persecuted by their own hostile projections of the depriving parent.

The task of psychotherapy within the institution can be seen as providing the opportunity for these needs and projections to be contained within a process of reverie, whereby sensations, impulses, and infantile feelings are understood and responded to appropriately, rather than defended against. In so doing, the psychotherapist supports the development of alpha functioning in the patient and also provides a model to support the development of the alpha function in other staff members.[14]

Notes

1. W. Bion, *Learning From Experience* (London: Heinemann, 1962).
2. A.S. Neill, *Summerhill* (London: Victor Gollancz, 1962).
3. See B. E. Dockar-Drysdale, *Therapy in Child Care* (London: Longman's, 1968); *Consultation in Child Care* (London: Longmans, 1973); *The Provision of Primary Experience: Winnicottian Work with Children and Adolescents* (London: Free Association Books, 1990).
4. Caldecott Community, *A Healing Experience* (Chalvington, England, Caldecott Community, 1988). Other residential therapeutic communities include Highdene Association, Kilworthy House, Mulberry Bush School, New Barns School, Peper Harow, Raddery, Thornby Hall, Cotswold Community.
5. R. Balbernie, *Residential Work with Children* (London: Pergamon, 1966).
6. M. Rose, *Healing Hurting Minds* (London: Routledge and Kegan Paul, 1990).
7. B. Bettelheim, *Love is Not Enough* (New York: Free Press, 1950); *A Home for the Informed Heart* (New York: Free Press, 1960).
8. B. Copley and B. Forryan, *Therapeutic Work with Children and Young People* (London: Robert Royce, 1987).
9. J. Woods, "The Boundary Between Psychotherapy and Therapeutic Teaching," *Jungian Child Psychotherapy* 12,2.
10. S. Dyke, "Referral and Assessment for Psychotherapy in a School for Children with Emotional and Behavior Difficulties." *Jungian Child Psychotherapy* 11,1.
11. J. Jackson "Child Psychotherapy in a Day School for Maladjusted Children," *Jungian Child Psychotherapy* 2,4.
12. S. Dyke, 1985.
13. J. Woods, 1986.
14. Two additional works on which this paper is based are: G. Henry, "Difficulties about Thinking and Learning," in *Psychotherapy with Severely Deprived Children* (London: Routledge and Kegan Paul, 1983); P. Wilson, "Individual Psychotherapy in a Residential Setting," in *The Adolescent Unit,* ed. Derek Steinberg (New York: John Wiley, 1986).

Index